C000111391

DATE DUE

A TRUE WOMAN

A TRUE WOMAN

BY

BARONESS ORCZY

AUTHOR OF
"THE ELUSIVE PIMPERNEL," "I WILL REPAY,"
"THE SCARLET PIMPERNEL," ETC.

"For like as the ground is given unto the wood
and the sea to his floods: even so they that dwell
upon the earth may understand nothing but that
which is upon the earth."—2 *Esdras* iv. 21.

London: HUTCHINSON & CO.
Paternoster Row ❧ ❧ ❧ 1911

178

TO KATHERINE
LADY DEMPSTER METCALFE

Friends such as you are indeed the gift
of heaven.

To you therefore I inscribe this book,
both in remembrance of the 7th day of
November, 1894, which you helped to make
the happiest of my life, and because I feel
that, given the circumstances in life, you
would always act as and remain a true
woman.

EMMUSKA ORCZY.

SNOWFIELD,
    March, 1911.

CONTENTS

CONTENTS

A TRUE WOMAN

CHAPTER I

WHICH TELLS OF A VERY COMMONPLACE INCIDENT

NO! no! she was not going to gush!—Not even
though there was nothing in the room at this
moment to stand up afterwards before her as dumb
witness to a moment's possible weakness. Less than
nothing, in fact: space might have spoken and
recalled that moment . . . infinite nothingness might
at some future time have brought back the memory of
it . . . but these dumb, impassive objects! . . . the
fountain pen between her fingers! the dull, uninteresting hotel furniture covered in red velvet—an
uninviting red that repelled dreaminess and peace!—
the ormolu clock which had ceased long ago to mark
the passage of time, wearied—as it no doubt was, poor
thing—by the monotonous burden of a bronze Psyche
gazing on her shiny brown charms, in an utterly blank
and unreflective bronze mirror, while obviously be-
moaning the fracture of one of her smooth bronze
thighs! Indeed, Louisa might well have given way to
that overmastering feeling of excitement before all

B

these things. They would neither see nor hear. They would never deride, for they could never remember.

But a wood fire crackled in the small hearth . . . and . . . and those citron-coloured carnations were favourite flowers of his . . . and his picture did stand on the top of that ugly little Louis Philippe bureau. . . . No! no! it would never do to gush—for these things would see . . . and though they might not remember they would remind.

And Louisa counted herself one of the strong ones of this earth. Just think of her name! Have you ever known a Louisa who gushed, who called herself the happiest woman on earth, who thought of a man—just an ordinary man, mind you—as the best, the handsomest, the truest, the most perfect hero of romance that ever threw a radiance over the entire prosy world of the twentieth century?

Louisas, believe me, do no such thing. The Mays and the Floras, the Lady Barbaras and Lady Edithas look beatific and charming when—clasping their lily-white hands together and raising violet eyes to the patterned ceiling paper above them—they exclaim: "Oh! my hero and my king!"

But Louisa would only look ridiculous if they behaved like that . . . Louisa Harris, too! . . . Louisa, the eldest of three sisters . . . the daughter of a wealthy English gentleman with a fine estate in Kent, an assured position, no troubles, no cares, nothing in her life to make it sad, or sordid, or interesting . . . Louisa Harris and romance! . . . Why, she was not even pretty. She had neither violet eyes nor hair of ruddy gold. The latter was brown and the former were grey. . . . How could romance come in the way of grey eyes, and of a girl named Louisa ?

Can you conceive, for instance, one of those adorable detrimentals of low degree and empty pockets, who have a way of arousing love in the hearts of the beautiful daughters of irascible millionaires, can you conceive such an interesting personage, I say, falling in love with Louisa Harris ?

I confess that I cannot. To begin with dear, kind, Squire Harris was not altogether a millionaire, and not at all irascible, and penniless owners of romantic personalities were not on his visiting list.

Therefore Louisa, living a prosy life of luxury, got up every morning, ate a copious breakfast, walked out with the dogs, hunted in the autumn, skated in the winter, did the London season and played tennis in the summer, just like hundreds and hundreds of other well-born, well-bred English girls of average means, average positions, average education, hunt, dance, and play tennis throughout the length and breadth of this country.

There was no room for romance in such a life, no time for it . . . the life itself was so full already—so full of the humdrum of daily rounds, of common tasks, that the heart which beat with such ordinary regularity in the seemingly ordinary breast of a very ordinary girl, did so all unconscious of the intense pathos which underlay this very ordinary existence.

Vaguely Louisa knew that somewhere beyond even the land of dreams, there lay all unknown, all mysterious, a glorious world of romance : a universe peopled by girlish imaginings, and the sensitive, creating thoughts of poets, by the galloping phantasies of super-excited brains, and the vague longings of ambitious souls, a universe wherein dwelt alike the memories of those who have loved and the hopes of those who suffer. But when she thought of it all she did so as one who from the arid plain gazes on the cool streams and golden minarets which the fairy Fata Morgana conjures on the horizon far away. She looked on it as all unreal and altogether beyond her ken. She shut her eyes to the beautiful mirage, her heart against its childish yearnings.

Such things did not exist. They were not for her— Louisa Harris. The little kitchenmaid at the Court, who on Sunday evenings went off giggling, her chubby face glowing with pride and the result of recent ablutions, on the arm of Jim the third gardener, knew more about that world of romance than well-bred, well-born young ladies ever dreamed of in their commonplace philosophy.

And Louisa Harris had always shut down the book which spoke of such impossible things, and counted herself one of the strong ones of the earth.

Therefore now with Luke's letter in her hand, in which he tells her in a very few words that he loves her beyond anything on earth and that he only waits the day when he can call her his own, his very own dearly loved wife, why should Louisa—prosy, healthy-minded, healthy-bodied Louisa—suddenly imagine that the whole world is transfigured—that the hotel room is a kind of ante-chamber to heaven—that the red velvet, uncompromising chairs are clouds of a roseate hue, and that the bronze Psyche with the broken thigh is the elusive fairy who with Morgana-like wand hath conjured up this mirage of glorious visions which mayhap would vanish again before long ?

She went up to the window and rested her forehead against the cool pane. She might be ever so strong, she could not help her forehead feeling hot and her eyes being full of tears . . . tears that did not hurt as they fell.

Outside the weather was indeed prosy and commonplace. Rain coming down in torrents and beating against the newspaper *kiosque* over the way, on the roofs of tramways and taxi-autos, making the electric light peep dimly through the veil of wet, drowning by its incessant patter, to which the gusts of a November gale made fitful if loud accompaniment, the shouts of the *cochers* on their boxes, the rattle of wheels on the stone pavement, even at times the shrill whistle for cabs emanating from the porch of the brilliantly lighted Palace Hotel.

It was close on half-past six by the clock of the Gard du Nord opposite. The express from Ostend had just come in—very late, of course, owing to the gale which had delayed the mail boat. Louisa, straining her eyes, watched the excited crowd pouring out of the station in the wake of porters and of piles of luggage jabbering, shouting and fussing like an army of irresponsible pigmies : men in blouses and men in immaculate bowler hats, women wrapped in furs, clinging to gigantic headgear that threatened to leave the safe

refuge of an elaborate coiffure or of well-fixed gargantuan hatpins, *midinettes* in fashionable skirts and
high-heeled shoes, countrywomen in wool shawls that
flapped round their bulky forms like the wings of an
overfed bat . . . all hurrying and jostling one another
in a mad endeavour to avoid the onrush of the innumerable taxi-autos, which in uncountable numbers
wound in and out of the slower-moving traffic like the
erratic thread of some living tangled skein.

Just the everyday prosy life of a small but ambitious
capital, struggling in the midst of an almost over-
powering sense of responsibility towards the whole of
Europe in view of its recent great Colonial expansion.

Louisa gave an impatient sigh.

Even the strong ones of the earth get wearied of the
daily round, the common task at times. She and aunt
were due to dine at the British Embassy at eight
o'clock ; it was only half-past six now, and obviously
impossible to sit another hour in this unresponsive
hotel room in the company of red velvet chairs and
the bronze Psyche.

Aunt, in conjunction with her maid, Annette, was
busy laying the foundations of an elaborate toilette.
Louisa was free to do as she pleased. She got a
serviceable ulster and a diminutive hat and sallied
forth into the streets. She did not want to think or to
dream, nor perhaps did she altogether wish to work
off that unusual feeling of excitement which had so
unaccountably transformed her ever since Luke's letter
had come.

All she wanted was to be alone, and to come out of

herself for a while. She had been alone all the after-noon, save for that brief half-hour when aunt discussed the obvious over a badly brewed cup of tea ; it was not that kind of " alone "-ness which Louisa wanted now, but rather the solitude which a crowded street has above all the power to give.

There is a kind of sociability in any room, be it ever so uncompromising in the matter of discomfort, but a crowded street can be unutterably lonely, either cruelly so or kindly, as the case may be.

To Louisa Harris, the commonplace society girl, accustomed to tea-fights, to dances and to dinner parties, the loneliness of this crowded little city was eminently welcome. With her dark ulster closely buttoned to the throat, the small hat tied under her chin, with everything on her weatherproof and un-fashionable, she attracted no notice from the passer-by.

Not one head was turned as, with a long breath of delight, she sallied forth from under the portico of the hotel out into the muddy, busy street ; not one glance of curiosity or interest so freely bestowed in the streets of foreign capitals on a solitary female figure if it be young and comely, followed this very ordinary-looking English miss.

To the crowd she was indifferent. These men and women hurrying along, pushing, jostling and scurrying, knew nothing of Luke, nor that she, Louisa Harris, was the happiest woman on earth.

She turned back towards the Boulevards, meaning to take a brisk walk all along the avenue of trees which makes a circuit round the inner part of the town and which ultimately would lead her back to the Gard du Nord and the Palace Hotel. It was a walk she had often done before : save for one or two busy corners on the way, it would be fairly solitary and peaceful.

Louisa stepped out with an honest British tread, hands buried in the pockets of her serviceable ulster, head bent against the sudden gusts of wind. She did not mind the darkness of the ill-lighted, wide Boulevard, and had every intention of covering the two miles in a little more than half an hour.

How the time sped ! It seemed as if she had only just left the hotel, and already surely not a quarter of a mile away she could see glimmering the lights of the Place Namur, the half-way point of her walk.

She was in the Boulevard Waterloo, there where private houses with closed *portes-cochères* add nothing to the municipal lighting of the thoroughfare.

Trams had been rushing past her in endless succession ; but now there was a lull. Close by her a taxi-auto whizzed quickly past and came to a standstill some hundred yards away, near to the pavement, and not far from an electric light standard.

Louisa, with vacant eyes attached on that cab, but with her mind fixed on a particular room in a particular house in Grosvenor Square, where lived a man of the name of Luke de Mountford, continued her walk. Those same vacant eyes of hers presently saw the chauffeur of the taxi-auto get down from his box and open the door of the cab, and then her absent mind was suddenly brought back from Grosvenor Square, London, to the Boulevard Waterloo in Brussels, by a terrible cry of horror which had broken from that same chauffeur's lips. Instinctively Louisa hurried on, but even as she did so a small crowd, which indeed seemed to have sprung from nowhere, had already gathered round the vehicle.

Murmurs of " What is it ? what is it ? " mingled with smothered groans of terror, as curiosity caused one or two of the more bold to peer into the gloomy depths of the cab. Shrill calls brought a couple of *gardiens* to the spot. In a moment Louisa found herself a unit in an eager, anxious crowd asking questions, conjecturing, wondering, horror-struck as soon as a plausible and graphic explanation came from those who were in the forefront and were privileged to see,

" A man . . . murdered . . ."

" But how ? "

" The chauffeur got down from his box . . . and looked in . . . ah, *mon Dieu !* "

" What did he see ? "

" A man . . . he is quite young . . . only about twenty years of age . . ."

" Stabbed through the neck. . . ."

" Stabbed ? . . . Bah . . . ! "

" Right through the neck, I tell you . . . just below the ear. . . . I can see the wound, quite small, as if done with a skewer. . . ."

" *Allons !* . . . *voyons !* . . . *voyons !* " came in gruff accents from the two portly *gardiens* who worked vigorously with elbows and even feet to keep the crowd somewhat at bay.

Louisa was on the fringe of the crowd. She could

see nothing, of course . . . she did not wish to see that which the chauffeur saw when first he opened the door of his cab . . . but she stood rooted to the spot, feeling that strange, unexplainable fascination which one always feels, when one of those great life dramas of which one reads so often and so indifferently happens to be enacted within the close range of one's own perception.

She gleaned a phrase here and there . . . saw the horror-stricken faces of those who had seen, the placid, bovine expression of the two *gardiens*, more inured to such sights, and calmly taking notes by the light of the electric standard.

" But to think that I drove that rascally murderer in my cab, and put him down safe and sound not ten minutes ago . . ." came with the adjunct of a loud oath from the irate chauffeur.

" How did it all occur ? "

The *gardiens* tried to stem the flow of the driver's eloquence ; such details should first be given to the police—*voyons !* . . . But what were two fat *mouchards* against twenty stalwart idlers all determined to hear ? . . . and then there were the women . . . they were determined to know more.

Louisa bent her ear to listen. She was just outside the crowd—not a part of it—and there was really no morbid curiosity in her. It was only the call of the imagination which is irresistible on those occasions— a prosy, matter-of-fact, high-bred girl could not, just then, tear herself away from that cab and the tragedy which had been enacted therein in the mysterious darkness whilst the unconscious driver sped along, ignorant of the gruesome burden which he was dragging to its destination.

" *Voilà !* " he was saying with many ejaculations and expletives, and a volley of excited gestures. " Outside the Parc, near the theatre, two bourgeois hailed me, and one of them told me to draw up on the top of the Galerie St. Hubert, which I did. The same one— the one who had told me where to go, got out, clapped the door to and spoke a few words to his friend who had remained inside."

" What did he say ? "

" Oh ! I couldn't hear, and I didn't listen . . . but after that he told me to drive on to Boulevard Waterloo, No. 34, and here I am."

" You suspected nothing ? "

" Nothing, how should I ? Two bourgeois get into my cab. I see nothing . . . I hear nothing . . . one of them gets out and tells me to drive on further. . . . How should I think there's anything wrong ? "

" What was the other man like . . . the one who spoke to you . . . ? "

" *Ma foi !* I don't know. . . . It was raining so fast and pitch dark just outside the Parc lights . . . and he did seem to keep in the shadow . . . now I come to think of it . . . and his cap—he wore a cap—was pulled well over his face . . . and the collar of his coat was up to his nose. It was raining so, I didn't really see him properly . . . I saw the other one better . . . the one who has been murdered. . . ."

But the rotund *gardiens* had had enough of this.

Moreover, they would hear all about it at full length presently; as for the crowd . . . it had no business to know too much.

They hustled the excited driver back on to his box, and themselves got into the cab beside It . . . the dead man, stabbed in the neck from ear to ear . . . the wound quite small as if it had been done with a skewer.

The *gardiens* ordered the chauffeur to drive to the Commissariat, and Louisa turned away with a slight shiver down her spine and her throat choked with the horror of what she had only guessed.

CHAPTER II

YOU don't suppose for a moment, I hope, that a girl like Louisa would allow her mind to dwell on such horrors. Mysterious crimes in strange cities, and in London too for the matter of that—are alas! of far too frequent occurrence to be quite as startling as they should be.

A day or two later Louisa Harris and her aunt, Lady Ryder, crossed over to England. They had spent five weeks in Italy and one in Brussels, not with a view to dreaming over the beauties of the Italian Lakes, or over the art treasures collected in the museums of Brussels, but because Lady Ryder had had a bronchial catarrh which she could not shake off, and so her doctor had ordered her a thorough change. Bellaggio was selected, and Louisa accompanied her. They stayed at the best hotels both in Bellaggio and in Brussels, where Lady Ryder had several friends whom she wished to visit before she went home.

Nothing whatever happened that should not have happened ; everything was orderly and well managed ; the courier and the maid saw to tickets and to luggage, to hotel rooms and sleeping compartments. It was obviously their mission in life to see that nothing untoward or unexpected happened—but only the obvious.

It was clearly not their fault that Miss Harris had seen a cab in which an unknown man happened to have been murdered.

Louisa, with a view to preventing her aunt from going to sleep after dinner and thereby spoiling her night's rest, had told her of the incident which she had witnessed in the Boulevard Waterloo, and Lady Ryder was genuinely shocked. She vaguely felt that her niece had done something unladylike and odd, which was so unlike Louisa.

The latter had amused herself by scanning a number of English papers in order to find out what was said in London about that strange crime, which she had almost witnessed—the man stabbed through the neck, from ear to ear, and the wound so small it might have been done with a skewer. But with characteristic indifference London paid but little heed to the mysterious dramas of a sister city. A brief account of the gruesome discovery . . . a figurative shrug of the shoulders as to the incompetence of the Belgian police, who held neither a clue to the perpetrator of the crime nor to the identity of the victim. . . . Just a stranger—an idler. Brussels was full of strangers just now. His nationality ? Who knows ? His individuality ? . . . there seemed no one to care. The police were active, no doubt, but so far they had discovered nothing.

Two men ! The murderer and the murdered engulfed in that great whirlpool known as humanity, small units of no importance, since no one seemed to care. Interesting to the detective whose duty it was to track the crime to its perpetrator. Interesting to the reporter who could fill a column with accounts of depositions, of questionings, of examinations. Interesting to the after-dinner talker who could expatiate over the moral lessons to be drawn from the conception of such a crime.

But the murdered man goes to his grave unknown ; and the murderer wanders Cain-like on the face of the earth . . . as mysterious, as unknown, as silent as his victim.

CHAPTER III

EVERYTHING went on just as convention—whose mouthpiece for the moment happened to be Lady Ryder—desired, just as Louisa surmised that everything would : the letters of congratulation, the stately visits from and to Lord Radclyffe—Luke's uncle—the magnificent diamond tiara from the latter, the rope of pearls from Luke, the silver salvers and inkstands, and enamel parasol handles from everybody who was anybody in London society.

Louisa's portrait and that of Luke hastily and cheaply reproduced in the halfpenny dailies, so that she looked like a white negress with a cast in her eye, and he like the mutilated hero of " *L'homme qui rit*," the more elegant half-tone blocks in the sixpenny weeklies under the popular, if somewhat hackneyed heading of " The Earl of Radclyffe's heir and his future bride, Miss Louisa Harris," it was all there, just as it had been for hundreds of other girls and hundreds of other young men before Louisa had discovered that there was only one man in the whole wide world, and that beyond the land of diamond tiaras and of society weddings, there was a fairy universe, immense and illimitable, whereon the sun of happiness never set, and whither no one dared venture alone, only hand in hand with that other being, the future mate, the pupil and teacher of love, the only one that mattered.

And the wedding was to be in four weeks from this day. The invitations were not out yet, for Louisa— closely pressed by Luke—had only just made up her mind half an hour ago about the date. Strangely enough she had been in no hurry for the wedding day to come. Luke had been so anxious, so crestfallen when she put him off with vague promises, that she herself could not account for this strange reticence within her . . . so unworthy a level-headed, conventional woman of the world.

But the outer lobby of the fairy universe was surpassingly beautiful, and though the golden gates to the inner halls beyond were ajar, and would yield to the slightest pressure of Louisa's slender fingers, yet she was glad to tarry awhile longer. Were they not hand in hand ? What mattered waiting, since eternity called beyond those golden gates ?

This morning, however, convention—still voiced by Lady Ryder—was more vigorous than was consistent with outward peace. Louisa, worried by aunt, and with the memory of Luke's expression of misery and disappointment when last night she had again refused to fix the wedding day, chided herself for her silly fancies, and at eleven o'clock set out for a stroll in Battersea Park, her mind made up, her unwonted fit of sentimentality smothered by the louder voice of common sense.

c

She and Luke always took their walks abroad in Battersea Park. In the morning hours they were free there from perpetual meetings with undesired company—all outside company being undesirable in the lobby of the fairy universe. Louisa had promised to meet Luke in the tropical garden at half-past eleven. She was always punctual and he always before his time ; she smart and business-like in her neat tailor-made gown and close hat which defied wind and rain, he always a little shamefaced when he took her neatly gloved hand in his, as most English young men are apt to be when sentiment for the first time happens to overmaster them.

To-day she saw him coming towards her just the same as on other days. He walked just as briskly and held himself as erect as he always did, but the moment that he was near enough for her to see his face she knew that there was something very wrong in the world and with him. Some one from the world of eternity beyond had seen fit to push the golden gates closer together, so that now they would not yield quite so easily to the soft pressure of a woman's hand.

" What is it, Luke ? " she asked very quietly, as soon as her fingers rested safely between his.

" What is what ? " he rejoined foolishly and speaking like a child would, and with a forced, almost inane-looking smile on his lips.

" What has happened ? " she reiterated more impatiently.

"Nothing," he replied, "that need worry you, I think. Shall we sit down here ? You won't catch cold ? " And he indicated a seat well sheltered against the cold breeze and the impertinent gaze of the passers-by.

"I never catch cold," said Louisa, smiling in spite of herself at Luke's funny, awkward ways. "But we won't sit down. Let us stroll up and down, shall we ? You can talk better then, and tell me all about it."

"There's not much to tell at present. And no occasion to worry."

"There's nothing that worries me so much as your shilly-shallying, Luke, or the thought that you are making futile endeavours to keep something from me," she retorted almost irritably this time, for strangely enough her nerves—she never knew before this that she had any—were slightly on the jar this morning.

"I don't want to shilly-shally, little girl," he replied gently, "nor to keep anything from you. There, will you put your hand on my arm. 'Arry and 'Arriet, eh ? . . . Well ! never mind. . . . There's no one to see."

He took her hand—that neatly-gloved small hand of hers, and put it under his arm. For one moment it seemed as if he would kiss that tiny and tantalizing place just below the thumb where the pink palm shows in the opening of the glove. Luke was not a demonstrative lover, he was shy and English and abrupt, but this morning—was it the breath of spring in the air, the scent of the Roman hyacinths in that bed over there, or merely the shadow of a tiny cloud on the uniform blue of his life's horizon that gave a certain rugged softness to his touch, as his hand lingered over that neat glove which nestled securely in among the folds of his coat sleeve ?

"Now," she said simply.

"Have you," he asked with abrupt irrelevance, "read your paper all through this morning?"

"Not all through. Only the important headlines."

"And you saw nothing about a claim to a peerage?"

"Nothing."

"Well! that's all about it. A man has sprung up from nowhere in particular, who claims to be my uncle Arthur's son, and therefore heir-presumptive to the title and all."

Luke heaved a deep sigh, as if with this brief if ungrammatical statement his own heart had been unburdened of a tiresome load.

"Your uncle Arthur?" she repeated, somewhat bewildered.

"Yes. You never knew him, did you?"

"No," she said, "I never knew him, though as a baby I must have seen him. I was only three, I think, when he died. But I never heard that he had been married. I am sure father never knew."

"Nor did I, nor did Uncle Rad, nor any of us. The whole thing is either a thunderbolt or a . . . an imposture."

"Tell me," she said, "a little more clearly, Luke dear, will you? I am feeling quite muddled." And now it was she who led the way to the isolated seat beneath that group of silver birch, whose baby leaves trembled beneath the rough kiss of the cool April breeze.

They sat down together, and on the gravelled path in front of them a robin hopped half shyly, half im-

pertinently about and gazed with tiny inquisitive
eyes on the doings of these big folk. All round them
the twitter of bird throats filled the air with its magic,
its hymn to the reawakened earth, and drowned in
this pleasing solitude the distant sounds of the busy
city that seemed so far away from this secluded nook
inhabited by birds and flowers, and by two dwellers
in Fata Morgana's land.

"Tell me firstly," said Louisa, in her most prosy,
most matter-of-fact tone of voice, "all that is known
about your uncle Arthur."

"Well! up to now, I individually knew very little
about him. He was the next eldest brother to Uncle
Rad, and my father was the youngest of all. When
Uncle Rad succeeded to the title, Arthur was heir-
presumptive, of course. But, as you know, he died—
as was supposed unmarried—nineteen years ago, and
my poor dear father was killed in the hunting field
the following year. I was a mere kid then and the
others were babies—orphans the lot of us. My mother
died when Edith was born. Uncle Rad was said to be
a confirmed bachelor. He took us all to live with him.
. . . And was father, mother, elder brother, elder
sister to us all. Bless him. . . ."

Luke paused abruptly, and Louisa too was silent.
Only the song of a thrush soaring upwards to the skies
called for that blessing which neither of them at the
moment could adequately evoke.

"Yes!" said Louisa at last, "I knew all that."

Lord Radclyffe and his people were all of the same
world as herself. She knew all about the present man's

touching affection for the children of his youngest brother, but more especially for Luke, on whom he bestowed an amount of love and tender care which would have shamed many a father by its unselfish intensity. That affection was a beautiful trait in an otherwise not very lovable character.

"I dare say," resumed Luke after a little while, "that I have been badly brought up. I mean in this way, that if . . . if the whole story is true . . . if Uncle Arthur did marry and did have a son, then I should have to go and shift for myself and for Jim and Frank and Edith. . . . Of course, Uncle Rad would do what he could for us, but I should no longer be his heir . . . and we couldn't go on living at Grosvenor Square and . . ."

"Aren't you rambling on a little too fast, dear ? " said Louisa gently, whilst she beamed with an almost motherly smile—the smile that a woman wears when she means to pacify and to comfort—on the troubled face of the young man.

"Of course I am," he replied more calmly, "but I can't help it. . . . For some days now I've had a sort of feeling that something was going to happen . . . that . . . well ! that things weren't going to go right. And this morning when I got up, I made up my mind that I would tell you."

"When did you hear first, and from whom ? "

"The first thing we heard was last autumn. There came a letter from abroad for Uncle Rad. It hadn't the private mark on it, so Mr. Warren opened it along with the rest of the correspondence. He showed it to

me. The letter was signed Philip de Mountford,
and began ' My dear uncle.' I couldn't make head or
tail of it ; I thought it all twaddle. . . . You've no
idea what sort of letters Uncle Rad gets sometimes
from every kind of lunatic or scoundrel you can think
of, who wants to get something out of him. Well !—
this letter at first looked to me the same sort of thing.
. . . I had never heard of any one who had the right
to say ' dear uncle ' to Uncle Rad . . . but it had a
lot in it about blood being thicker than water and all
the rest of it, with a kind of request for justice and talk
about the cruelty of Fate. . . . The writer, however,
asserted positively that he was the only and legitimate
son of Mr. Arthur de Mountford, who—this he pro-
fessed to have only heard recently—was own brother
to the Earl of Radclyffe. The story which he went on
to relate at full length was queer enough in all conscience. I remember every word of it, for it seemed
to get right away into my brain, then and there, as if
something was being hammered or screwed straight
into one of the cells of my memory never really to
come out again."

   " And yet when . . . when we were first engaged,"
rejoined Louisa quietly, " you never told me anything
about it."

   " I'll tell you directly how that was. I remembered
and then forgot—if you know what I mean—and now
it has all come back. At the time I thought the letter
of this man who called himself Philip de Mountford
nothing but humbug—so did Mr. Warren, and yet he
and I talked it over and discussed it between us for

ever so long. It all sounded so strange. Uncle Arthur
—so this man said who called himself Philip de Mountford—had married in Martinique a half-caste girl
named Adeline Petit, who was this same Philip's
mother. He declares that he has all the papers—
marriage certificates or whatever they are called—to
prove every word he says. He did not want to trouble
his uncle much, only now that his mother was dead,
he felt all alone in the world and longed for the companionship and affection of his own kith and kin. All
he wanted, he said, was friendship. Then he went on
to say that, of course, he did not expect his lordship to
take his word for all this, he only asked for an opportunity to show his dear uncle all the papers and other
proofs which he held that he was in real and sober
truth the only and legitimate son of Mr. Arthur de
Mountford, own brother to his lordship."

"How old is this man—this Philip de Mountford—
supposed to be ? "

"Well, he said in that first letter that the marriage
took place in the parish church of St. Pierre in Martinique on the 28th of August, 1881. That he himself
was born the following year, and christened in the same
church under the name of Philip Arthur, and registered
as the son of Mr. Arthur Collingwood de Mountford
of Ford's Mount, in the county of Northampton,
England, and of Adeline de Mountford, *née* Petit, his
wife."

"Twenty-four years ago," said Louisa thoughtfully,
"and he only claims kinship with Lord Radclyffe
now. . . ."

"That's just," rejoined Luke, "where the curious part of the story comes in. This Philip de Mountford—I don't know how else to call him—said in his first letter that his mother never knew that Mr. Arthur de Mountford was anything more than a private English gentleman travelling either for profit or pleasure, but in any case not possessed of either wealth or social position. Between you and me, dear, I suppose that this Adeline Petit was just a half-caste girl, without much knowledge of what goes on in the world, and why she should have married Uncle Arthur I can't think . . ."

"If she did marry him, you mean. . . ."

"If she did marry him, as you say," said Luke with a singular want of conviction, which Louisa was not slow to remark.

"You think that this young man's story is true, then?"

"I don't know what to think, and that's the truth."

"Tell me more," added Louisa simply.

"Well, this Philip's story goes on to say that his father—Uncle Arthur—apparently soon tired of his exotic wife, for it seems that two years after the marriage he left Martinique and never returned to it to the day of his death."

"Pardon," said Louisa in her prim little way, "my interrupting you; but have any of you—Lord Radclyffe, I mean, or any of your friends—any recollection of your uncle Arthur living at Martinique for a while? Two years seems a long time. . . ."

"As a matter of fact, Uncle Arthur was a bit of a wastrel, you know. He never would study for anything. He passed into the navy—very well, too, I believe—but he threw it all up almost as soon as he got his commission, and started roaming about the world. I do know for a fact that once his people had no news of him for about three or four years, and then he turned up one fine day as if he had only been absent for a week's shooting."

" When was that ? "

" I can't tell you exactly. I was only a tiny kid at the time, not more than three years old I should say. Yes, I do remember, now I come to think of it, that Uncle Arthur was home the Christmas after my third birthday. I have a distinct recollection of my dad telling me that Uncle Arthur was one of my presents from Father Christmas, and of my thinking what a rotten present it was. Later on in the nursery all of us children were rather frightened of him, and we used to have great discussions as to where this uncle came from. The Christmas present theory was soon exploded, because of some difficulty about Uncle Arthur not having been actually found in a stocking, and his being too big anyway to be hidden in one, so we fell back on Jim's suggestion that he was the man in the moon come down for a holiday."

" You," she said, " had your third birthday in 1883."

" Yes."

" That was the year, then, that your uncle Arthur came home from his wanderings about the world, during which he had never given any news of himself or his doings to any member of his family."

" By Jove ! Loo, what a splendid examining

magistrate you'd make ! " was Luke's unsophisticated comment on Louisa's last remark.

But she frowned a little at this show of levity, and continued quietly :

" And your uncle, according to this so-called Philip de Mountford, was married in 1881 in Martinique, his son was born in 1882, and he left Martinique in 1883 never to return."

" Hang it all, Loo ! " exclaimed the young man almost roughly, " that is all surmise."

" I know it is, dear, I was only thinking."

" Thinking what ? "

" That it all tallies so very exactly, and that this . . . this Philip de Mountford seems in any case to know a great deal about your uncle Arthur, and his movements in the past."

" There's no doubt of that ; and . . ."

Luke paused a moment, and a curious blush spread over his face. The Englishman's inborn dislike to talk of certain subjects to his women-folk had got hold of him, and he did not know how to proceed.

As usual in such cases, the woman—unmoved and business-like—put an end to his access of shyness.

" The matter is—or may be—too serious, dear, for you to keep any of your thoughts back from me at this juncture."

" What I meant was," he said abruptly, " that this Philip might quite well be Uncle Arthur's son, you know, but it doesn't follow that he has any right to call himself Philip de Mountford, or to think that he is Uncle Rad's presumptive heir."

" That will, of course, depend on his proofs—his papers and so on . . ." she assented calmly. " Has any one seen them ? "

" At the time—it was some time last November—that he first wrote to Uncle Rad, he had all his papers by him. He wrote from St. Vincent—have I told you that ? "

" No."

" Well ! it was from St. Vincent that he wrote. He had left Martinique, I understand, in 1902, when St. Pierre, if you remember, was totally destroyed by volcanic eruption. It seems that when Uncle Arthur left the French colony for good, he lodged quite a comfortable sum in the local bank at St. Pierre in the name of Mrs. de Mountford. Of course, he had no intention of ever going back there, and anyhow he never did, for he died about three years later. The lady went on living her own life quite happily. Apparently she did not hanker much after her faithless husband. I suppose that she never imagined for a moment that he meant to stick to her, and she certainly never bothered her head as to what his connections or friends over in England might be. Amongst her own kith and kin, the half-caste population of a French settlement, she was considered very well off, almost rich. After a very few years of grass-widowhood, she married again, without much scruple or compunction, which proves that she never thought that her English husband would come back to her. And then came the catastrophe."

" What catastrophe ? "

" The destruction of St. Pierre. You remember the awful accounts of it. The whole town was destroyed. Every building in the place—the local bank, the church, the presbytery, the post-office—were burnt to the ground ; everything was devastated for miles around. And thousands perished, of course."

" I remember."

" Mrs. de Mountford and her son Philip were amongst the very few who escaped. Their cottage was burned to the ground, but she, with all a Frenchwoman's sense of respect for papers and marks of identification, fought her way back into the house, even when it was tottering above her head, in order to rescue those things which she valued more than her life, the proofs that she was a respectable married woman and that Philip was her lawfully begotten son. Her second husband—I think from reading between the lines that he was a native or at best a half-caste—was one of the many who perished. But Mrs. de Mountford and Philip managed to reach the coast unhurt and to put out to sea in an open boat. They were picked up by a fishing smack from Marie Galante and landed there. It is a small island—French settlement, of course—off Guadeloupe. They had little or no money, and how they lived I don't know, but they stayed in Marie Galante for some time. Then the mother died, and Philip made his way somehow or other to Roseau in Dominica, and thence to St. Vincent."

" When was that ? "

" Last year, I suppose."

" And," she said, meditating on all that she had

heard, "it was in St. Vincent that he first realized
who he was . . . or might be."

"Well! in a British colony it was bound to happen.
Whether somebody put him up to it out there, or
whether he merely sucked the information in from
nowhere in particular, I can't say; certain it is
that he did soon discover that the name he bore was
one of the best-known in England, and that his father
must, as a matter of fact, have been own brother to the
Earl of Radclyffe. So he wrote to Uncle Rad."

Louisa was silent. She was absorbed in thought,
and for the moment Luke had come to the end of what
he had to say—or rather of what he meant to say just
now. That there was more to come, Louisa well knew.
Commonplace women have a way of intuitively getting
at the bottom of the thoughts of people for whom they
care. Louisa guessed that beneath Luke's levity and
his schoolboyish slang—which grew more apparent
as the young man drew to the end of his narrative—
that beneath his outward flippancy there lay a deep
substratum of puzzlement and anxiety.

The story as told by Luke sounded crude enough,
almost melodramatic—right out of the commonplace
range of Louisa's usual everyday life. Whilst she sat
listening to this exotic tale of secret and incongruous
marriage and of those earthquakes and volcanic
eruptions which had seemed so remote when she had
read about them nine years ago in the newspapers, she
almost thought that she must be dreaming, that she
would wake up presently in her bed at the Langham
Hotel where she was staying with aunt, and that she

would then dress and have her breakfast and go out to meet Luke, and tell him all about the idiotic dream she had had about an unknown heir to the Earldom of Radclyffe, who was a nigger—or almost so—and was born in a country where there were volcanoes and earthquakes.

How far removed from her at this moment did aunt seem, and father, and the twins. Surely they could not be of the same world as this exotic pretender to Uncle Radclyffe's affection, and to Luke's hitherto undisputed rights. And as father and aunt, and Mabel and Chris were very much alive and very real, then this so-called Philip de Mountford must be a creature of dreams.

" Or else an impostor."

She had said this aloud, thus breaking in on her own thoughts and his.   A feeling of restlessness seized her now. She was cold too, for the April breeze was biting and had searched out the back of her neck underneath the sable stole and caused her to shiver in the spring sunshine.

" Let us walk," she said, " a little . . . shall we ? "

CHAPTER IV

THEY walked up the gravel walk under the chest-nut trees, whereon the leafbuds, luscious-looking, with their young green surface delicately tinged with pink, looked over-ready to burst into fan-shaped full-ness of glory. The well-kept paths, the orderly flower beds and smoothly trimmed lawns looked all so simple, so obvious beside the strange problem which fate had propounded to these two young people walking up and down side by side . . . and with just a certain distance between them as if that problem was keeping them apart.

And that intangible reality stood between them, causing in Luke a vague sense of shame-facedness, as if he were guilty towards Louisa . . . and in her a feeling of irritation against the whole world around her, for having allowed this monstrous thing to happen —this vague shadow on life's pathway, on the life of the only man who mattered.

People passed them as they walked—the curious, the indifferent ; men with bowler hats pulled over frowning brows, boys with caps carelessly worn at the back of their heads, girls with numbed fingers thrust in worn gloves, tip-tilted noses blue with cold, thin, ill-fitting clothes scarce shielding attenuated shoulders against the keen spring blast.

Just the humdrum, everyday crowd of London : the fighters, the workers, toiling against heavy odds of feeble health, insufficient food, scanty clothing, the poor that no one bothers about, less interesting than the unemployed labourers, less picturesque, less noisy . . . they passed and had no time to heed the elegantly clad figure wrapped in costly furs, or the young man in perfectly tailored coat, who was even now preparing himself for a fight with destiny, beside which the daily struggle for halfpence would be but a mere skirmish.

Instinctively they knew—these two—the society girl and the easy-going, wealthy man—that it was reality with which they would have to deal. That instinct comes with the breath of Fate : a warning that her decrees are serious, not to be lightly set aside but pondered over, that her materialized breath would not be a phantom or a thing to be derided.

Truth or imposture ? Which ?

Neither the man nor the girl knew as yet, but Reality—whatever else it was.

They walked on for a while in silence. Another instinct—the conventional one—had warned them that their stay in the Park had been unduly prolonged ; there were social duties to attend to, calls to make, luncheon with Lord Radclyffe at Grosvenor Square.

So they both by tacit consent turned their steps back towards the town.

A man passed them from behind, walking quicker than they did. As he passed, he looked at them both

D

intently, as if desirous of arresting their attention. Of course, he succeeded, for his look was almost compelling. Louisa was the first to turn towards him, then Luke did likewise ; and the passer-by raised his hat respectfully with a slight inclination of head and shoulders that suggested foreign upbringing.

Once more convention stepped in, and Luke mechanically returned the salute.

" Who was that ? " asked Louisa, when the passer-by was out of earshot.

" I don't know," replied Luke. " I thought it was some one you knew. He bowed to you."

" No ! " she said, " to you, I think. Funny you should not know him."

But silence once broken, constraint fled with it. She drew nearer to Luke and once more her hand sought his coat sleeve, with a light pressure quickly withdrawn.

" Now, Luke," she said abruptly, reverting to the subject, " how do you stand in all this ? "

" I ? "

" Yes. What does Lord Radclyffe say ? "

" He laughs the whole thing to scorn, and declares that the man is an impudent liar."

" He saw," she asked, " the first letter ? The one that came from St. Vincent ? "

" Yes. Mr. Warren and I did not think we ought to keep it from him."

" Of course not," she assented. " Then he said that the letter was a tissue of lies ? "

" From beginning to end."

"He refused," she insisted, "to believe in the marriage of your uncle Arthur out there in Martinique ? "

"He didn't go into details. He just said that the whole letter was an impudent attempt at blackmail."

"And since then ? "

"He has never spoken about it."

"Until to-day ? " she asked.

"He hasn't spoken," he replied, insisting on the word, "even to-day. Two or three times I think letters came for him in the same handwriting. Mr. Warren did not open them, of course, and took them straight to Uncle Rad. They always bore foreign postmarks, some from one place, some from another, but Uncle Rad never referred to them after he had read them, nor did he instruct Mr. Warren to reply. Then the letters ceased, and I began to forget the whole business. I didn't tell you, because Uncle Rad told me not to talk about the whole thing. It was beneath contempt, he said, and he didn't want the tittle-tattle to get about."

"Then," she asked, "what happened ? "

"A week ago a letter came with a London postmark on it. The address and letter were both typewritten, and the latter covered four sheets of paper, and was signed Philip de Mountford. Bar the actual story of the marriage and all that, the letter was almost identical to the first one which came from St. Vincent. Mr. Warren had opened it, for it looked like a business one, and he waited for me in his office to ask my opinion about it. Of course, we had to give it to Uncle

Rad. It had all the old phrases in it about blood being thicker than water, and about longing for friendship and companionship and all that. There was no hint of threats or demand for money or anything like that."

" Of course not," she said, " whilst Lord Radclyffe is alive, the young man has no claim."

" Only," he rejoined, " that of kinship."

" Lord Radclyffe need not do anything for him."

Already there was a note of hostility in Louisa's even voice. The commonplace woman was donning armour against the man who talked of usurping the loved one's privileges.

" I wish," he insisted, " that I could have got the letter from Uncle Rad to show you. It was so simple and so sensible. All he asks is just to see Uncle Rad personally, to feel that he has kindred in the world. He knows—he says—that beyond goodwill, he has no claim now. As a matter of fact he has something more substantial than that, for Uncle Arthur had a little personal property about £15,000 which he left to us four children—Jim and Frank and Edie and me—and which I for one wouldn't touch if I knew for certain that this Philip was his son."

" But," she argued, " you say that the man does not speak of money."

She hated the talk about money, for she had all that contempt for it which women have who have never felt the want of it. It would have been so simple if the intruder had only wanted money. She would not have cared a little bit if Luke had none, or was not going to have any. It was his right which she would not hear of being questioned. His right in Lord Radclyffe's affections, in his household, and also his rights in the future when Lord Radclyffe would be gone.

"You are sure," she insisted, "that he does not want money ? "

"I don't think," he replied, "that he does, just now. He seems to have a little ; he must have had a little, since he came over from St. Vincent and is staying at a moderately good hotel in London. No. He wants to see Uncle Rad, because he thinks that if Uncle Rad saw him, blood would cry out in response. It appears that now he has lodged all his papers of identification with a London lawyer—a very good firm, mind you—and he wants Uncle Rad's solicitor to see all the papers and to examine them. That seems fair to me. Doesn't it to you ? "

" Very fair indeed," she mused.

"What I mean," he added with great conviction, " is that if those papers weren't all right and that, he wouldn't be so anxious for Uncle Rad's solicitors to have a look at them, would he ? "

" No."

And after a while she reiterated more emphatically—

" Certainly not."

" I must say," he concluded, " that the whole thing simply beats me."

" But what does Lord Radclyffe say now ? "

" Nothing."

" How do you mean, nothing ? "

"Just what I say. He won't talk about the thing. He won't discuss it. He won't answer any question which I put to him. 'My dear boy, the man is a palpable impudent impostor, a blackmailer.' And that's all I can get out of him."

"He won't see the man?"

"Won't hear of it."

"And won't he let his solicitor—Mr. Dobson, isn't it?—meet the other lawyer?"

"He says he wouldn't dream of wasting old Dobson's time."

"Then what's going to happen?"

"I don't see," he said, "what is going to happen."

"Won't you have a talk about it with old Mr. Dobson, and see what he says?"

"I can't very well do that. Strictly speaking, it's none of my business . . . as yet. I couldn't consult Uncle Rad's lawyers, without Uncle Rad's consent."

"Another one, then."

He shrugged his shoulders, obviously undecided what to do. He had thought very little about himself or his future in all this; his thoughts had dwelt mostly on Lord Radclyffe—father, mother, brother, sister to them all. Bless him! . . . and then he had thought of her. He looked round him with eyes that scarcely saw, for they really were turned inwards to his own simple soul, and to his loving heart. Right up against that very simplicity of soul, a duty stood clear and uncompromising, a duty yet to be performed, the real aim and end of all that he had said so far. But he did not know how best to perform such a duty.

Simple souls—unlike the complex physiological phenomena of modern times—are apt to be selfless, to think more of the feelings of others than of analysing their own various sensations, and Luke knew that what he considered his duty would not be quite so obvious to Louisa, and that by fulfilling it he would give her pain.

CHAPTER V

BUT it was she who gave him an opening.

"Luke," she said, "it's all very well, but the matter does concern you in a way, far more so, in fact, than it does Lord Radclyffe. Nothing can make any difference to Lord Radclyffe, but if what this young man asserts is all true, then it will make a world of difference to you."

"I know that—that's just the trouble."

"You were thinking of yourself?"

"No. I was thinking of you?"

"Of me?"

"Yes," he said now very abruptly, quite roughly and crudely, not choosing his words lest they helped to betray what he felt, and all that he felt. "If what this man says is true, then I am a penniless nonentity whom you are not going to marry."

"You are talking nonsense, Luke, and you know it," was all that she said. And she said it very quietly, very decisively. He was talking nonsense, of course, for whatever happened or didn't happen, there was one thing in the world that was absolutely, undeniably impossible, and that was that she should not marry Luke.

Whilst she, Louisa Harris, plain, uninteresting, commonplace Louisa Harris was of this world, her marriage with Luke must be. People—in this present-day, matter-of-fact world—didn't have their hearts wrenched out of them, they were not made to suffer impossible and unendurable tortures; then why should she—Louisa Harris—be threatened with such a cataclysm ?

"I am not," he was saying rather tonelessly, "talking nonsense, Loo. I have thought all that over. It's over eight days since that letter came ; eight times twenty-four hours since I seemed in a way to see all my future through a thick black cloud, and I've had time to think. I saw you too through that thick black cloud . . . I saw you just as you are, exquisite, beautiful, like a jewel that should for ever remain in a perfect setting. I . . . "

He broke off abruptly, and—mechanically—his hand went up to his forehead and eyes. Where was he ? He gave a sudden, quaint laugh.

"What a drivelling fool you must think me, Loo."

She looked straight at him : pure of soul, simple of heart, with a passion of tenderness and self-abnegation as yet dormant beneath the outer crust of a conventional education, and of commonplace surroundings, but with the passion there, nevertheless. And it was expressed in the sudden, strange luminosity of her eyes—I would not have you think that they were tears—as they met and held his own.

They didn't say anything more just then. People of their type and class in England do not say much, you know, under such circumstances. They have been drilled not to. Drilled and drilled from childhood upwards, from the time when, after a fall and a cut lip or broken tooth, the tears have to be held back, lest the words " snivel " or " cry-baby " be mentioned. But quietude does not necessarily mean freedom from pain. A cut lip hurts worse when it is not wetted with tears.

It was only the shadow that was hovering over these two as yet : nothing really tangible. And the shadow was not between them. She would not let it come between them. If it covered him, it should wrap her too. The commonplace woman had no fear of its descent, only as far as it affected him.

"Nothing," she said after a while, "could make a difference to our marriage, Luke. Except, of course, if you ceased to care."

" Or you, Loo," he suggested meekly.

" Do you think," she retorted, " that I should ? Just because you had no money ? "

" Not," he owned, " because of that. But I should be such a nonentity. I have no real profession, and there are the others . . . Jim in the Blues costs a fearful lot a year, and Frank in the diplomatic service must have his promised allowance . . . I have read for the Bar, but beyond that what am I ? . . . '

" Your uncle's right hand," she retorted firmly, " his agent, his secretary, his factotum all rolled into one. You manage his estates, his charities, his correspondence. . . . You write his speeches and control his household. . . . Lord Radclyffe—every one says it in London—would not be himself at all without Luke de Mountford behind him. . . ."

" That's not what I mean, Loo."

" What do you mean ? "

" I mean that . . ."

He paused a moment, then added with seeming irrelevance—

" We all know that Uncle Rad is a curious kind of man. . . . If this story turns out to be true, he would still say nothing . . . but he would fret and fret . . . and worry himself into his grave. . . ."

" The story," she argued obstinately, " will not turn out to be true . . . It's not like you, Luke, to jump at conclusions, or to be afraid of a nightmare."

" I am not afraid," he rejoined simply. " But I must look at possibilities. Yes, dear," he continued more forcibly, " it is possible that this story is true. . . . No good saying that it is impossible . . . improbable, if you like, but not impossible. Look at it how you like, you must admit that it is not impossible. Uncle Arthur may have married in Martinique . . . he was out there in 1881 . . . he may have had a son. . . . His telling no one about his marriage is not to be wondered at. . . . He was always reticent and queer about his own affairs. . . . This Philip may possibly be Uncle Rad's sole and rightful heir . . . and I may possibly be a beggar."

She uttered an exclamation of incredulity. Luke ! . . . a beggar ! . . . Luke ! the one man in all the world, different to every other man ! . . . Luke ousted by that stranger upstart ! . . .

God had too much sense of humour to allow so ridiculous a Fate to work her silly caprice.

"And," she said with scorn, "because of all these absurd possibilities you talk of breaking off your engagement to me. . . . Do you care so little as all that, Luke?"

He did not reply, but continued to walk beside her, just a yard or so apart from her, turning his steps in the direction of the gates, towards the Albert Bridge, their nearest way home. She—meekly now, for already she was sorry—turned to look at him. Something in his attitude, the stoop of the shoulders, usually so square and erect, the hands curiously clasped behind his back, told her that her shaft—very thoughtlessly aimed—had struck even deeper than it should.

"I am so sorry, dear," she said gently.

His look forgave her, even before the words were fully out of her mouth, but with characteristic reticence, he made no reply to her taunt. Strangely enough, she was satisfied that he should say nothing. The look, which did not reproach even whilst it tried to conceal the infinite depth of the wound so lightly dealt, had told her more than any words could do. Whatever Luke decided to do, it would be from a sense of moral obligation, that desire for doing the right thing—in the worldly sense of the term—which is inherent in Englishmen of a certain class. No sentiment save that of a conventional one of honour would be allowed to sway her destiny and his.

Conventionality—that same strained sense of honour and duty—decreed that under certain mundane

circumstances a man and woman should not mate.
Differences of ancestry, of parentage, of birth and of
country, divergence of taste, of faith, of belief . . . all
these matter not one jot. But let the man be beggared
and the woman rich, and convention steps in and says,
" It shall not be ! "

These two bowed to that decree : unconventional
in so far as that they both made the sacrifice out of the
intense purity of their sentiment to one another. They
made an absolutely worldly sacrifice for a wholly un-
worldly motive. Luke would as soon have thought of
seeing Louisa in a badly fitting serge frock, and paying
twopence for a two-mile ride in an omnibus, as he
would expect to see a diamond tiara packed in a
cardboard box : it would be unfair on the jeweller
who had made the tiara thus to subject it to rough
treatment ; and it would be equally unfair on the
Creator of Louisa to let her be buffeted about by the
cruder atoms of this world.

Louisa only thought of Luke, and that perhaps he
would feel happier in his mind if she allowed him to
make this temporary sacrifice.

There is such wonderful balm in self-imposed sacrifice !

" What," she asked simply, " do you want me to
say, Luke ? "

" Only that . . . that you won't give me up altogether unless . . ."

Here he checked himself abruptly. Was there ever
an Englishman born who could talk sentiment at
moments such as this ? Luke was no exception to

that rule. There was so much that he wanted to say to Louisa, and yet the very words literally choked him before he could contrive to utter them.

"Don't," she said quietly, "let us even refer to such things, Luke. I do not believe in this shadow . . . and I cannot even understand why you should worry about it . . . but whatever happens, I should never give you up. Never. We will put off fixing the day of our wedding—since we have made no announcement this won't matter at all; but I only agree to this because I think that it is what you would like. . . . I fancy that it would ease your mind. . . . As for breaking our engagement in the future—in case the worst happens—well, it shall not be with my consent, Luke, unless you really ceased to care."

They had reached the gate close to the bridge. Life pulsated all round them, the life of the big city, callous, noisy, and cruel. Omnibuses, cabs, heavy vans rattled incessantly past them. People jostled one another, hurrying and scurrying, pigmies and ants adding their tiny load of work, of care, of sorrow to the titanic edifice of this living world.

Louisa's last words remained unanswered. Luke had—by silence—said everything that there was to say. They stood on the pavement for a moment, and Luke hailed a passing taxi-cab.

At the corner opposite, an omnibus pulled up on its way westwards. A man stepped off the kerb ready to enter it. Louisa caught his eye, and he raised his hat— the man who had passed them in the Park just now.

CHAPTER VI

JUST A DISAGREEABLE OLD MAN

THE luncheons at Grosvenor Square were always rather dull and formal. But Louisa did not mind that very much. She was used to dull and formal affairs: they were part and parcel of her daily life. London society is full of it. The dull and formal dominate, the others—vulgar if more lively—were not worth cultivating.

Then, she almost liked Lord Radclyffe, because he was so fond of Luke. And even then " almost " was a big word. No one—except Luke—could really like the old man. He was very bad-tempered, very dictatorial, a perfect tyrant in his own household. His opinions no one dared contradict, no one cared to argue with him, and his advanced Tory views were so rabid that he almost made perverts from the cause, of all those whom he desired to convince.

And even these were few, for Lord Radclyffe had no friends and very few acquaintances. He had a strange and absolute dislike for his fellow-men. He did not like seeing people, he hated to exchange greetings, to talk or to mingle with any crowd that was purely on pleasure bent. He went up to the House and made speeches— political, philanthropic, economic speeches which Luke

prepared for him and which he spoke without enthusiasm or any desire to please. This he did not because
he liked it or took any interest in things political,
philanthropic, or economic, but only because he considered that a man in his position owed certain duties
to the State—duties which it would be cowardly to
shirk.

But he really cared nothing for the thoughts of
others, for their opinions, their joys or their sorrows.
He had schooled himself not to care, to call philanthropy
empty sentiment, politics senseless ambition, economics
grasping avarice.

His was a life entirely wrapped up in itself. In youth
he had been very shy : a shyness caused at first by a
serious defect of speech which, though cured in later
years, always left an unconquerable diffidence, an
almost morbid fear of ridicule in its train.

Because of this, I think, he had never been a sportsman—or rather never been an athlete, for he was
splendid with a gun and the finest revolver shot in
England, so I've been told, and an acknowledged
master of fence—but with bat, ball or racquet he was
invariably clumsy.

He had always hated to be laughed at, and therefore
had never gone through the rough mill of a tyro in
athletics or in games. Arthur, one of his brothers, had
been a blue at Oxford, the other one, James—you
remember James de Mountford ?—was the celebrated
cricketer; but he, the eldest, always seemed to remain
outside that magic circle of sport, the great ring of many
links which unites Englishmen one to another in a way

that no other conformity of tastes, of breeding, or of religion can ever do.

Because of this diffidence too, no doubt, he had never married. I was told once by an intimate friend of his, that old Rad—as he was universally called—had never mustered up sufficient courage to propose to any woman. And as he saw one by one the coveted matrimonial prizes—the pretty girls whom at different times he had admired sufficiently to desire for wife—snapped up by more enterprising wooers, his dour moroseness grew into positive chronic ill-humour.

He liked no one and no one liked him ; and during sixty years of life he had succeeded in eliminating from his entire being every feeling of sentiment—save one. He had to all appearances an absolutely callous heart ; he cared neither for dog nor horse—he ordered a splendid mare to be shot without the slightest compunction, after she had carried him in the hunting field and in the Park faithfully and beautifully for over eight years, just because she had shied at a motor-car and nearly thrown him. He was not cruel, you know, just callous in all respects save one : void of all sentiment—he called it sentimentality—save in his affection for Luke.

Luke had been—ever since he was a growing lad—the buffer in the establishment, between the irascible master and the many subordinates. From Mr. Warren —the highly paid and greatly snubbed secretary—down to the maids below stairs, one and all brought troubles, complaints, worries to Mr. Luke. No one dared approach his lordship. A word out of season

E

brought instant dismissal; and no one thought of leaving a place where, besides excellent wages, there was the pleasure of waiting on Mr. Luke.—Never Mr. de Mountford, you notice . . . always Mr. Luke. He had grown up amongst the household; Winston, the old coachman, had taught him to ride—Mary, now housekeeper, then a nurse, had bathed him in a wash-hand basin when he was less than eighteen inches long.

Therefore the atmosphere of the gloomy old house pleased Louisa Harris. With the perfect and unconscious selfishness of a woman in love, she gauged everything in life just as it affected Luke. She even contrived to like Lord Radclyffe. He trod on every one of her moral and spiritual corns, it is true; he had that lofty contempt for the entire feminine sex which pertains to the Oriental more than to the more civilized Western races; he combated her opinions, both religious and political, without any pretence at deference; he smoked very strong cigars in every room in the house, without the slightest regard for the feelings of his lady visitors; he did or left undone a great many other things which would tend to irritate and even to offend a woman accustomed to the conventional courtesies of daily social life; but when Luke entered a room where but a moment ago Lord Radclyffe had been venting his chronic ill-humour on an offending or innocent subordinate, the old man's dour face would become transfigured, irradiated with a look of pride and of joy at sight of the man on whom he had lavished all the affection of which his strong nature was capable.

Luke could do no wrong. Luke was always right He could argue with his lordship, contradict him, obtain anything he liked from him. Eternal contradictions of human nature : the childless man in perfect adoration before a brother's son, the callous, hard-hearted misanthrope soft as wax in the hands of one man.

CHAPTER VII

AND it was into this atmosphere of gloom and of purposeless misanthropy that Louisa Harris brought this morning the cheering sunshine of her own indomitable optimism.

She knew, of course, from the first that the subject which interested every one in the house more than any other subject could ever do was not to be mentioned in Lord Radclyffe's presence. But she was quite shrewd enough to see that dear old Luke—unsophisticated and none too acute an observer—had overestimated his uncle's indifference to the all-absorbing matter.

The old man's face—usually a mirror of contemptuous cynicism—looked, to the woman's keener insight, distinctly troubled, and his surly silence was even more profound than hitherto.

He hardly did more than bid Louisa a curt " How de do ? " when she entered, and then relapsed into moroseness wholly unbroken before luncheon was announced.

Jim—" in the Blues "—was there when she arrived, and Edie came in a few moments later, breathless and with hat awry and tawny hair flying in all directions, straight from a tussle with the dogs and the sharp east wind in the Park.

Evidently no secret had been made before these two of the strange events which had culminated this very morning in their brother's avowal to Louisa, and the postponement *sine die* of the wedding. But equally evidently these young creatures, absorbed in their own life, their own pursuits and amusements, were not inclined to look on the matter seriously.

Their sky had been so absolutely cloudless throughout their lives that it was impossible for them at the moment to realize that the dark shadow on the distant horizon might possibly conceal thunder in its filmy bosom.

Edie—just over twenty years of age and already satiated with the excitement of three London seasons, her mind saturated with novel-reading and on the look-out for some new sensations—was inclined to look on the affair as an exhilarating interlude between the Shrove Tuesday dance at Wessex House and the first Drawing-room in May. Jim—" in the Blues "—very eligible as a possible husband for the daughters of ambitious mammas, a trifle spoilt, a little slow of wit, and not a little self-satisfied—dismissed the whole incident as " tommy-rot."

When Louisa first greeted them, Edie had whispered excitedly—

" Has he told you ? "

And without waiting for a direct reply had continued with unabated eagerness—

" Awfully exciting, don't you think ? "

But Jim, with the elegant drawl peculiar to his kind, had suppressed further confidences by an authoritative—

"Awful rot, I call it, don't you? Luke is soft to worry about it."

Strangely enough, at luncheon it was Lord Radclyffe who brought up the subject-matter. Edie, with the tactlessness of youth, had asked a point-blank question—

"Well!" she said, "when is that wedding to be, and what are we bridesmaids going to wear? I warn you I won't have white—I hate a white wedding."

Then, as no answer came, she said impatiently—

"I wish you'd name the day, you two stupids. Awfully soft, I call it, hanging about like this."

Luke would have said something then, but Louisa interposed.

"It is all my fault, Edie," she said. "You know I want to take the twins out myself this season. I must give them a real good time before I marry."

"Bosh!" remarked Edith unceremoniously. "Mabel and Chris will have a far better time when you are married and can present them yourself. Tell them from me that it's no fun being 'out,' and the longer they put it off the better they'll enjoy themselves later on. Besides, Colonel Harris will take them about."

"Father hates sitting up late. . . ." hazarded Louisa, somewhat lamely.

"The truth of the matter is," here broke in Lord Radclyffe dryly, "that Luke has persuaded you to put off the wedding because of this d—d impostor who seems to have set you all off by the ears."

Edie laughed and said "Bosh!" Jim growled and murmured "Rot!"

Luke and Louisa were silent, the while Lord Radclyffe's closely-set dark, piercing eyes wandered from one young face to the other. Louisa, feeling uncomfortable beneath that none too amiable scrutiny, did not know what to say, but Luke quietly remarked after a while—

"You're right, uncle. It is my doing, but Loo agrees with me, and we are going to wait until this cloud is properly cleared up."

If any one else had spoken so clearly and decisively in direct contradiction to the old man's obvious wishes in the matter, the result would have been an outburst of ill-humour and probably a volley of invectives, not unmixed with more forcible language. But since it was Luke who had spoken—and Luke could do no wrong— Lord Radclyffe responded quite gently—

"My dear boy," he said, and it was really touching to hear the hard voice soften and linger on the endearing words, "I have told you once and for all that the story of this so-called Philip de Mountford is a fabrication from beginning to end. There is absolutely no reason for you to fret one single instant because of the lies a blackmailer chooses to trump up. As for your putting off your wedding one single hour because of this folly, why, it is positive nonsense. I should have thought you had more common sense . . . and Miss Harris too, for the matter of that."

Luke was silent for a moment or two, while Edie tossed her irresponsible head with the gesture of an absolute "I told you so." Jim muttered something behind his heavy cavalry moustache. Louisa, with head bent and fingers somewhat restless and fidgety, waited to hear what Luke would say.

"If only," he said, "you would consent, Uncle Rad, to let Mr. Dobson go through this man's papers."

"What were the good of wasting Mr. Dobson's time?" retorted Lord Radclyffe, with surprising good humour. "I know that the man is an impostor. I don't think it," he reiterated emphatically, "I know it."

"How ?"

Before the old man had time to reply, the butler—sober, solemn Parker—came in with a card on a salver, which he presented to his master. Lord Radclyffe took up the card, and grunted as he glanced at it. He always grunted when he was threatened with visitors.

"Why," he said gruffly, and he threw the card back on to the salver, "haven't you told Mr. Warren ? "

"Mr. Warren," said solemn Parker, "is out, my lord."

"Then ask Mr. Dobson to call another time."

"It's not Mr. Dobson hisself, my lord. But a young gentleman from his office."

"Then tell the young gentleman from the office that I haven't time to bother about him."

"Shall I see him, sir ? " asked Luke, ready to go.

"Certainly not," retorted the irascible old man.

"Stay where you are. You have got Miss Harris to entertain."

"The young gentleman," resumed Parker with respectful insistence, "said he wouldn't keep your lordship five minutes. He said he'd brought some papers for your lordship's signature."

"The Tower Farm lease, Uncle Rad," remarked Luke.

"I think, Mr. Luke," assented the butler, "that the young gentleman did mention the word lease."

"Why has that confounded Warren taken himself off just when I want him?" was Lord Radclyffe's gruff comment as he rose from the table.

"Let me go, sir," insisted Luke.

"No, hang it, boy, you can't sign my name—not yet, anyway . . . I am not yet a helpless imbecile. . . . Show the young man into the library, Parker. . . . I can't think why Dobson is always in such a con-founded hurry about leases . . . sending a fool of a clerk up at most inconvenient hours. . . ."

Still muttering half audibly, he walked to the library door, which Parker held open for him, and even this he did not do without surreptitiously taking hold of Luke's hand and giving it a friendly squeeze. For a moment it seemed as if Luke would follow him, despite contrary orders. He paused, undecided, standing in the middle of the room. Louisa's kind grey eyes following his slightest movement.

Jim stolidly pulled the cigar-box towards him, and Edie with chin resting in both hands looked sulky and generally out of sorts.

Parker—silent and correct of mien—had closed the library door behind his master, and now with noiseless tread he crossed the dining-room and opened the other door—the one that gave on the hall. Louisa instinctively turned her eyes from Luke and saw—standing in the middle of the hall—a young man in jacket suit and overcoat, who had looked up, with palpitating eagerness expressed in his face, the moment he caught sight of Parker.

It was the same man who had lifted his hat to Luke and to herself in Battersea Park this very morning. Luke saw him too, and apparently also recognized him.

"That's why he bowed to us, Luke . . . in the Park . . . you remember ? " she said as soon as the door had once more closed on Parker and the visitor

"Funny that you didn't know him . . ." she continued, since Luke had made no comment.

"I didn't," he remarked curtly.

"Didn't what ? "

"I did not, and do not know this man."

"Not Mr. Dobson's clerk ? "

Luke did not answer, but went out into the hall. Parker was standing beside the library door, which he had just closed, having introduced the visitor into his lordship's presence.

"Parker," said Luke abruptly, "what made you tell his lordship that that young gentleman came from Mr. Dobson ? "

The question had come so suddenly that Parker—

pompous, dignified Parker—was thrown off his balance, and the reply, which took some time in coming, sounded unconvincing.

" The young gentleman," he said slowly, " told me, Mr. Luke, that he came from Mr. Dobson."

" No, Parker," asserted Luke unhesitatingly, " he did nothing of the sort. He wanted to see his lordship and got you to help him concoct some lie whereby he could get what he wanted."

A greyish hue spread over Parker's pink and flabby countenance.

" Lord help me, Mr. Luke," he murmured tonelessly, " how did you know ? "

" I didn't," replied Luke curtly. " I guessed. Now I know."

" I didn't think I was doing no harm."

" No harm by introducing into his lordship's presence strangers who might be malefactors ? "

Already Luke, at Parker's first admission, had gone quickly to the library door. Here he paused, with his hand on the latch, uncertain if he should enter. The house was an old one, well-built and stout; from within came the even sound of a voice speaking quite quietly, but no isolated word could be distinguished. Parker was floundering in a quagmire of confused explanations.

" Malefactor, Mr. Luke ! " he argued; " that young man was no malefactor. He spoke so nicely. And he had plenty of money about him. I didn't see I was doing no harm. He wanted to see his lordship, and asked me to help him to it. . . ."

" And," queried Luke impatiently, " paid you to
help him, eh ? "

" I thought," replied the man, loftily ignoring the
suggestion, " that taking in one of Mr. Dobson's cards
that was lying in the tray could do no harm. I thought
it couldn't do no harm. The young gentleman said his
lordship would be very grateful to me when he found
out what I'd done."

" And how grateful was the young gentleman to you,
Parker ? "

" To the tune of a five-pound note, Mr. Luke."

" Then, as you have plenty of money in hand, you
can pack up your things and get out of this house
before I've time to tell his lordship."

" Mr. Luke . . . ."

" Don't argue. Do as I tell you."

" I must take my notice from his lordship," said
Parker, vainly trying to recover his dignity.

" Very well. You can wait until his lordship has
been told."

" Mr. Luke . . ."

" Best not wait to see his lordship, Parker. Take my
word for it."

" Very well, Mr. Luke."

There was a tone of finality in Luke's voice which
apparently Parker did not dare to combat. The man
looked confused and troubled. What had seemed to
him merely a venial sin—the taking of a bribe for a
trivial service—now suddenly assumed giant pro-
portions . . . a crime almost, punished by a stern
dismissal from Mr. Luke.

He went without venturing on further protest, and Luke, left standing alone in the hall, once more put his hand on the knob of the library door. This time he tried to turn it. But the door had been locked from the inside.

CHAPTER VIII

AND THUS THE SHADOW DESCENDED

FROM within, the hum of a man's voice—speaking low and insistently—still came softly through. Luke, with the prodigality of youth, would have given ten years of his life for the gift of second sight, to know what went on between those four walls beyond the door where he himself stood expectant, undecided, and more than vaguely anxious.

" Luke ! "

It was quite natural that Louisa should stand here beside him, having come to him softly, noiselessly, like the embodiment of moral strength, and a common sense which was almost a virtue.

" Uncle Rad," he said quietly, " has locked himself in with this man."

" Who is it, Luke ? "

" The man who calls himself Philip de Mountford."

" How do you know ? "

" How does one," he retorted, " know such things?"

" And Parker let him in ? "

" He gave Parker a five-pound note. Parker is only a grasping fool. He concocted the story of Mr. Dobson and the lease. He is always listening at keyholes, and he knows that Mr. Dobson often sends up a clerk with papers for Uncle Rad's signature. Those things are not very difficult to manage. If one man is determined and the other corruptible, it's done sooner or later."

"Is Lord Radclyffe safe with that man, do you think ? "

"God grant it," he replied fervently.

Jim and Edie made a noisy irruption into the hall, and Luke and Louisa talked ostentatiously of indifferent things . . . the weather, Lent, and the newest play, until the young people had gathered up coats and hats and banged the street door to behind them, taking their breeziness, their optimism away with them out into the spring air, and leaving the shadows of the on-coming tragedy to forgather in every angle of the luxurious house in Grosvenor Square.

And there were Luke de Mountford and Louisa Harris left standing alone in the hall ; just two very ordinary, very simple-souled young people, face to face for the first time in their uneventful life with the dark problem of a grim " might be." A locked door between them and the decisions of Fate, a world of possibilities in the silence which now reigned beyond that closed door.

They were, remember, wholly unprepared for it, untrained for any such eventuality. Well-bred and well brought up, yet were they totally uneducated in the great lessons of life. It was as if a man absolutely untutored in science were suddenly to be confronted with a mathematical problem, the solution or nonsolution of which would mean life or death to him.

The problem lay in silence beyond the locked door : silence broken now and again by the persistently gentle hum of the man's voice—the stranger's—but never by a word from Lord Radclyffe.

" Uncle Rad," said Luke at last, in deep puzzlement, " has never raised his voice once. I thought that there would be a row . . . that he would turn the man out of the house. . . . Dear old chap ! he hasn't much patience as a rule."

" What shall we do, Luke ? " she asked.

" How do you mean ? "

" You can't go on standing like that in the hall as if you were eavesdropping. The servants will be coming through presently."

" You are right, Loo," he said, " as usual. I'll go into the dining-room. I could hear there if anything suspicious was happening in the library."

" You are not afraid, Luke ? "

" For Uncle Rad, you mean ? "

" Of course."

" I hardly know whether I am or not. No," he added decisively, after a moment's hesitation, " I am not afraid of violence , . . the fellow whom we saw in the Park did not look that sort."

He led Louisa back into the dining-room, where a couple of footmen were clearing away the luncheon things. The melancholy Parker placed cigar-box and matches on a side table, and then retired silent and with a wealth of reproach expressed in his round, beady eyes.

Soon Luke and Louisa were alone. He smoked

and she sat in a deep arm-chair close to him saying nothing, for both knew what went on in the other's mind.

Close on an hour went by, and then the tinkle of a distant bell broke the silence. Voices were heard somewhat louder of tone in the library, and Lord Radclyffe's sounded quite distinct and firm.

" I'll see you again to-morrow," he said, " at Mr. . . . tell me the name and address again, please."

The door leading from library to hall was opened. A footman helped the stranger on with coat and hat. Then the street door banged to again, and once more the house lapsed into silence and gloom.

" I think I had better go now."

Louisa rose, and Luke said in matter-of-fact tones—

" I'll put you into a cab."

" No," she said, " I prefer to walk. I am going straight back to the Langham. Will you go to the Ducies' At Home to-morrow ? "

" Yes," he said, " just to see you."

" You'll know more by then."

" I shall know all there is to know."

" Luke," she said, " you are not afraid ? "

It was the second time she had put the question to him, but this time its purport was a very different one. He understood it nevertheless, for he replied simply—

" Only for you."

" Why for me ? "

" Because, Loo, you are just all the world to me . . .

F

and a man must feel a little afraid when he thinks he may lose the world."

"Not me, Luke," she said, "you would not lose me   whatever happened."

"Let me get you a cab."

He was English, you see, and could not manage to say anything just then. The flood-gates of sentiment might burst asunder now with the slightest word uttered that was not strictly commonplace. Louisa understood, else she had not loved him as she did. It never occurred to her to think that he was indifferent. Nay, more ! his sudden transition from sentiment to the calling of a cab—from sentiment to the trivialities of life, pleased her in its very essence of incongruity.

"I said I would walk," she reminded him, smiling.

Then she gave him her hand. It was gloveless, and he took it in his, turning the palm upwards so that he might bury his lips in its delicately perfumed depths. His kiss almost scalded her flesh, his lips were burning hot. Passion held in check will consume with inward fire, whilst its expression often cools like the Nereid's embrace.

He went to the door with her, and watched her slender, trim figure walking rapidly away until it disappeared round the corner of the Square.

When he turned back into the hall, he found himself face to face with Lord Radclyffe. Not Uncle Rad— but an altogether different man, an old man now with the cynical lines round the mouth accentuated and deepened into furrows, the eyes hollow and colourless, the shoulders bent as if under an unbearable load.

"Uncle Rad," said Luke, speaking very gently, forcing his voice to betray nothing of anxiety or surprise, "can I do anything for you?"

But even at sight of his nephew, of the man who had hitherto always succeeded in dissipating, by his very presence, every cloud on the misanthrope's brow, even at sight of him Lord Radclyffe seemed to shrink within himself, his face became almost ashen in its pallor, and lines of cruel hardness quite disfigured his mouth.

"I want to be alone to-day," he said dryly; "tell them to send me up some tea in the afternoon. I'll go to my room now. . . . I shan't want any dinner."

"But, sir, won't you . . . ?"

"I want to be alone to-day," the old man reiterated tonelessly, "and to be left alone."

"Very well, sir."

Lord Radclyffe walked slowly towards the staircase. Luke—his heart torn with anxiety and sorrow—saw how heavy was the old man's step, how listless his movements. The younger man's instinct drew him instantly to the side of the elder. He placed an affectionate hand on his uncle's shoulder.

"Uncle Rad," he said appealingly, "can't I do anything for you?"

Lord Radclyffe turned, and for a moment his eyes softened as they rested on the face he loved so well. His wrinkled hand sought the firm, young one which lingered on his shoulder. But he did not take it, only put it gently aside, then said quietly—

"No, my boy, there's nothing you can do, except to leave me alone."

Then he went upstairs and shut himself up in his own room, and Luke saw him no more that day.

CHAPTER IX

AND now a month and more had gone by, and the whole aspect of the world and of life was changed for Luke. Not for Louisa, because she, womanlike, had her life in love and love alone. Love was unchanged, or if changed at all it was ennobled, revivified, purified by the halo of sorrow and of abnegation which glorified it with its radiance.

For Luke the world had indeed changed. With the advent of Philip de Mountford that spring afternoon into the old house in Grosvenor Square, life for the other nephew—for Luke, once the dearly loved—became altogether different.

That one moment of softness, when Lord Radclyffe—a bent and broken old man—went from the library up the stairs to his own room, determined to be alone, and gently removed Luke's affectionate hand from his own bowed shoulders, that one moment of softness was the last that passed between uncle—almost father—and nephew. After that, coldness and cynicism : the same as the old man had meted out to every one around him—save Luke—for years past. Now there was no exception. Coldness and cynicism to all, and to the intruder, the new-comer, to Philip de

Mountford, an unvarying courtesy, constant deference that at times verged on impassive submission.

And the change, I must own, did not come gradually. Have I not said that only a month had gone by ? and Arthur's son, from the land of volcanoes and earthquakes, had already conquered all that he had come to seek. He who had been labelled an impostor and a blackmailer took—after that one interview—his place in the old man's mind . . . if not in his heart. Heaven only knows—for no one else was present at that first interview—what arguments he held, what appeals he made. He came like a thief, bribing his way into his uncle's presence, and stayed like a dearly loved son, a master in the house.

And Luke was shut out once and for all from Lord Radclyffe's mind and heart. Can you conceive that such selfless affection as the older man bore to the younger can live for a quarter of a century and die in one hour ? Yet so it seemed. Luke was shut out from that innermost recess in Uncle Rad's heart which he had occupied, undisputed, from childhood upwards. Now he only took his place amongst the others : with Jim and Edie and Frank, children of the younger brother, of no consequence in the house of the reigning peer.

Luke with characteristic pride—characteristic indolence, mayhap, where his own interests were at stake—would not fight for his rightful position—his by right of ages, twenty years of affection, of fidelity and comradeship.

The day following the first momentous interview Lord Radclyffe spent in lawyers' company. Mr.

Davies in Finsbury Court, then Mr. Dobson in Bedford Row. The latter argued and counselled. Though papers might be to all appearances correct and quite in order, there was no hurry to come to a decision. But Lord Radclyffe—with that same dictatorial obstinacy with which he had originally branded the claimant as an impostor and a black-mailer, now clung to his reversed opinion. Convinced—beyond doubt apparently—that Philip de Mountford was his brother Arthur's son, he insisted on acknow-ledging him openly as his heir, and on showering on him all those luxuries and privileges which Luke had enjoyed for so many years.

Indignant and mentally sore, Jim and Edie protested with all the violence of youth, violence which proved as useless as it was ill-considered. Luke said nothing, for he foresaw that the end was inevitable. He set about making a home for his younger brothers and sister to be ready for them as soon as the cataclysm came, when Philip de Mountford, usurping every right, would turn his cousins out of the old home.

Frank, absent at Santiago—a young attaché out at his first post—had been told very little as yet. Luke had tried to break the news to him in a guarded letter, which received but the following brief and optimistic answer—

"Why, old man! what's the matter with you? Worrying over such rubbish? Take my advice and go to Carlsbad. Your liver must be out of order."

But the catastrophe came nevertheless; sooner even than was expected. Edie's language grew very un-

guarded in Philip's presence, and Jim " in the Blues "
did not watch over his own manners when the new
cousin was in the house.

One evening when Luke was absent—as was very
often the case now—and the family gathering con-
sisted of Lord Radclyffe—sullen and morose—Philip—
pleasantly condescending—and Jim and Edie—snubbed
and wrathful—a difference in political opinion between
the young people set a spark to the smouldering ashes.

Philip—still pleasantly condescending—did not say
much that evening, though he had been called a cad
and an upstart, and told to go back to his nigger
relations ; but the next morning Jim and Edie received
a curt admonition from Lord Radclyffe, during which
they were told that if such a disgraceful exhibition of
impertinence occurred again, they would have to go
and pitch their tent elsewhere.

They brought their grievance to Luke : told him all
that they had treasured up in their rebellious young
hearts against the usurper, and much that they had
hitherto kept from the elder brother, who already,
God knows ! had a sufficient load of disappointment to
bear

What could Luke do but promise that Jim and Edie
should in future have a house of their own, wherein
neither usurper nor upstart would have access, and
where they could nurse their wrath in peace and un-
snubbed ?

For the first time since many, many days Luke was
alone with his uncle in the library. Philip was out,
and Lord Radclyffe was taken unawares.

What Luke never would have dreamed of doing for himself, he did for his brothers and sister : he made appeal to his uncle's sense of right, of justice, and of mercy.

"Uncle Rad," he said, "you have told us all so often that this should be a home for us all. It doesn't matter about me, but the others—Jim and Edie—they haven't offended you, have they ? "

Lord Radclyffe was fretful and irritable. When Luke first came in it had almost seemed as if he would order him to go. Such an old man he looked—sour and morose : his clothes hung more loosely than before on an obviously attenuated frame. He seemed care-worn and worried, and Luke's heart, which could not tear itself away from the memories of past kindness, ached to see the change.

"Would you," he asked insistently, "would you rather we went away, Uncle Rad ? "

The old man shifted about uneasily in his chair. He would not meet Luke's eyes any more than he would take his hand just now.

"Jim and Edie," he said curtly, "are very ill-mannered, and Philip feels . . ."

He passed his tongue over his lips, which were parched and dry. A look—it was a mere flash—almost of appeal passed from his eyes to Luke.

"Then," said Luke simply, "it is this . . . this Philip whom Jim and Edie have offended ? . . . Not you, Uncle Rad ? "

"Philip is your uncle Arthur's son," rejoined Lord Radclyffe, speaking like a fretful child in a thin voice that cracked now and again; "he will be the head of the family presently . . ."

"Not," interposed Luke earnestly, "before many years are past, I trust and pray for all our sakes, Uncle Rad . . ."

"The sooner," continued the old man, not heeding the interruption, "those young jackanapes learn to respect him, the better it will be for them."

"Jim and Edie have been a little spoilt by your kindness, sir. They are finding the lesson a little hard to learn. Perhaps they had better go and study elsewhere."

Lord Radclyffe made no reply. Silence was full of potent meaning : of submission to another's more dominant personality, of indifference to everything save to peace and quiet.

Suppressing a sigh of bitter disappointment, Luke rose to go.

"Then," he said, "the sooner I make all arrangements the better. There's only the agreement for the flat to sign, and we can move in next week."

"Where's the flat ? " queried the old man hesitatingly.

"In Exhibition Road, Kensington ; close to the Park. Edie loves the Park, and it won't be far from barracks for Jim."

"But you've no furniture. . . . How will you furnish a flat ? . . . Don't go yet," continued Lord Radclyffe, seeing that Luke was preparing to take his leave. " Philip won't be here till tea-time."

"I am afraid, sir, that I don't care to steal a few

minutes of your company, just when Philip is absent.
. . . I would rather not see you at all than see you on
sufferance."

"You are very obstinate and tiresome . . . and you
make it so difficult for me. . . . I want to hear about
the furniture . . . and how you are going to manage."

"Loo is helping Edie to get what is wanted," replied
Luke, smiling despite the heavy weight of disappointment in his heart. It was pitiable to see the old man's
obvious feeling of relief in the absence of the man who
was exercising such boundless influence over him.

"But have you money, Luke?" he asked.

"Not overmuch, sir, but enough."

"The £15,000 your father left you?"

"Yes. And that's about all."

"And the £15,000 from your uncle Arthur?"

"I don't know about that, sir. I think that should
go back to Uncle Arthur's son."

"Nonsense! nonsense!" retorted Lord Radclyffe
querulously. "I've talked to Dobson about that.
Your uncle Arthur left that money to you . . . and
not to his son. . . . He had his own reasons for doing
this. . . . Dobson thinks so too."

"It is very kind of Mr. Dobson to trouble about
my affairs, but . . ."

"The money was left to you," persisted the old
man, "and to Jim and Edie and Frank."

"They will do whatever they like with their share,
but I could not touch a penny of Uncle Arthur's
money."

"What will you do?"

"I don't know yet, uncle. I have only had a month in which to think of so much . . . and there was the new flat to see to."

Lord Radclyffe rose and shuffled towards Luke. He dropped his voice, lest the library walls had ears.

"I'll not forget you, Luke . . . presently . . . when I am gone . . . and that won't be long. . . . I'll provide for you . . . my will. . . ."

"Don't, Uncle Rad, for God's sake!" and the cry was wrung from a heart overburdened with pity and with shame.

And without waiting to take more affectionate leave, Luke hurried from the room.

CHAPTER X

LIFE MUST GO ON JUST THE SAME

THEY met at dances and at musical At Homes, for the world wagged just as it had always done, and here—don't you think ?—lies the tragedy of the commonplace. Luke and Louisa, with the whole aspect of life changed for them, with a problem to face of which hitherto they had no conception, and the solution of which meant a probing of soul and heart and mind, Luke and Louisa had to see the world pass them by, the same as heretofore, with laughter and with tears, with the weariness of pleasure, and the burdens of disappointment.

The world stared at them—curious and almost interested — searching wounds that had only just begun to ache, since indifferent hands had dared to touch them. And convention said : " Thou shalt not seem to suffer, thou shalt pass by serene and unmoved, thou shalt dance and sing and parade in Park or ballroom ; thou art my puppet and I have nought to do with thy soul."

So Luke and Louisa did as convention bade them, and people stared at them and asked them inane questions that were meant to be delicate, but were supremely tactless. People, too, wondered what they

meant to do, when the engagement would be duly
broken off or what Colonel Harris's — Louisa's
father's — attitude would be in all this. Somehow after the first excitement consequent on Lord
Radclyffe's open acknowledgment of the claimant,
things had tamed off somewhat : Luke de Mountford
looked just the same as before, although a while ago he
had been heir to one of the first peerages in England
and now was a penniless son of a younger son. I don't
know whether people thought that he ought to look
entirely different now, or whether he should henceforth
wear shabby dress clothes and gloves that betrayed the
dry cleaner : certain it is that when Luke entered a
reception room, a dozen lips were ready—had they
dared or good breeding allowed—to frame the questions—

"Well ! and what are you going to do now ? "

Or—

"Do tell us how it feels to find oneself a beggar all of
a sudden."

Enterprising hostesses made great attempts to
gather all parties in their drawing-rooms. With
strategy worthy of a better cause they manœuvred to
invite Philip de Mountford and Lord Radclyffe, and
Luke and Louisa—all to the same dinner-party, promis-
ing themselves and their other guests a subtle enjoyment at sight of these puppets dancing to rousing
tunes, beside which the most moving problem play
would seem but tame entertainment.

But Philip de Mountford—though as much sought
after now as Luke had been in the past—declined to be

made a show of for the delectation of bored society women : he declined all invitations on his own and Lord Radclyffe's behalf.

So people had to be content to watch Luke and Louisa.

They were together at the Ducies' At Home. There was a crush, a Hungarian band from Germany, a Russian singer from Bayswater, a great many diamonds, and incessant gossip.

" Luke de Mountford is here . . . and Miss Harris. Have you seen them ? "

" Oh yes ! we met on the stairs, and had a long chat."

" How do they seem ? "

" Oh ! quite happy."

"They don't care."

" Do they mean to break off the engagement ? "

" I have heard nothing. Have you ? "

" Louisa Harris has a nice fortune of her own."

" And Lord Radclyffe will provide for Luke."

" I don't think so. He practically turned him out of the house, you know.'

" Not really ? "

" I know it for a positive fact. My sister has just got a new butler, who left Lord Radclyffe's service the very day Philip de Mountford first walked into the house."

" Old Parker; I remember him."

" He says Lord Radclyffe turned all the family out, bag and baggage. They were so insolent to Philip."

" Then it's quite true ? "

" That this Philip is the late Arthur de Mountford's son ? "

" Quite true, I believe. Lord Radclyffe openly acknowledges it. He is satisfied, apparently."

" So are the lawyers, I understand."

" Oh ! how do you do, Miss Harris ? So glad to see you looking so well."

This very pointedly, as Louisa, perfectly gowned, smiling serenely, ascended the broad staircase.

" I have not been ill, Lady Keogh."

" Oh no ! of course not. And how is Mr. de Mountford ? "

" You can ask him yourself."

And Louisa passed on to make way for Luke. And the same remarks, the same questions repeated *ad infinitum*, until a popular waltz, played by the Hungarian gentlemen from Germany, drew the fashionable crowd round the musicians' platform.

Then Luke and Louisa contrived to make good their escape, and to reach the half-landing above the heads of numerous young couples that adorned the stairs. The hum of voices, the noise of shrill laughter, and swish of skirts and fans masked their own whisperings. The couples on the stairs were absorbed in their own little affairs—they were sitting out here so that they might pursue their own flirtations.

Luke and Louisa could talk undisturbed.

They spoke of the flat in Exhibition Road and of the furniture that Louisa had helped Edie to select.

" There are only a few odds and ends to get now," Louisa was saying, " coal-scuttles and waste-paper baskets : that sort of thing. I hope you don't think that we have been extravagant. Edie, I am afraid, had rather luxurious notions. . . ."

" Poor Edie ! "

" Oh ! I don't think she minds very much. Life at Grosvenor Square in the past month has not been over-cheerful."

Then, as Luke made no comment, she continued, in her own straightforward, matter-of-fact way—the commonplace woman facing the ordinary duties of life—

" Now that the flat is all in order you can all move in whenever you like . . . and then, Luke, you must begin to think of yourself."

" Of you, Loo," he said simply,

" Oh ! there's nothing," she said, " to think about me."

" There you are wrong, Loo, and you must not talk like that. Our engagement must be officially broken off. . . . Colonel Harris has been too patient as it is."

" Father," she rejoined, " does not wish the engagement broken off."

" All these people," he said, nodding in the direction of the crowd below, " will expect some sort of announcement."

" Let them."

" Loo, you must take back your word."

" How does one take back one's word, Luke ? Have you ever done it ? I shouldn't know how to."

She looked at him straight, her eyes brilliant in the glare of the electric lamps, not a tear in them or in

G

his, her face immovable, lest indifferent eyes happened to be turned up to where these two interesting people sat. Only a quiver round the lips, a sign that passion palpitated deep down within her heart, below the Bond Street gown and the diamond collar, the soul within the puppet.

She held his glance, forcing him into mute acknowledgment that his philosophy, his worldliness, was only veneer, and that he had not really envisaged the hard possibility of actually losing her.

Oh ! these men of this awful conventional world, how cruel they can be in that proud desire to do what is right . . . what their code tells them is right ! No law of God or nature that !—only convention, the dictates of other men ! Hard on themselves, selfless in abnegation, but not understanding that the dearest gift they can bestow on a woman is the right for her to efface herself, the right for her to be the giver of love, of consolation, of sacrifice.

Commonplace, plain, sensible Louisa understood everything that Luke felt ; those great luminous eyes of hers, tearless yet brilliant, read every line on that face drilled into impassiveness.

No one else could have guessed the precise moment at which softness crept into the hard determination of jaw and lips ; no ear but hers could ever have perceived the subtle change in the quivering breath, from hard obstinacy that drew the nostrils together, and set every line of the face, to that indrawing of the heavy air around caused by passionate longing which hammered at the super-excited brain, and made the sinews crack in the mighty physical effort at self-repression.

But, to all outward appearance, perfect calm, correct demeanour :—the attitude and tone of voice prescribed by the usages of this so-called society.

"Loo," he said, "it is not fair to tempt me. I should be a miserable cur if I held you to your word. I am a penniless beggar—a wastrel now, without a profession, without prospects, soon to be without friends."

He seemed to take pleasure in recalling his defects, and she let him ramble on. Women who are neither psychological puzzles nor interesting personalities have a way of listening patiently whilst a tortured soul eases its burden by contemplating its own martyrdom.

"I am a penniless beggar," he reiterated. "I have no right to ask any woman to share my future dull and humdrum existence. A few thousands is all I have. I think that Edie will marry soon, and then I can go abroad. . . . I must go abroad. . . . I must do something. . . ."

"We'll do it together, Luke."

"I feel," he continued, rebellious now and wrathful, all the primary instincts alive in him of self-preservation and the desire to destroy an enemy, "I feel that if I stayed in England I should contrive to be even with that blackguard. . . . His rights ? By God ! I would never question those . . . the moment I knew that he was Uncle Arthur's son I should have been ready to shake him by the hand, to respect him, to stand aside, as was his due. . . . But his attitude !

. . . the influence he exercises over Uncle Rad ! . . .
His rancour against us all ! Jim and Edie ! what had
they done ? . . . to be all turned out of the house like
a pack of poor relations . . . and poor Uncle Rad.
. . ."

He checked himself, for she had put a hand on his
coat-sleeve.

" Luke, it is no use," she said.

" You are right, Loo ! and I am a miserable wretch.
. . . If you only knew how I hate that man ! . . ."

" Don't," she said, " let us think of him."

" How can I help it ? He robs me of you."

" No," she rejoined, " not that."

Her hand still rested on his arm, and he took it
between both his. The couples in front of them, all
down the length of stairs, paid no heed to them, and
through the hum of voices from a distant room beyond
came softly wafted on the hot, still air the strains of
the exquisite Barcarolle from the "Contes d'Hoffmann."

Louisa smiled confidently, proudly. He held her
hand, and she felt that his—hot and dry—quivered
in every muscle at her touch. The commonplace
woman had opened the magic book of Love. She had
turned its first pages, the opening chapters had been
simple, unruffled, uncrumpled by the hand of men or
Fate. But now at last she read the chapter which all
along she knew was bound to reach her ken. The
leaves of the book were crumpled, Fate with cruel
hand had tried to blur the writing ; the psychological
problem of to-day—the one that goes by the name of
" modern woman "—would no doubt ponder ere she

tried to read further ; she would analyse her feelings, her thoughts, her sensations, she would revel over her own heartache and delight in her own soul-agony. But simple-minded, conventional Louisa did none of these things. She neither ruffled her hair nor dressed in ill-made serge clothes ; her dress was perfect and her hand exquisitely gloved. She did nothing out of the way, she only loved one man altogether beyond herself, and she understood his passionate love for her, and all that troubled him in this world in which they both lived.

" I love that Barcarolle, don't you ? " she said after a while.

" I did not hear it," he replied.

" Luke ! "

" It's no use, Loo," he said under his breath, " you must despise me for being a drivelling fool ; but I have neither eyes nor ears now. I would give all I have in the world to lie down there on the floor now before you and to kiss the soles of your feet."

" How could I despise you, Luke, for that ? "

" Put your hand on my knee, just for a moment, Loo ; I think I shall go mad if I don't feel your touch."

She did as he asked her, and he was silent until the last note of the Barcarolle died away in a soft murmured breath.

" What a cowardly wretch I am," he said, under cover of the wave of enthusiastic applause which effectually covered the sound of his voice to all save hers. " I think I would sell my soul for a touch of your hand, and all the while I know that with every word I am playing the part of a coward. If Colonel Harris heard me he would give me a sound thrashing. A dog-whip is what I deserve."

"I have told you," she rejoined simply, "that father does not wish our engagement to be broken off. He sticks to your cause, and will do so through thick and thin. He still believes that this Philip is an impostor, and thinks that Lord Radclyffe has taken leave of his senses."

She spoke quite quietly, matter-of-factedly now, pulling by her serene calm Luke's soul back from the realms of turbulent sensations to the prosy facts of to-day. And he—in answer to her mute dictate and with a movement—wholly instinctive and mechanical —drew himself upright, and passed his hand over his ruffled hair, and the jeopardized immaculateness of shirt front and cuffs.

"Philip de Mountford," he said simply, "is no impostor, Loo. He has been perfectly straightforward ; and Mr. Dobson for one, who has seen all his papers, thinks that there is no doubt whatever that he is Uncle Arthur's son. His clerk—Mr. Downing—went out to Martinique, you know, and his first letters came a day or two ago. All inquiries give the same result, and Downing says that it is quite easy to trace the man's life—step by step—from his birth in St. Pierre, past the dark days of the earthquake and the lonely life at Marie Galante. Mrs. de Mountford was a half-caste native, as we all suspected, but the marriage was unquestionably legal. Downing has spoken to people in Martinique and also in Marie Galante, who knew her and her son, or at any rate of them. I cannot tell you everything clearly, but there are a great many links in a long chain of evidence, and so far Mr. Dobson and his clerk have not come across a broken one. That the Mrs. de Mountford who died at Marie Galante was Uncle Arthur's wife, and that Philip is his son, I am afraid no one can question. He has quite a number of letters in his possession, which Uncle Arthur wrote after he had practically abandoned wife and child. I think it was the letters that convinced Uncle Rad."

"Lord Radclyffe," she remarked dryly, "has taken everything far too much for granted."

"He is convinced, Loo . . . and that's all about it."

"He is," she retorted more hotly than was her wont, "acting in a cruel and heartless manner. Even if this Philip is your uncle Arthur's son, even if he is heir to the peerage and the future head of the family, there was no reason for installing him in your home, Luke, and turning you and the others out of it."

"I suppose," rejoined Luke philosophically, "the house was never really our home. What Uncle Rad gave freely, he has taken away again from us. I don't suppose that we have the right to complain."

"But what will become of you all ? "

"We must scrape along. Frank must have his promised allowance or he'll never get along in the service, and five hundred pounds a year is a big slice out of a thousand. Jim, too, spends a great deal: Uncle Rad never stinted him with money, for it was he who wanted Jim to be in the Blues. Now he may have to exchange into a less expensive regiment. I think Edie will marry soon. . . . Reggie Duggan has been in love with her for the past two years . . . she may make up her mind now."

" But you, Luke ? "

He did not know if he ought to tell her of his plans :— the ostrich farm out in Africa — the partnership offered to him by a cousin of his mother's who was doing remarkably well, but who was getting old and wanted the companionship of one of his kind. . . . It was a living anyway . . . but a giving up of everything that had constituted life in the past . . . and the giving up of his exquisite Loo. . . . How could he ask her to share that life with him ? . . . the primitive conditions . . . the total absence of luxuries . . . the rough, everyday existence ?

And Loo so perfectly dressed, so absolutely modern and dainty . . . waited on hand and foot. . . .

But she insisted, seeing that he was hesitating and was trying to keep something from her.

" What about you, Luke ? "

He had not time to reply, for from the hall below a shrill voice called to them both by name.

" Mr. de Mountford, Miss Harris, the young people want to dance . . . you'll join in, won't you ? "

Already he was on his feet, every trace of emotion swept away from his face, together with every crease from his immaculate dress clothes, and every stray wisp of hair from his well-groomed head. Not a man, torn with passion, fighting the battle of life against overwhelming odds, casting away from him the hand which he would have given his last drop of blood to possess—only the man of the world, smiling while his very soul was being wrung—only the puppet dancing to the conventional world's tune.

"Dancing ? " he said lightly.   "Rather . . . Lady Ducie, may I have this first waltz ?   No ? . . . oh, I say, that's too bad. . . . The first Lancers, then ? . . . Good ! Loo, may I have this dance ? "

And the world went on just the same.

CHAPTER XI

THE first November fog.

The world had wagged on in its matter-of-fact way for more than six months now, since that day in April when Philip de Mountford—under cover of lies told by Parker—had made his way into Lord Rad-clyffe's presence—more than five months since the favoured nephew had been so unceremoniously thrust out of his home.

Spring had yielded to summer, summer given way to autumn : and already winter was treading hard on autumn's heels. The autumn session had filled London with noise and bustle, with political dinner-parties and monster receptions, with new plays at all the best theatres, and volumes of ephemeral literature.

And all that was—to-night—wrapped in a dense fog, the first of the season, quite a stranger too in London, for scientists had asserted positively that the era of the traditional " pea-souper " was over : the metro-polis would know it no more.

Colonel Harris was in town with his daughter Louisa, and swearing at London weather in true country fashion. He declared that fogs paralysed

his intellect, that he became positively imbecile, not
knowing how to fight his way in the folds of such a
black pall. Taxi-cab drivers he mistrusted : in fact he
had all an old sportsman's hatred of mechanically
propelled vehicles, whilst he flatly refused to bring
valuable horses up to town to catch their death of
cold whilst waiting about in the fog.

So Luke had promised to pilot the party as far as
the Danish Legation, where they were to dine to-night
—this was the only condition under which Colonel
Harris would consent to enter one of those confounded
motors.

Colonel Harris had remained loyal to the core to
Luke and to his fortunes. It is a way old sportsmen
have ; and he had never interfered by word or in-
nuendo in Louisa's actions with regard to her engagement. His daughter was old enough, he said, to know
her own mind. She liked Luke, and it would be shabby
to leave him in the lurch, now that the last of the society
rats were scurrying to leave the sinking ship. They
were doing it too in a mighty hurry. The invitations,
which the penniless younger son received towards the
end of the London season, were considerably fewer than
those which were showered on him at its beginning,
before the world had realized that Philip de Mountford
had come to stay, and would one day be Earl of Radclyffe with a rent roll of £80,000 a year, and the sore
need of a wife.

It had begun with the bridge parties. Luke would no
longer play—since he could no longer afford to lose a
quarter's income at one sitting. Uncle Rad used to

shrug indifferent shoulders at such losses, and place
blank cheques at the dear boy's disposal. Imagine
then how welcome Luke was at bridge parties, and how
very undesirable now.

Then he could no longer make return for hospitable
entertainments. He had no home to which to ask
smart friends : Lord Radclyffe, though a monster of
ill-humour, gave splendid dinner-parties at which
Luke was quasi host. Now it was all give and no take ;
and the givers retired one by one, quite unregretted
by Luke, who thus was spared the initiative of turning
his back on his friends. They did the turning, quite
politely but very effectually. Luke scarcely noticed
how he was dropping out of his former circle. He was
over-absorbed and really did not care. Moreover his
dress clothes were getting shabby.

To-night at the Langham, when he arrived at about
seven o'clock so as to have an undisturbed half-hour
with Loo, Colonel Harris greeted him with outstretched
hand and cordial welcome—

" Hello ! Luke my boy ! how goes it with you ? "

Louisa said nothing, but her eyes welcomed him,
and she drew him near to her, on to the sofa in front
of the fire, and allowed her hand to rest in his, for she
knew how he loved the touch of it. People were
beginning to say that Louisa Harris was getting old :
she never had been good-looking, poor thing ! but
always smart, very smart . . . now she was losing
her smartness, and what remained ?

She had come up to town this autumn in last
autumn's frocks ! and the twins were after all being

chaperoned by their aunt. Would that absurd engagement never be broken off ? Fancy Louisa Harris
married to a poor man ! Why ! she did not know how
to do her hair, and dresses were still worn fastened at
the back, and would be for years to come ! Louisa
Harris and no French maid, cheap corsets and cleaned
gloves ! it was unthinkable.

Perhaps the engagement was virtually broken
off . . . anyhow the wedding could never take
place.

Unless Philip de Mountford happened to die.

But it did not look as if the engagement was broken
off. Not at any rate on this raw November evening,
when there was a dense fog outside, but a bright, cheery
fire and plenty of light in the little sitting-room at the
Langham, and Luke sat on the sofa beside Louisa, and
plain Louisa—in last autumn's gown—looking at
him with her candid, luminous eyes.

" How is Lord Radclyffe ? " asked Colonel Harris.

" Badly," replied Luke, " I am afraid. He looks
very feeble, and his asthma, I know, must bother him.
He was always worse in foggy weather."

" He ought to go to Algeciras. He always used
to."

" I know," assented Luke dejectedly.

" Can't something be done ? Surely, Luke, you
haven't lost all your influence with him."

" Every bit, sir. Why, I hardly ever see him."

" Hardly ever see him ? " ejaculated Colonel Harris,
and I am afraid that he swore.

" I haven't been to Grosvenor Square for over six

weeks. I am only allowed to see him when Philip is out, or by special permission from Philip. I won't go under such conditions."

" How that house must have altered ! "

" You wouldn't know it, sir. All the servants have gone, one after the other ; they had rows with Philip and left at a month's notice. I suppose he has no idea how to set about getting new ones. . . . I know I shouldn't ! . . . There's only a man and his wife, a sort of charwoman who cleans and cooks, and the man is supposed to look after Uncle Rad, but he doesn't do it, for he is half seas over most of the time."

" Good God ! " murmured Colonel Harris.

" They have shut up all the rooms, except the library where Uncle Rad and Philip have their meals when they are at home. But they lunch and dine at their club mostly. . . ."

" What club do they go to ? I called in at the Athenæum last night, thinking to find Radclyffe there, but the hall-porter told me that he never went there now."

" No. He and Philip have joined some new club in Shaftesbury Avenue—The Veterans', I think it's called."

" Some low, mixed-up kind of place ! Old Radclyffe must be out of his senses ! "

" He likes it, so he tells me, because people don't come and bother him there."

" I should think not, indeed ! I wouldn't set foot in such a place."

" He goes there most evenings, and so does Philip

. . . and it's so bad for Uncle Rad to be out late these foggy nights."

" You ought to make an effort and stop it, Luke."

" I have made many efforts, sir. But, as a matter of fact, I had made up my mind to make a final one to-night. Uncle Rad ought to go abroad, and I thought I would try to impress this on Philip. He can't be a bad man. . . ."

" Oh ! can't he ? " was Colonel Harris's muttered comment.

" At any rate, if I have no influence, he has, and he must exert it and get Uncle Rad down to Algeciras or anywhere else he likes, so long as it is well south."

Luke paused awhile, his face flushed with this expression of determination, which must have caused his pride many a bitter pang. Then he resumed, more quietly—

" It's rather humiliating, isn't it, to go to that man as a suppliant ? "

" Don't go as a suppliant, my boy. You must insist on your uncle being properly looked after."

Colonel Harris thought all that sort of thing so easy. One always does before one has had a genuine tussle with the unpleasant realities of life ; to the good country squire with an assured position, an assured income, assured influence, it seemed very easy indeed to insist. He himself never had to insist : things occurred round him and at his word, as it were, of themselves.

But Louisa, knowing how matters stood, made no

suggestion. She knew that Luke would do his best, but that that best was but of little avail now. As Philip de Mountford arranged, so it would all come about.

Friends and well-wishers could but pray that the intruder was not a bad man, and that he had his uncle's health at heart.

She gave the signal to go, saying simply—

" We mustn't be late for dinner, father, must we ? "

And she rose to go, held back by the hand, by Luke's fervent insistence.

He could not accustom himself to part from her, as he often had to do. It seemed absurd, but undeniable. He was supremely happy in her company, and snatched as much of it as ever he could ; but the wrench was always awful, and Louisa—subtly comprehensive— was conscious of the terrible pain which she gave him at every parting. She felt the repercussion of it in all her nerves, although her sound common sense con- demned the sensation as unreal.

To-night the feeling was even stronger than it had ever been before. At her first suggestion that it was time to go, an elusive current passed from him to her. He had been holding her hand, and his had been cool and only slightly on the quiver from time to time, when her own fingers pressed more markedly against his. But now, all at once, it seemed as if a sudden current of lava had penetrated his veins ; his hand almost scorched her own, and though visibly it did not move, yet she felt the pulses throbbing and trem- bling beneath the flesh. The look of misery in his face made her own heart ache, though she tried to smile with easy gaiety.

"To-morrow we go to the Temple Show together, don't forget, Luke."

Her words seemed to recall him from another world, and he quickly enough pulled himself together and helped her on with her cloak. Colonel Harris, with the gentle tactfulness peculiar to kind hearts, had loudly announced that he would be waiting in the hall.

"Anything the matter, Luke?" she asked as soon as her father had gone from the room.

He contrived to smile and to look unconcerned.

"Not particularly," he replied.

"You seem different to-night, somehow."

"How different?"

"I can't explain. But you are not yourself."

"Myself more than ever. My adoration for you is more uncontrolled—that is all."

She wrapped herself up in her furs; for it was silence that gave the best response. And then he said, quite calmly—

"Will you go first? I'll switch off the light."

"Father will be waiting downstairs," she rejoined.

Then she went past him and out through the door, and he had to go back to the mantelpiece where one of the electric light switches was. He turned off the light; the room remained in darkness, save where the dying embers of the fire threw a red glow on the sofa where she had sat with him, and the footstool on which her evening shoe had rested.

And the conventional man of the world, schooled

H

from childhood onwards to discipline and self-control, fell on both knees against that mute footstool, and, leaning forward, he pressed his burning lips against the silk cushions of the sofa, which still bore the impress and the fragrance of her exquisite shoulders.

Then he too went out of the room.

CHAPTER XII

SHALL A MAN ESCAPE HIS FATE?

ON the way to the Danish Legation Colonel Harris asked Luke what his plans were for the evening.

"I shall," replied Luke, "call at Grosvenor Square. I may find Uncle Rad, or Philip, or both at home. I mean to have a good tussle about this wintering abroad. . . . It's really most important."

"I call it criminal," retorted Colonel Harris, "keeping a man in London who has been used to go south in the winter for the past twenty years at least."

"Uncle Rad is still fairly well now, though I do think he looks more feeble than usual. He ought to go at once."

"But," suggested Louisa, "he oughtn't to go alone."

"No. He certainly ought not."

"Would Mr. de Mountford go with him?"

"I don't think so."

"This new man of his, then?"

"That," said Luke hotly, "would be madness. The man is really a drunkard."

"But somebody ought to go."

"Edie would be only too willing . . . if she is allowed."

"Edie ? " exclaimed Louisa.

And she added, with a smile—

"What will Reggie Duggan have to say to that ? "

"Nothing," he replied quietly. "Reggie Duggan has cried off."

"You don't mean that."

"He has given up Edie, who has little or nothing a year, and become engaged to Marian Montagu, who has eight thousand pounds a year of her own."

"Poor Edie ! " murmured Louisa ; whilst Colonel Harris's exclamation was equally to the point and far more forcible, and more particularly concerned the Honourable Reginald Duggan.

"Yes ! " rejoined Luke, "it has hit her hard, coming on the top of other things. There's no gainsaying the fact, is there, Colonel Harris, that we four brothers and sister owe something to Uncle Arthur's son ? "

"The handle of a riding whip," came from out the depths of Colonel Harris's fur coat. "Stupid way parsons have of saying that to wish a man dead is tantamount to murder. I am committing murder now for the matter of that, for I wish that blackguard were buried in one of his native earthquakes."

"Would to God," added Luke, " that wishing alone would do it."

There was so much wrath, such hatred and contempt, contained in those words that Louisa instinctively whispered—

"Hush, Luke! don't talk like that."

And Colonel Harris somewhat ostentatiously cleared his throat and said—

"Don't let us think of that confounded Philip."

Luke took leave of Colonel Harris and of Louisa at the door of the Danish Legation. He waited on the carpeted kerb beneath the awning until he saw her white evening cloak disappear in the doorway.

The fog had become very dense. Just here, where a number of carriage lamps threw light around, one could distinguish faces and forms immediately close to one; but as Luke turned away from the brilliant lights he realized how thick was the pall which enveloped London to-night. He looked at his watch; it was close upon eight. The next few minutes brought him to the door of Lord Radclyffe's house.

He rang, but obtained no answer; he rang again and again, and finally came to the conclusion that his uncle and cousin were, as usual, dining out, and that the elderly couple who did perfunctory service in the house were either asleep or out of earshot, or had taken the opportunity of seeking amusement in a neighbouring public-house.

But Luke was worried about Lord Radclyffe; moreover, he had made up his mind that he would speak to him and to Philip to-night with regard to the imperative wintering abroad for the old man.

The Veterans' Club was unknown to Luke, but Shaftesbury Avenue was not. He turned into Oxford

Street, and as taxi-cabs were now a forbidden luxury he hailed a passing omnibus and jumped into it, and thus was rapidly conveyed into the very heart of the fog, which had found its haven around Piccadilly Circus.

CHAPTER XIII

AS to what occurred in the heart of the fog on that night in November, four years ago, most of you, no doubt, will remember. Those who do not I must refer to the morning papers of the following day.

A perfect harvest for journalists. Gossip and detail sufficient to fill column upon column of newspaper : gossip that grew as the hours sped on, and the second day of fog pursued its monotonous course.

A man had been found murdered in a taxi-cab, his throat stabbed through from ear to ear, the jugular pierced, life absolutely extinct—the murderer vanished.

Drama in the midst of reality.

Such things are, you know. No amount of so-called realistic literature, no amount of sneers at what is dubbed melodrama, will prevent this fact occurring— and occurring very frequently in the streets of a mighty city.

Just a man murdered, and the murderer disappeared. A very real thing that, and London has had to face such facts often enough, more often than has an audience at Drury Lane or the Adelphi. The superior-minded critic who spells British Drama with a capital B and D, and pronounces it Pritish Trama, sat in the stalls of a London theatre on this very same foggy evening in November, four years ago. The play was one that did not appeal to the superior-minded critic ; it was just a simple tale of jealousy which led to the breaking of that great commandment : "Thou shalt do no murder ! "

And the superior-minded critic yawned behind a well-gloved hand and dubbed the play melodramatic, unreal, and stagey, quite foreign to the life of to-day. But just at that hour—between nine and ten o'clock— a man was murdered in a taxi-cab, and his murderer vanished in the fog.

London doesn't dub such events melodrama, she does not sneer at them or call them unreal. She knows that they are real : there is nothing stagey or artificial about them : they have even become commonplace.

They occur so often ; and most often whilst society dines or dances, and the elect applaud with languid grace the newest play by Mr. Bernard Shaw.

Only in this case the event gained additional interest. The murdered man was a personality. Some one whom everybody that was anybody had talked about, gossiped, and discussed for the past six months. Some one whom few had seen, but many had heard about—Philip de Mountford, the son of the late Arthur de Mountford—Radclyffe's newly found heir, you know.

The news spread as only such news can spread, and when society poured out from theatres, from houses in Grosvenor Square, or from the dining-room of the Carlton, every one had heard the news.

It was as if the sprite of gossip had been busy whispering in over-willing ears.

" Philip de Mountford has been murdered."

" He was found in a taxi-cab ; his throat was cut from ear to ear."

" No, no ! not cut, I understand. Pierced through with a sharp instrument—a stiletto, I presume."

" How horrible ! "

" Poor Lord Radclyffe . . . such a tragedy ! . . ."

" He'll never live through it."

" He has looked very feeble lately."

" The scandal round the late Arthur's name broke him up, I think."

" It seems Arthur de Mountford had married a negress."

" No, no ! Philip did not look like a half-caste. I saw him once or twice. He was dark, but nice-looking."

" Still ! there was some scandal about the marriage."

" Nothing to what this scandal will be ! "

" What scandal ? "

" Seek whom the crime benefits, you know."

" Then you think . . . ? You really think Luke de Mountford did it ? "

" I thought so the moment I heard the story."

" I've always thought that Luke de Mountford a queer sort of fellow."

" And he took his cousin's advent very badly."

" Well, one can't wonder at that exactly . . . to lose a future peerage all of a sudden . . . and he has no private fortune either . . ."

"Poor beggar."

"I heard there were awful rows between the cousins until Lord Radclyffe himself turned Luke and the others out of the house."

"And now Philip de Mountford has been murdered."

"And the police will seek him whom the crime benefits."

"It certainly looks very suspicious."

"A real *cause célèbre*. . . . Won't it be exciting?"

"Something to read about in one's morning papers."

"I shall try and get reserved seats for the trial. . . . I hate a crush, don't you?"

"Will they hang him, do you think?"

"If he is found guilty . . . English justice is no respecter of persons."

"How awful."

And tittle-tattle, senseless talk, inane remarks were wafted on the grimy wings of the fog. They penetrated everywhere, in the lobbies of the theatres, the boudoir of madame, and the smoking-room of my lord. They penetrated to the magnificent reception rooms of the Danish Legation, and Louisa heard the remarks even before she knew the full details of the story. Louisa had a well-trained contralto voice, and had been asked to sing in the course of the evening. Just as she stood in an outer room selecting her music, she heard a group of idlers—men and women—talking over the mysterious murder in the taxi-cab.

They had at first been unconscious of her presence. She had her back towards them, turning over the leaves of her song. Suddenly there was a hush in the conversation; one of the chatterboxes must have pointed her out to the others.

Whereupon Louisa, serene and smiling, a roll of music in her hand, joined the merry group.

" Please," she said, " don't stop. I have heard nothing yet. And of course I want to know."

One of the men laughed inanely, and the ladies murmured silly nothings.

" Oh!" said some one, " it mayn't be true. Such lots of wild rumours get about."

" What," asked Louisa placidly, " mayn't be true ? Some one said just now that Philip de Mountford has been murdered."

" Well," murmured one of the ladies, " they say it was Mr. de Mountford, but they can't be sure, can they ? "

The group was dissolving ; almost, it seemed, as if it had vanished into thin air. When Louisa first heard them talking there were about a dozen men and women, a brilliant throng of gaily plumaged birds ; now the ladies remembered that they wanted to hear the latest infant prodigy, who had been engaged to entertain the guests at the post-dinner reception to-night, and the men, too, feeling uncomfortable and awkward, made good their escape.

People—the pleasure-loving people of to-day—have no use for latent tragedy ; excitement, yes ! and drama, but only from the secure distance of a private seat at an Old Bailey trial. The murder of Philip de Mountford could be discussed with quite an amount of enjoyment between a dinner-party and a ball supper, but not in Louisa Harris's presence! By Gad! too much of a good thing you know!

Within a very few minutes Louisa found herself almost alone, just the one or two near her to whom she had directly spoken, and—fortunately— Colonel Harris in the doorway, come to look for his daughter.

"The infant with the violin," he said as soon as he caught sight of Louisa, "is just finishing his piece, poor little rat! You promised you would sing next, Loo. What songs have you got?"

"I was just making a selection when you came, father. What would you like me to sing?"

With an unexpressed sigh of relief the last two of the original group of gossips dwindled away into the reception room beyond, congratulating themselves on having successfully engineered their exit.

"Dooced awkward, don't you know, Miss Harris asking questions."

"I suppose she doesn't realize . . ."

"She will soon enough . . ."

"She ought to have broken off her engagement long ago."

"Isn't it awful? . . . poor thing!"

Louisa, left alone with her father, could allow her nerves to ease their fearful tension. She had no need to hide from him the painful quiver of her lips, or the anxious frown across her brow.

"Do you know," she asked, "anything about this awful business, father?"

"There's a lot of gossip," he replied; his voice was

not only gruff, but hoarse, which showed that he was strangely moved.

"But," she insisted, "some truth in the gossip?"

"They say Philip de Mountford has been murdered."

"Who says so?"

"Some people have come on from the theatres, and men from the clubs. The streets are full of it . . . and evening papers have brought out midnight editions, which are selling like hot cakes."

"And do they say that Luke has killed Philip de Mountford?"

"No"—with some hesitation—"they don't say that."

"But they hint at it."

"Newspaper tittle-tattle."

"How much is actual fact?"

"I understand," he explained, "that at nine o'clock or thereabouts two men in evening dress hailed a passing taxi-cab just outside the Lyric Theatre in Shaftesbury Avenue and told the chauffeur to drive to Hyde Park Corner, just by the railings of the Green Park. The driver drew up there and one of the two men got out. As he reclosed the door of the cab he leaned toward the interior and said cheerfully, "Slong, old man. See you to-morrow." Then he told the chauffeur to drive on to 1 Cromwell Gardens, opposite the Museum, and turning on his heel disappeared in the fog. When the chauffeur drew up for the second time no one alighted from the cab. So he got down from his box and opened the door."

"The other man," murmured Louisa vaguely, "was in the cab . . . dead! . . ."

" That's about it."

" With his throat pierced from ear to ear by a sharp instrument which might have been a skewer."

" You have heard it all, then ? "

" No ! no ! " she said hurriedly.

The room was swaying round her ; the furniture started hopping and dancing. Louisa, who had never fainted in her life, felt as if the floor was giving way under her feet. Memory was unloading one of her store-houses, looking over the contents of a hidden cell, wherein she had put away a strange winter scene in Brussels, a taxi-cab, the ill-lighted boulevard, the chauffeur getting down from his box and finding a man crouched in the further corner of the cab—dead—with his throat pierced from ear to ear by an instrument which might have been a skewer. And memory was raking out that cell, clearing it in every corner ; trying to find the recollection of a certain morning in Battersea Park a year ago when Louisa recounted her impressions of that weird scene, told the tale of this crime, which she had almost witnessed. Memory found a distinct impression that she had told the tale at full length, and with all the details which she knew. She remembered talking it all over, and that when she did so, the ground in Battersea Park was crisp with the frost under her feet, and an inquisitive robin perched himself on the railings and then flew away, accompanying her and another all the way along as far as the gates.

Two pictures, vivid and distinct : that evening in Brussels, and the morning in Battersea Park, her first

meeting with Luke after his letter to her—the letter
which had come to her in the Palace Hotel and which
had made her the happiest woman in all the world.
Memory—satisfied—had at last emptied the storehouse of that one cell and left Louisa Harris standing
here, staring at her father, her ears buzzing with
the idle and irresponsible chatter of society jack-
daws, her mind seeing all that had happened outside
1 Cromwell Gardens : the cab stopping, the chauffeur
terrified, the crowd collecting, the police taking notes.
Her mind saw it as if her bodily eyes had been there,
and all that her father told her seemed but the re-
capitulation of what she knew already.

"Where," she said after a while, "is the dead man
now ? "

"I don't know," he replied, "I should imagine
they would keep the body at the police station until
the morning. I don't suppose they'd be such mugs
as to disturb Lord Radclyffe at this time of night;
the shock might kill the old man."

"I suppose they are quite sure that it is Philip de
Mountford who was killed ? "

"Why, yes ! he had his pocketbook, his cards, his
letters on him, and money too . . . robbery was not
the object of the crime. . . . "

"It was Philip de Mountford then ? "

"Good God, yes ! of whom were you thinking ? "

"I was thinking of Luke," she replied simply.

The old man said nothing more. Had he spoken
at all then it would have been to tell her that he too
was thinking of Luke, and that there was perhaps

not a single person in the magnificent house at that moment who was not—in some way or other—thinking of Luke.

The hostess came in, elegant and worldly, with banal words to request the pleasure of hearing Miss Harris sing

" It is so kind of you," she said, " to offer. I have never heard you, you know, and people say you have such a splendid voice. But perhaps you would rather not sing to-night ? "

She spoke English perfectly, but with a slight Scandinavian intonation, which seemed to soften the banality of her words. Being foreign, she thought less of concealing her sympathy, and was much less fearful of venturing on delicate ground.

She held out a small exquisitely-gloved hand and laid it almost affectionately on the younger woman's arm.

" I am sure you would rather not sing to-night," she said kindly.

" Indeed, Countess, why should you think that ? " retorted Louisa lightly. " I shall be delighted to sing. I wonder which of these new songs you would like best. There is an exquisite one by Guy d'Hardelot. Shall I sing that ? "

And Her Excellency, who so charmingly represented Denmark in English society, followed her guest into the reception room : she admired the elegant carriage of the English girl, the slender figure, the soft abundant hair.

And Her Excellency sighed and murmured to herself—

"They are stiff, these English! and oh! they have no feelings, no sentiment!"

And a few moments later, when Louisa Harris's really fine voice, firm and clear, echoed in the wide reception room, Her Excellency reiterated her impressions—

"These English have no heart! She sings and her lover is suspected of murder! Bah! they have no heart!"

CHAPTER XIV

AND whilst the morning papers were unfolded by millions of English men and women, and the details of the mysterious crime discussed over eggs and bacon and buttered toast, Philip de Mountford, the newly found heir-presumptive to the Earldom of Radclyffe, was lying in the gloomy mortuary chamber of a London police court, whither he had been conveyed in the same cab whose four narrow walls jealously guarded the secret of the tragedy which had been enacted within their precincts.

Lord Radclyffe had been aroused at ten o'clock the previous night by representatives of the police, who came to break the news to him. It was not late, and the old man was not yet in bed. He had opened the front door of his house himself ; his servants, he explained curtly, were spending their evening more agreeably elsewhere.

The house—even to the police officer—appeared lonely and gloomy in the extreme, and the figure of the old man—who should have been surrounded by every luxury that rank and wealth can give—looked singularly pathetic as he stood in his own doorway, evidently unprotected and uncared for, and sus-

piciously demanding what his late visitors' business
might be.

Very reluctantly, on hearing the latter's status, he
consented to admit them. He did not at first appear
to suspect that anything wrong might have happened, or that anything untoward could occasion this
nocturnal visit ; in fact, he seemed unconscious of the
lateness of the hour.

He walked straight into the library, where he had
obviously been sitting, for an arm-chair was drawn to
the fire, a reading-lamp was alight on the table, and
papers and magazines lay scattered about.

The police officer in plain clothes, who stood with
his subordinate, somewhat undecided, hardly knew
how to begin. It was a hard task to break such awful
news to this lonely old man.

At last it was done ; the word " accident " and
" your nephew " were blurted out by the man in command. But hardly were these out of his lips than
Lord Radclyffe—livid and trembling—had jumped to
his feet.

" Luke ! " he contrived to exclaim, and his voice
was almost choked, his lips and hands trembled, beads
of perspiration stood upon his forehead : " something
has happened to Luke."

" No, no, my lord ! that's not the name. . . .
Philip was on the card and on the letters. . . . Philip
de Mountford . . . that was, I think, the poor gentleman's name."

" And an accident has happened to Mr. Philip de
Mountford ? "

The voice was quite different now. No longer choked with anxiety : calm, and as if mildly interested in passing events. It was obvious, even to the strangers present, that one nephew was of far greater moment than the other.

"I am afraid, my lord, that it's worse than an accident. . ."

The officer paused a moment, satisfied that he was doing all that was necessary and possible to mitigate the suddenness of the blow.

"It's foul play," he said at last, "that's what it was."

"Foul play ? What do you mean by that ? "

"Mr. Philip de Mountford has been murdered, my lord . . . his body now lies at the police station. . . . Would you wish him conveyed home at once, my lord ? . . . or wait until after the inquest ? "

There was silence in the room for a moment or two, while the old-fashioned clock ticked stolidly on. At the awful announcement—which, indeed, might have felled a younger and more vigorous man—Lord Radclyffe had not moved. He was still standing, his hand resting on the table beside the piled-up newspapers. The light of the lamp, veiled by a red shade, illumined the transparent delicacy of the high-bred hand, the smooth, black surface of the coat, and the glimmering whiteness of the shirt-front, with its single pearl stud. The face itself was in shadow, and thus the police officer saw little or nothing of that inward struggle for self-mastery which was being put so severely to the test.

Lord Radclyffe, face to face with the awful event, strove by every power at his command to remain dignified and impassive. The lessons taught by generations of ancestors had to bear fruit now, when a representative of the ancient name stood confronting the greatest crisis that one of his kind has ever had to face. The brutal, vulgar fact of a common murder, the realities of a sordid life brought within the four walls of a solemn, aristocratic old house.

For a moment before he spoke again the old man looked round about him—the tall mahogany bookcases filled with silent friends, the busts of Dryden and of Milton, the globes in their mahogany casings : all heirlooms from the generations of de Mountfords who had gone before.

It seemed as if the present bearer of the historic name called all these mute things to witness this present degradation. A crime had smirched the family escutcheon ; for to some minds—those who dwell on empyrean heights to which the matter-of-fact sordidness of everyday life never reaches—to those minds the victim is almost as horrible as the assassin.

Lord Radclyffe, however, fought his own battle silently. Not with one tremor or one gasp would he let the two men see what he felt. Conventionality wielded her iron rod in this shabby old library, just as she had done in the ballroom of the Danish Legation, and whilst not two hundred yards away Louisa Harris sang Guy d'Hardelot's songs and smilingly received praise and thanks for her perfect performance, so here the old man never flinched.

He gave to his nerves the word of command, and as soon as he had forced them to obey, he looked straight at the police officer and said quite calmly—

"Please tell me all that I ought to know."

He sat in his high-backed chair, curtly bidding the two men to sit down; he made no attempt to shade his face and eyes; once the battle fought and won he had nothing more to hide : his own face rigid and still, his firm mouth and smooth brow were mask enough to conceal the feelings within.

The officer gave the details at full length : he told Lord Radclyffe all that was known of the mysterious crime. The old man listened in silence until the man had finished speaking, then he asked a few questions.

"You have a clue of course ? "

"I think so, my lord," replied the officer guardedly.

"Can I help in any way ? "

"Any information, my lord, that you think might help us would, of course, be gladly welcomed."

"The man who hailed the cab in Shaftesbury Avenue. . . . What was he like ? . . . I could help you if I knew."

"I'll have his description properly written out, my lord, and bring it you in the morning."

"Can't you tell me now ? Every moment lost is irretrievable in cases like these."

"I am afraid, my lord, that I cannot tell you definitely now. There's a dense fog outside . . . and . . ."

"The chauffeur's descriptions are vague," interposed Lord Radclyffe, with a sneer; "the eternal excuses for incompetence."

" My lord ! " protested the man.

" All right ! all right ! No offence meant, I assure you. . . . You must pardon an old man's irritability . . . the news you have brought me does not make for evenness of temper. . . . I rely on your department to clear this matter up with the least possible scandal. . . ."

" I am afraid that scandal is inevitable," retorted the officer dryly, for he still felt sore at Lord Radclyffe's ill-tempered thrust ; " we shall have to rake up a great deal of what might be unpleasant to many parties."

" Why should it be unpleasant ? "

" We shall have to know something of the murdered man's past, of his associates before . . . before he was able to establish his claim to your lordship's consideration."

" I have no doubt that the late Philip de Mountford had many undesirable associates in the past," remarked Lord Radclyffe curtly.

The silence which followed was tantamount to a dismissal. The officer rose to go. He felt nettled at the old man's obvious sneers : they had been like a cold douche over his enthusiasm, for the case had already drifted into his hands and it promised to be the most interesting and most sensational criminal case of modern times.

"You have not," he said before taking his leave, "told me, my lord, what you wish done about the body."

" Surely," replied Lord Radclyffe querulously, " it is too late now to make any arrangements. What is the time ? "

"Half-past ten, my lord."

"Surely to-morrow morning we can discuss all that."

"Just as you wish, of course."

"To-morrow morning . . . as early as you like. . . . My servants will be at home then . . . the house will be ready . . . and I can make arrangements . . . or else we'll wait, as you say, until after the inquest."

The sound of a bell broke the silence that ensued.

"You must excuse me," said his lordship dryly; "my servants are out, and there's some one at the front door."

"I can hear footsteps below stairs, my lord," remarked the officer.

"Ah! I believe you're right. Those two blackguards must have come home and I didn't know it. . . . They do pretty much as they like."

Shuffling, uncertain footsteps were heard across the hall. The officer said hurriedly—

"One more thing, my lord . . . you will pardon me asking, but . . . you had not thought of—er— offering a reward . . . ? "

"What for ? "

"The apprehension of the murderer . . . or useful information that would lead to conviction. . . ."

"Oh! ah! yes! a reward, by all means. . . . Of course, I'll give a reward to stimulate incompetence, eh ? "

"What will your lordship make it ? " asked the officer, determined this time to show no resentment.

" Two hundred . . . five hundred . . . have what you like . . . so long as you get that brute."

" Five hundred, my lord, would stimulate us all."

" Very well ! " said Lord Radclyffe briefly. " Good evening."

" Good evening, my lord. And to-morrow morning we'll be ready for the body to be taken away, if you wish it. . . . But the inquest will be the day after, so perhaps it might be best to wait until then . . . the Coroner's Court, Victoria, my lord . . . South Kensington, you know . . . everything will be all right. . . . Good evening, my lord."

The two men took their leave, glad enough to have done with the unpleasant interview.

As they walked to the door that gave from the library on the hall it was opened from the outside, and a seedy-looking man, dressed in shabby evening clothes that bore many traces of past libations, walked unceremoniously midway into the room.

" Will you see Mr. Luke de Mountford ? " he muttered, addressing his master.

"Certainly not," replied his lordship. "It's much too late. Ask Mr. Luke to call again to-morrow. And you and your wife can go to bed."

CHAPTER XV

BY the time the police officers reached the outer hall door, Luke had received his order of dismissal. He stood on the step for a moment—undecided what to do—and saw the two men coming out of his uncle's study.

They raised their hats as they met him on the doorstep, and one of them said politely—

"Mr. Luke de Mountford?"

"That is my name," replied Luke.

"Mine is Travers—attached to Scotland Yard. Could I ask you a few questions? . . ."

"Certainly . . . but not in my uncle's house, I think. . . ."

"Of course not . . . where do you suggest?"

"Here on the doorstep if you like. . . ,"

"Hardly. Might I trouble you to step into a cab with me and to come as far as Victoria Police Court?"

"It's very late, isn't it? . . . I have an engagement at eleven . . . close by here. . . ."

He was going to fetch Colonel Harris and Louisa at the Danish Legation and pilot them home to the Langham.

"It's an important matter, Mr. de Mountford," retorted the man. " Are you lodging anywhere near here ? "

" In Exhibition Road, Kensington."

" Ah ! close to Cromwell Road ? "

" Not far."

" Then where shall it be, Mr. de Mountford ? "

" Why not in the cab ? " remarked Luke.

" Just as you like."

The taxi-cab which had brought the police officers was standing some few paces further on, its strong lights only just piercing the intensity of the fog : and its throbbings, as the taxi-meter marked off two-pences with unerring rapidity, filled the night with their strangely familiar sound.

The three men got into the cab, the officer telling the chauffeur to remain stationary until told to move on.

" I know very little about the business, Mr.—er— Travers," remarked Luke as soon as all three of them had stowed themselves fairly comfortably in the interior of the vehicle. " I suppose it is about this ghastly affair that you wanted to speak to me."

" Yes, sir. It was about that. I thought you could give us some information about the late Mr. de Mount-ford's past life, or his former friends."

" I know nothing," retorted Luke dryly, " of my cousin's past or present life. He did not confide in me."

" But you were good friends ? " interposed the other quickly.

" We knew each other very little."

" And to-night ? "

" I saw him at his Club."

" Where was that ? "

" The Veterans' in Shaftesbury Avenue."

" About what time ? "

" Between eight and nine."

" You had some talk with him ? "

" Yes."

" Pleasant talk ? " asked the officer indifferently.

" Family affairs," rejoined Luke dryly.

" And you parted from him ? "

" Somewhere about nine."

" In the Club ? "

" In the Club."

" The doorstep ? "

" No. The lobby."

" He was alone then ? I mean . . . besides yourself there was no one with him ? "

" No one. The hall-porter stood there, of course."

" No one joined him afterwards ? "

" That I cannot say. When I parted from him he was alone."

" You know that Mr. Philip de Mountford was murdered in a taxi-cab between Shaftesbury Avenue and Hyde Park Corner, soon after nine o'clock ? "

" I have heard most of the details of that extraordinary crime."

" And you can throw no light on it at all ? "

" None. How could I ? "

" Nothing," insisted the police officer, " occurs to you at this moment that might help us in any way to trace the murderer ? "

" Nothing whatever,"

The man was silent. It seemed as if he was meditating how best to put one or two more questions. Up to now these had been curt and to the point, and as they followed one another in quick succession there was a marked difference in the attitude both of the questioner and the questioned. The police officer had started by being perfectly deferential—just like a man accustomed to speak with people whose position in the world compelled a certain regard. He had originally addressed Luke as " sir," just as he had invariably said " my lord " to Lord Radclyffe, but now he spoke much more curtly; there was a note of demand in every question which he put, a peremptoriness of manner which did not escape the observation of his interlocutor.

As the one man became more aggressive, so did Luke also change his manner. There had been affable courtesy in his first reply to the questions put to him, a desire to be of help if help was needed, but with his senses attuned by anxiety and nerve strain to distinguish subtle differences of manner and of intention, he was quick enough to notice that he himself was, as it were, in a witness-box, with a counsel ready enough to bully, or to trip up any contradictory statement.

Not that Luke realized the reason of this change. The thought that he could be suspected of a crime was as far removed from his ken as the desire to visit the moon. He could not understand the officer's attitude, it puzzled him, and put him on his guard—

but it was just the instinct of self-preservation, of caution which comes to men who have had to fight the world, and who have met enemies where they least expected to find one.

"Do you remember," now resumed Travers after that slight pause, which had seemed very long to Luke, but as a matter of fact had only lasted a short minute, "whether you saw Mr. Philip de Mountford speaking with any one when you left him in the lobby of the Club ? "

"I told you," said Luke impatiently, "that he was alone, except for the hall-porter."

"Alone in the whole Club-house ? "

"Alone," reiterated Luke with measured emphasis, "in the lobby of the Veterans' Club."

"How many rooms has the Club ? "

"I don't know; it was the first time I had ever been there."

"Did you know any of the staff ? "

"No . . . since I had never been there before."

"You were not known to any member of the staff."

"Not that I know of."

"You were shown into the Club-rooms without being known there at all ? "

"The Veterans' Club is a new one, and its rules apparently are not very strict. I asked if Mr. de Mountford was in the Club and was told that I should find him in the smoking-room, and I did."

"How long did your interview with Mr. de Mountford last ? "

"About three-quarters of an hour, I should say."

" And it was of a perfectly amicable nature."

" Of a perfectly indifferent nature," corrected Luke.

" And after the interview what did you do ? "

" I walked out of the Club."

" But after that ? "

" I walked about."

" In the fog ? " This in an undisguised tone of surprise.

" In the fog."

" In what direction ? "

" Really," here rejoined Luke, with a sudden show of resentment, " Mr.—er—Travers, I fail to see how my movements can be of concern to you."

He was certainly not going to tell this man that he had made his way through the fog as far as the residence of the Danish Minister, and that he had walked up and down for over an hour outside that house like a love-sick fool, like a doting idiot, because he knew that if he waited patiently he would presently hear the faint echo of a well-trained contralto voice whose mellowness would come to him through the closed windows of the brilliantly illumined mansion, and would ease for a moment the wild longing of his heart.

What the man near him said in answer to his retort he really could not say. He had not heard, for in a moment his thoughts had flashed back to that lonely vigil in the fog, to the sound of her voice, which came, oh ! so faintly to his ear, and then to the first breath of gossip that came from the passers-by, the coachmen and chauffeurs who had drawn up in long rows along

the kerb, the idlers who always hang about outside in
the cold and the damp when a society function is in
progress, the pickers-up of unconsidered trifles, lost or
willingly bestowed.

From these he had first heard the news : vaguely at
first, for he did not—could not realize that the amazing
thing which was being commented on and discussed
had anything to do with him. The talk was of murder,
and soon the name of de Mountford was mentioned.
The details he got were very confused ; and the open
allusions as to " seek whom the crime will benefit "
never really reached his brain, which was almost numb
with the violence of the shock.

His first thought after that was to go and see Uncle
Rad ; he had, for the moment, almost forgotten Louisa.
Every other interest in life sank to nothingness beside
the one clear duty; Uncle Rad would be alone, the
awful news must be broken very gradually to Uncle
Rad. He had hurried to Grosvenor Square, only to
find that emissaries of the police had forestalled him
in his duty.

All this he could not explain to the man Travers.
It would have sounded lame and barely plausible.
Nowadays men do not walk outside houses wherein
their liege-lady dwells, and if they do, they do not
choose a foggy night for the sentimental dalliance.
He was thankful, therefore, that Travers put no
further questions to him, and merely said with a return
to his original politeness—

" I am greatly obliged to you, sir. I don't think I
need detain you any longer. . . . You said you had

an engagement later on . . . won't you keep this cab ? "

Luke thanked him, but refused the offer of the cab. " It is close by," he said.

" May I call on you to-morrow morning, sir ? "

" If it is necessary."

" I am afraid so. . . . You see, we don't like to trouble Lord Radclyffe, and we must try and obtain knowledge of certain facts and verify others."

" Quite so. Well, to-morrow then."

" Thank you, sir. Your address is . . . ? "

" Fairfax Mansions, Exhibition Road."

" Such a nice neighbourhood. . . , No fog there to-night, I think."

" I hope not. Good night."

" Good night, sir."

Luke made his escape from the cab. He was afraid of missing Louisa and her father. His thoughts were somewhat in a whirl, and—being overburdened with matters of paramount importance—were inclined to dwell on trifles.

" I ought," he reflected, " to have taken that man's cab. It might be difficult to get another, and Colonel Harris hates waiting in a crowded hall."

CHAPTER XVI

AND THE PUPPETS DANCED

AND so he went to meet Louisa and Colonel Harris at the Danish Legation, and found them a taxi-cab, and generally saw to their comparative comforts.

There was no restraint between the three of them. It was as natural to them all to avoid speaking of important matters on the doorstep of a neighbour's house as it was to eat or drink or breathe. So Luke asked if the dinner had been enjoyable and the reception crowded, and Colonel Harris comfortably complained of both. He hated foreign cooking, and society crushes, and had endured both to-night. No doubt the terrible events of this night, as yet mere shadows—hardly admitted to be real—were weighing on the kind old man's usual hearty spirits.

But so versed were they all in the art of make-believe, that each one individually was able to register in the innermost depths of an anxious heart the firm conviction that the other " had not heard."

Luke was convinced that the gruesome and sordid news could not have penetrated within the gorgeous mansion where Loo, in an exquisite gown, had sung modern songs in her pure contralto voice. He felt sure that neither Loo nor Colonel Harris had heard that

Philip de Mountford had been murdered in a taxi-cab,
and that police officers had thought fit to speak to him
—Luke—in tones of contemptuous familiarity. Nay
more ! now that he himself sat thus opposite good-
natured, prosy, sensible Colonel Harris, he began to
think that he must have been dreaming, that the
whole thing could not have occurred, but that he had
imagined it all whilst leaning against the garden-
railings trying to strain his ears so that they should
hear the soft, faint echo of that pure contralto voice.

Perhaps the wish had been father to the thought ;
whilst gazing up at those brilliantly illumined windows,
he might in his heart of hearts have wished the non-
existence of Philip . . . not his death, but the annihi-
lation of the past few months, the non-advent of the
intruder ; and, thus wishing, he may have imagined
the whole thing—the murder in the cab, the police
officer on the doorstep of the old home in Grosvenor
Square.

A sense of supreme well-being encompassed him
now. Loo sat opposite to him. He could not distinguish her face in the gloom, only the outline of her
head with the soft brown hair perfectly dressed by the
hand of an accomplished maid. Loo, the personifica-
tion of modernity, of ordinary commonplace life, but
exquisite—just the woman whom he loved with every
fibre of his heart, every tendril of his being, and every
sense within him. A soft perfume of sweet peas clung
to her gown and was wafted to his nostrils. He closed
his eyes, and drew in a long breath of supreme delight.
Now and then as the cab gave a jerk his knee came in

contact with hers, and down on the ground quite close to his own there rested a small neatly shod foot, the sole of which he would have given his heart's blood to kiss.

Oh yes! he was quite, quite happy; this was reality: his exquisite Louisa, the outline of her perfect head, the touch of her knee, the scent of sweet peas which intoxicated him and whipped his senses to madness and to dreams. . . . It was reality, and the other was only the wild phantasmagoria of a wild imagination—the insane thought born of insane desire. In the darkness which enveloped him and Loo, he could, you see, give free rein to himself. The world was not gaping, conventionality held no sway within these four narrow walls, the puppet could loosen the string which had forced it to dance; it could lie placid for a while, dead to the world, but enjoying its own existence and its own vitality.

And Loo, watching him in that same darkness which concealed him entirely, save to her eyes of watchfulness, believed that he had heard nothing as yet. She vaguely combated the desire to tell him everything then and there, so that he should hear the worst and the best from her lips rather than through indifferent channels later on.

But with that subtle perception peculiar to her— the modern, commonplace woman of the world—she divined that he was living for the moment in a world of his own, from which it were sacrilege to try and drag him away.

Just then the cab drew up outside the Langham

Hotel. The everyday world had returned with its flaring electric lights, its hall-porters, its noise and bustle, and chased away the illusions of the past few moments. Luke jumped out, ready to help Loo down —a happy second that, for her hand must needs rest in his.

The glare of the electric lamp above fell full on his face, which was serene, placid, the usual mask of supreme indifference ; only Louisa read beyond the mask, and as her hand rested in his for just a thought longer than conventionality allowed, she realized that he knew everything : the murder, the horror, and the suspicion which had touched him already with the tip of its sable wing.

Her eyes and the pressure of her hand bade him " good night," and she passed on into the lighted hall of the hotel. He followed Colonel Harris into the lobby.

" You have heard ? " he asked quickly and in a whisper, lest Loo should hear.

" Yes," replied the other.

" And Louisa ? Does she know ? "

" Gossip was all over the confounded place," was Colonel Harris's muttered comment.

" But you've heard no details ? "

" No. Have you ? "

" Very little. Only what the police officer chose to tell me."

" Then," queried the old man, " it's an absolute fact ? "

" Absolute, unfortunately."

" H'm ! As to that . . . Have you seen your uncle ? "

" No. I went round as soon as I knew, but the police had forestalled me and broken the news to him."

" But why didn't you see him ? "

" He sent word that he would rather I came back in the morning. Philip's influence still prevalent, you see."

" Well ! It's a confounded business," ejaculated Colonel Harris, with hearty conviction ; " but I'm not going to lament over it. After all said and done, it's a very simple way out of an impossible situation."

" A very horrible way."

" Bah ! "

And the good-natured old man shrugged his shoulders with a gesture of supreme indifference.

" Well ! " said Luke quietly, " it's late now, sir. You'll want to get to bed."

" Well ! " retorted the other, with a touch of joviality, " it's an ill wind . . . you know."

" Good night, sir."

" Good night, my boy. How will you get back ? "

" Oh ! a taxi is the quickest. Edie might have heard something, and be anxious. I must hurry home now."

Louisa was standing in the hall at the top of the steps. Luke raised his hat to her, and having shaken hands with Colonel Harris quietly turned to go, and was soon lost in the gloom beyond.

No one who had been standing in the lobby of the hotel would have guessed that these three people who had talked and bowed and shaken hands so quietly were facing one of life's most appalling, most over-whelming tragedies.

The world's puppets had been strung up again, because indifferent eyes were there to watch and gape, and in the presence of these modern Bulls of Bashan the puppets danced to the prevalent tune.

CHAPTER XVII

AND WHAT OF THE SECRET ?

WHEN Luke arrived at his uncle's house early the next morning, he was met in the hall by Dr. Newington, who was descending the stairs and who gravely beckoned to the young man to follow him into the library.

"They called me in last night," he said in reply to Luke's quick and anxious query. "The butler—or whatever he may be—told me that he was busy fastening up the front door, preparatory to going to bed, when he heard a heavy thud proceeding from the library. He found his master lying full length on the floor : the head had come in violent contact, as he fell, with the corner of this table ; blood was trickling from a scalp wound and Lord Radclyffe himself was apparently in a swoon. The man is a regular coward and a fool besides. He left his master lying just as he had fallen, but fortunately he knew me and knew where to find me, and within ten minutes I was on the spot, and had got Lord Radclyffe into bed."

"Is it," asked Luke, "anything serious ? "

"Lord Radclyffe has not been over strong lately. He has had a great deal to put up with, and at his age the system is not sufficiently elastic—or—how shall I put it ?—sufficiently recuperative to stand either constant nerve strain or nagging worries."

"I don't know," interposed Luke stiffly, "that my uncle has had either nerve strain or worry to put up with."

"Oh!" rejoined the doctor, whose gruff familiarity seemed to Luke's sensitive ear to be tainted with the least possible note of impertinence, "I am an old friend of your uncle's, you know, and of all your family; there isn't much that has escaped my observation during the past year."

"You have not yet told me, doctor," said Luke, a shade more stiffly than before, "what is the matter with Lord Radclyffe."

There was distinct emphasis on the last two words.

Dr. Newington shrugged his shoulders good-humouredly.

"Your uncle has had something in the nature of a stroke," he said bluntly, and he fixed his keen light-coloured eyes on those of Luke, watching the effect which the news—baldly and crudely put—would have on the young man's nerves. He was a man with what is known as a fashionable practice. He lived in Hertford Street, and his rounds were encircled by the same boundaries as those of the rest of Mayfair. He had had plenty of opportunity of studying those men and women who compose the upper grades of English society. They and their perfect sangfroid, their well-drilled calm under the most dire calamities or most unexpected blows, had often cost him astonishment when he was a younger man, fresh from hospital work, and from the haunts of humbler folk, who had no cause or desire to hide the depth of their feelings. Now he was used to his fashionable patients and had ceased to wonder, and Luke's impassiveness on hearing of his uncle's sudden illness did not necessarily strike him as indifference.

" Is it serious ? " asked Luke.

" Serious. Of course," assented the doctor.

" Do you mean that Lord Radclyffe's life is in danger ? "

" At sixty years of age, life is always in danger."

" I don't mean that," rejoined Luke with a slight show of impatience. " Is Lord Radclyffe in immediate danger ? "

" No. With great care and constant nursing, he may soon rally, though I doubt if he will ever be as strong and hearty as he was this time last year."

" Then what about a nurse ? "

" I'll send one down to-day, but . . ."

" Yes ? "

" Lord Radclyffe's present household is . . . well, hardly adequate to the exigencies of a long and serious illness . . . he ought to have a day and a night nurse . . . I can send both . . . but they will want some waiting on and, of course, proper meals and ordinary comforts. . . ."

" I can see to all that. . . . Thank you for your advice. . . ."

" A good and reliable cook is also necessary . . . who understands invalid cooking . . . all that is most important."

" And shall be attended to at once. . . . Is there anything else ? "

" Perfect rest and quiet, of course, is the chief thing."

" I shan't worry him, you may be sure . . . and no one else is likely to come near him."

" Except the police," remarked the doctor dryly.

" The police ? "

The grave events of the night before, and those that were ready to follow one another in grim array for the next few days, had almost fled from Luke's memory in face of the other—to him more serious— calamity : his uncle's illness.

" Oh ! ah ! yes ! " he said vaguely, " I had forgotten."

" The nurses," rejoined the doctor with a pompousness which somehow irritated Luke, " will have my authorization to forbid any one having access to Lord Radclyffe for the present. I will write out the certificate now, and this you can present to any one who may show a desire to exercise official authority in the matter of interviewing my patient."

" I dare say that I can do all that is necessary at the inquest and so on. . . . Lord Radclyffe need not be worried."

" He mustn't be worried. To begin with, he would not know any one, and he is wholly unable to answer questions."

" That settles the matter, of course. So, if you will write the necessary certificate, I'll see the police authorities at once on the subject. . . . Would Lord Rad-

clyffe know me, do you think ? " added the young
man after a slight pause of hesitancy.

" Well," replied the doctor evasively, " I don't
think I would worry him to-day. We'll see how he
gets on. . . ."

" He'll probably ask for me."

" That is another matter, and if he does, you must,
of course, see him. . . . But unless there is a marked
improvement during the day, he won't ask for any
one."

Luke was silent for a moment or two while the
doctor sat down at the writing-table and sought for
pen and ink.

" Very well," he said after a while, " we'll leave it
at that. Lord Radclyffe—I can promise you this—
shall on no account be disturbed without permission
from you. How soon will the nurse arrive ? "

" Within the hour. The night nurse will come after
tea."

Dr. Newington wrote out and signed the usual
medical certificate to the effect that Lord Radclyffe's
state of health demanded perfect quietude and rest
and that he was unable to see any one or to answer
any questions. He read his own writing through
very carefully, then folded the paper in half and
handed it to Luke.

" This," he said, " will make everything all right.
And I'll call again in a couple of hours' time. You
won't forget the cook ? "

" No, I won't forget the cook."

When the doctor had taken his leave, Luke stood

for a moment quietly in the library : he folded up the medical certificate which he had received at the hands of Dr. Newington and carefully put it away in his pocket-book.

" You won't forget the cook."

I don't think that ever in his life before had Luke realized the trivialities of life as he did at this moment. Remember that he was quite man of the world enough, quite sufficiently sensible and shrewd and English, to have noticed that the degree of familiarity in the doctor's manner had passed the borderland of what was due to himself ; the tone of contemptuous indifference savoured of impertinence. And there was something more than that.

Last night when Luke wandered up and down outside the brilliantly lighted windows of the Danish Legation, trying to catch a few muffled sounds of the voice he so passionately loved to hear, he heard the first rumours that an awful crime had been committed which, for good or ill, would have such far-reaching bearings on his own future ; but he had also caught many hints, vague suggestions full of hidden allusions, of which the burden was : " Seek whom the crime benefits."

Luke de Mountford was no fool. Men of his stamp —we are accustomed to call them commonplace— take a very straight outlook on life. They are not hampered by the psychological problems which affect the moral balance of a certain class of people of to-day, they have no sexual problems to solve. Theirs is a steady, wholesome and clean life, and the mirrors of nature have not been blurred by the breath of psychologists. Luke had never troubled his head about his neighbour's wife, about his horse or his ass or anything that is his, therefore his vision about the neighbour himself had remained acute.

Although I must admit that at this stage the thought that he might actually be accused of a low and sordid crime never seriously entered his head, he nevertheless felt that suspicion hovered round him, that some people at any rate held it possible that since he would benefit by the crime, he might quite well have contemplated it.

The man Travers thought so certainly, the doctor did not deem it impossible . . . and of course there would be others.

No wonder that he stood and mused. Once more the aspect of life had changed for him. He was back in that position from which the advent of the unknown cousin had ousted him so easily—the cousin who had come, had seen and had conquered the one thing needful : the confidence and help of Uncle Rad.

By what means he had succeeded in doing that had been the great mystery which had racked Luke's mind ever since he felt his uncle's affection slipping away from him.

Uncle Rad, who had loudly denounced the man as an impostor and a blackmailer before he set eyes on him, was ready to give him love and confidence the moment he saw him ; and Luke was discarded like an old coat that no longer fitted. The affection of years was turned to indifference ; and what meant more still, the habits of a lifetime, were changed. Lord Radclyffe, tyrannical and didactic, became a nonentity in his own household. The grand seigneur, imbued with every instinct of luxury and refinement, became a snuffy old hermit, uncared-for, not properly waited on, feeding badly and living in one room.

All this Philip de Mountford had accomplished entirely by his mere presence. The waving of a wand—a devil's wand—and the metamorphosis was complete! What magic was there in the man himself? what in the tale which he told? what subtle charm did he wield, that the news of his terrible death should strike the old man down as some withered old tree robbed of its support?

Now he lay dead, murdered! only God knew as yet by whom. People suspected Luke, because Fate had given a fresh turn to her wheel and reinstated him in the pleasing position from which the intruder had ousted him.

Luke de Mountford was once more heir-presumptive to the Earldom of Radclyffe, and the stranger had taken the secret of his success with him to the grave.

CHAPTER XVIII

SINCE Lord Radclyffe was too ill to attend to anything or to see any one, it devolved upon Luke to make what arrangements he thought fitting for the lying-in-state and the subsequent obsequies of the murdered man. For the present Philip de Mountford lay in the gloomy mortuary chamber of the Victoria police court. Luke had sent over massive silver candelabra, flowers and palms, and all the paraphernalia pertaining to luxurious death.

The dead man lay—not neglected—only unwatched and alone, surrounded by all the evidences of that wealth which he had come a very long way to seek, but which Fate and a murderer's hand had snatched with appalling suddenness from him.

And in the private sitting-room at the Langham, Louisa Harris sat opposite her father at breakfast, a pile of morning papers beside her plate, she herself silent and absorbed.

"That's a queer tale," Colonel Harris was saying, "the papers tell about that murder in Brussels a year ago . . . though I must say that to my mind there appears some truth in what they say. What do you think, Louisa?"

" I hardly know," she replied absently, " what to think."

" The details of that crime, which was committed about a year ago, are exactly the same as those which relate to this infernal business of last night."

" Are they really ? "

No one could have said—and Louisa herself least of all—why she was unwilling to speak on that subject. She had never told her father, or any one, for a matter of that, except . . . that she had been so near to the actual scene of that mysterious crime in Brussels, and that she had known its every detail.

" And I must say," reiterated Colonel Harris emphatically, " that I agree with the leading article in *The Times*. One crime begets another. If that hooligan—or whatever he was—in Brussels had not invented this new and dastardly way of murdering a man in a cab and then making himself scarce and sending the cab spinning on its way, no doubt Philip de Mountford would be alive now. Not that that would be a matter for great rejoicings. Still, a crime is a crime, and if we were going to allow blackguards to be murdered all over the place by other blackguards, where would law and order be ? "

He was talking more loudly and volubly than was his wont, and he took almost ostentatiously quantities of food on his plate, which it was quite obvious he never meant to eat. He also steadily avoided meeting his daughter's eyes. But at this juncture she put both elbows on the table, rested her chin in her hands, and looked straight across at her father.

L

" It's no use, dear," she said simply.

" No use what ? " he queried, with ungrammatical directness.

" No use your pretending to talk at random and to be eating a hearty breakfast, when your thoughts are just as much absorbed as mine are."

" H'm ! " he grunted evasively, but was glad enough to push aside the plateful of eggs and bacon which, indeed, he had no desire to eat.

" You have," she continued gently, " read all the papers, just as I have, and you know as well as I do what to read between the lines when they talk of ' clues ' and of ' certain sensational developments.' "

" Of course I do," he retorted gruffly ; " but it's all nonsense."

" Of course it is. But worrying nevertheless."

" I don't see how such rubbish can worry you."

" Not," she said, " for myself. But for Luke. He must have got an inkling by now of what is going on."

" Of course he has. And if he has a grain of sense he'll treat it with the contempt it deserves."

" It's all very well, father. But just think for a moment. Place yourself in Luke's position. The very idea that you might be suspected, must in itself be terrible."

" Not when you are innocent," he rejoined, with the absolute certitude of a man who has never been called upon to face any really serious problem in life. " I shouldn't care what the rabble said about me, if I had a clear conscience."

Louisa was silent for a moment or two, then she said—

"Luke is different somehow. He has been different lately"

"He has had a lot to put up with, with old Radclyffe going off his head in that ridiculous way."

But Louisa did not reply to that suggestion. She knew well enough that it was neither Lord Radclyffe's unkindness, nor the arrogance of the new cousin that had changed and softened Luke's entire nature.

The day that he had sat beside her on the stairs at Lady Ducie's ball, the completeness of the change had been fully borne in on her. When Luke said to her : "I would give all I have in the world to lie on the ground before you and to kiss the soles of your feet," she knew that Love had wrought its usual exquisite miracle, the absorption of self by another, the utter sinking of the ego before the high altar of the loved one. She knew all that, but dear old Colonel Harris had forgotten—perhaps he had never known.

That knowledge comes to so few nowadays. Life, psychology, and sexual problems have taken the place of the divine lesson which has glorified the world since the birth of Lilith.

All that Louisa now remarked to her kind and sensible father was—

"You know, dear, suspicion has killed a man before now. It was but a very little while ago that a noble-hearted gentleman preferred death to such dishonour."

"You've got your head," he retorted, "full of non-sense, Loo. Try and be a sensible woman now, and think of it all quietly. Is there anything you would like me to do, for instance ? "

" Yes, if you will."

" What is it ? "

" Couldn't you see Uncle Ryder ? "

" At Scotland Yard, you mean ? "

" He is at the head of the Criminal Investigation Department, isn't he ? "

" I've always understood so."

" Would he see you, do you think ? at his office ? "

" Tom not see me ? " exclaimed Colonel Harris, " Of course he would. What do you want me to see him about ? "

" He could tell you exactly how matters stood with regard to . . . to Luke, couldn't he ? "

" He could. But would he ? "

" You can but try."

" It's a great pity your aunt is out of town, you might have heard a good deal from her."

" Oh ! Sir Thomas never tells aunt anything that's professional," said Louisa, with a smile. " She'd be for ever making muddles."

" I am sure she would," he assented, with deep conviction.

" Do you think I might go with you ? "

" What ? To Tom's ? I don't think he would like that, Loo ; and it wouldn't quite do, you know."

" Perhaps not," she agreed, with hardly even a sigh of disappointment. She was so accustomed, you see, to being thwarted by convention, whenever impulse carried her out of the bounds which the world had prescribed. Moreover, she expected to see Luke soon. He would be sure to come directly after an early visit to Grosvenor Square.

She helped her father on with his coat. She was almost satisfied that he should go alone. She would have an hour with Luke, if he came early, and it was necessary that she should have him to herself, before too many people had shouted evil and good news, congratulations, opprobrium, and suspicions at him.

Colonel Harris, she knew, would get quite as much, if not more, information out of his brother-in-law, Sir Thomas Ryder, than he could do if she—a mere woman—happened to be present at the interview. Sir Thomas would trust Colonel Harris with professional matters which he never would confide to a woman, and Louisa trusted her father implicitly.

She knew that—despite the grumblings and crustiness peculiar to every Englishman when he is troubled with domestic matters whilst sitting at his own breakfast-table—her father had Luke's welfare just as much at heart as she had herself.

CHAPTER XIX

NOT ALL ABOUT IT

COLONEL HARRIS sent in his card to Sir Thomas Ryder. He had driven over from the Langham in a hansom—holding taxi-cabs in even more whole-hearted abhorrence than before. He inquired at once if Sir Thomas was in his private sanctum, and if so whether he might see him.

Curiously enough the Chief, usually quite inaccessible to the casual visitor—whether relative or stranger—received his brother-in-law immediately.

"Hello, Will," he said by way of greeting. The way Englishmen have of saying that they are pleased to see one another.

"Hello!" responded Colonel Harris in the same eloquent tone.

And the two old boys shook hands.

Sir Thomas then resumed his official chair behind his huge desk and motioned his brother-in-law to an arm-chair close by.

"Have a cigar," said the host.

"Thanks," rejoined the other.

The box was handed across, a havana selected.

The cigars were lighted, and for quite three minutes the two men smoked in silence. One of them had come here to find out how much of his daughter's happiness lay in jeopardy, the other knew what was in the balance, the danger of his niece's happiness, the terrible abyss of misery which yawned at her feet.

But both sat there and enjoyed their cigar. They were dressed with scrupulous care, in the uniform prescribed by the world in which they lived as being suitable for gentlemen of their position and of their age : frock-coats and dark grey trousers, immaculate collar and tie with pearl pin. Both wore a seal ring on the little finger of the left hand, and a watch chain of early Victorian design. They might be twins but for their faces . . . convention had put a livery on them which they would on no account have discarded.

But the faces were very different. Colonel Harris carried his sixty years as easily as if they had been forty. There were not many lines on his round, chubby face, with its red cheeks and round, childlike eyes. The heavy cavalry moustache—once auburn, now almost white—hid the expression of the mouth, but one felt, judging by the eyes and the smooth forehead which continued very far now on to the back of his head, that if one were allowed a peep below that walrus-like face adornment that one would see a mouth that was kind and none too firm, the mouth of a man who had led other men perhaps, but who had invariably been led by his womenfolk.

Now Sir Thomas Ryder was—or rather is, for he is still in perfect health and full vigour—a very different type of man. You have no doubt seen him about town, for he takes a constitutional in the Park every day on his way to his work, and he goes to most first nights at the theatres, and if so you will have admired the keen, sharp face, the closely set eyes, the mobile mouth free from moustache or beard : the face is furrowed all over, especially round the eyes, yet he does not look old—that is because of the furrows : they form a wonderful network round his eyes, giving them an expression of perpetual keen amusement. The hair is pale in colour—not white, but faded—and scanty. Sir Thomas wears it carefully brushed across the top of his head, with a parting on the left side.

He has a trick when he is thinking deeply of passing his hand—which is white, slender, and tapering—over that scanty covering of what,—but for it,—would be a bald cranium.

Some people said that Sir Thomas Ryder was a man without any sentiment, others that he was a slave to red tape ; but no one denied the incontrovertible fact that he was the right man in the right place.

He looked the part and always acted it, and fewer blunders had undoubtedly been committed in the detective department of the Metropolitan Police since Sir Thomas Ryder took the guiding reins in his hands.

" I suppose," he said at last, " that you've come to see me about this de Mountford business."

" I have," replied Colonel Harris simply.

" Well! it's not a pleasant business."

" I know that. The papers are full of it, and it's all a confounded damnable business, Tom, and that's all about it."

" Unfortunately it's not 'all about it,'" rejoined Sir Thomas dryly.

" That's what Louisa says. Women are so queer about things of that sort, and the papers are full of twaddle. She is anxious about Luke."

" I don't wonder."

" But it's all nonsense, isn't it ? "

" What is ? "

Colonel Harris did not reply immediately ; for one thing he did not know exactly how to put his own fears and anxieties into words. They were so horrible and so far-fetched that to tell them plainly and baldly to his brother-in-law, to this man with whom he was soberly smoking a cigar in a sober-looking office, whilst hansoms and taxi-cabs were rattling past in the street below within sight and hearing, seemed little short of idiocy. He was not a man of deep pene-tration — was Colonel Harris—no great reader of thoughts or of character. He tried to look keenly at Sir Thomas's shrewd face, but all he was conscious of was a network of wrinkles round a pair of eyes which seemed to be twinkling with humour.

Humour at this moment! Great heavens above !

" I wish," he blurted out somewhat crossly at last, " you'd help me out a bit, Tom. Hang it all, man, all this officialism makes me dumb."

" Don't," said Sir Thomas blandly, " let it do that,

Will "; and the speaker's eyes seemed to twinkle even
more merrily than before.

"Well then, tell me something about Luke."

"Luke de Mountford," mused the other, as if the
name recalled some distant impression.

"Yes, Luke de Mountford, who is engaged to
Louisa, your niece, man, and she's breaking her
heart with all the drivel these newspapers talk and
I couldn't bear it any longer, so I've come to you,
Tom, and you must tell me what truth there is in the
drivel, and that's all I want to know."

Sir Thomas Ryder seemed, whilst the other thus
talked volubly, to have suddenly made up his mind
to say more than had originally been his intention.
Anyway, he now said with abrupt directness—

"If, my good Will, by 'drivel' you mean that in
the matter of the assassination of Philip de Mountford,
in a taxi-cab last night, grave suspicion rests on his
cousin Luke, then there's a great deal of truth in the
drivel."

Colonel Harris received the sudden blow without
much apparent emotion. He had been sitting in an
arm-chair with one hand buried in his trouser-pocket,
the other holding the cigar.

Now he merely glanced down at the cigar for a
moment and then conveyed it to his lips.

"What," he asked, "does that mean exactly ? "

"That unless Luke de Mountford will within the
next forty-eight hours answer certain questions more
satisfactorily than he has done hitherto, he will be
arrested on a charge of murder."

" That is impossible," protested Colonel Harris hotly.

" Impossible ?   Why ? "

" Because . . . because . . . Hang it all, man ! you know Luke de Mountford. Do you believe for a moment that he would commit such a dastardly crime ? Why, the boy wouldn't know how to plan such villainy, let alone carry it through."

" My dear Will," rejoined the other quietly, " the many years that I have spent at this desk have taught me many things. Among others I have learnt that every man is more or less capable of crime, it only depends what the incentive—the temptation if you like to call it so—or the provocation happens to be."

" But here there was no provocation, no temptation, no . . ." Colonel Harris paused abruptly. He felt rather than saw his brother-in-law's eyes in their framework of wrinkles resting with obvious sense of amusement upon his wrathful face. No temptation ? and what of a peerage and a fortune lost, that could only be regained by the death of the intruder ? No provocation, and what of the brother and sister turned out of the old home ? The good, simple-minded man had sense enough to see that here—if he wished to speak up for Luke—he was on the wrong track.

" What questions," he said abruptly, " does Luke not answer satisfactorily ? "

" How he spent certain hours of yesterday evening."

" He was dancing attendance on Louisa and me."

" Oh ! was he ? Well, that's satisfactory enough. At what time did you part from him ? "

" Well ! he escorted us to the Danish Legation, where we were dining."

" At what time was that ? "

" Eight o'clock dinner."

" But he was not dining at the Danish Legation ? "

" No. He came and fetched us again soon after eleven."

" That's right, but between whiles ? "

" Between whiles ? "

" Yes. Between eight and soon after eleven ? "

" Well ! . . . I suppose . . . I don't know . . . Yes, of course I do ! what a stupid ass I am. . . . Luke told me himself that he was going to see his uncle at the Something Club in Shaftesbury Avenue. . . ."

" The Veterans' ? "

" Yes, that's it . . . the Veterans'. Luke wanted to persuade old Radclyffe to go abroad for the benefit of his health . . . Algeciras—that was it. . . ."

" Quite so," rejoined Sir Thomas dryly, " and Luke de Mountford went to the Veterans' Club in Shaftesbury Avenue, and he asked to see Lord Radclyffe, who was more or less of an habitué at that hour. On being told that Lord Radclyffe was not there that evening, but that Mr. de Mountford was in the smoking-room, Luke elected to go in and presumably to have a talk with his cousin."

" I didn't know that," said Colonel Harris.

" No. But we did. Let me tell you what followed. The hall-porter of the Club showed Luke into the smoking-room, and less than five minutes later he heard loud and angry words proceeding from that room. That a quarrel was going on between the two cousins was, of course, obvious. One or two members of the Club remarked on the noise, and one gentleman actually opened the smoking-room door to see what was going on. He seems to have heard the words ' blackguard ' and ' beggar ' pleasingly intermingled and flying from one young man to the other. This witness knew Philip de Mountford very well by sight, but he had never seen Luke. But remember that Luke denies neither the interview nor the quarrel. The former lasted close on an hour, and Lord Radclyffe's journey to Algeciras was the original topic of discussion. At about nine o'clock Luke emerged from the smoking-room. The hall-porter saw him. He was then very pale, and almost tottered as he walked. Men do get at times intoxicated with rage, you know, Will."

" I know that, and I can well imagine what happened at that interview. Radclyffe had become such a confounded fool that he would not move or do anything without this Philip's permission : and Luke was determined to get him down to Algeciras at once. As Philip was at the Club, he thought that he would tackle him then and there."

" Quite so. He did tackle him. And equally of course the two men quarrelled."

" But hang it all, one's not going to murder every man with whom one quarrels."

" Stop a moment, Will. As you say, one does not

murder every man with whom one quarrels. But you must admit that this is altogether an exceptional case. There was more than a mere quarrel between these two men. There was deadly enmity . . . justified enmity, I'll own, on Luke's side. . . . We have already come across—it was not very difficult—two or three of the servants who were in Lord Radclyffe's house before Luke and his brother and sister were finally turned out of it. They all have tales to tell of the terrible rows which used to go on in the house between the cousins. You, Will, must know how Luke hated this Philip de Mountford."

Again Colonel Harris was silent. What was the use of denying such an obvious truth ?

"You wanted," continued the other man quietly, "to hear the truth, Will, and you've got it. For Louisa's sake, for all our sakes in fact, I made up my mind to tell you all . . . or most . . . that is officially known to me at this moment. You must get Louisa out of town at once—take her abroad if you can, and keep English newspapers away from her."

" She won't come," said Colonel Harris firmly.

" Oh, yes she will, if you put it the right way."

Which saying on the part of the acute chief of our Criminal Investigation Department was but a further proof—if indeed such proofs were still needed nowadays—of how little clever men know of commonplace women.

" The case will be extremely unpleasant," resumed Sir Thomas, who was quite unconscious of the ignorance which he had just displayed. "It will be hateful for you, and quite impossible for Louisa."

"Always supposing," retorted the other, "that Luke is guilty, which neither I nor Louisa will admit for a moment."

"That," rejoined Sir Thomas, "is as you please."

He put down his cigar, crossed one leg over the other, leaned back in his chair, and folded his tapering hands together, putting finger to finger, with the gesture of one who is dealing with a youthful mind, and has much to explain.

"Look here," Will, he resumed, "I have three men standing in my outer office at the present moment. Two of them have come back after having questioned the past servants of the Grosvenor Square household. There was the butler Parker, and an elderly housekeeper, both of whom are in service in the West End. The woman tried to screen Luke and to make light of the many quarrels which broke out between the cousins on all possible occasions : but she broke down under our fellows' sharp questions. She had to admit that the arrogance of the one man often drove the other to unguarded language, and that she had on more than one occasion heard the men servants of the house say that they would not be astonished if murder ensued one day. Well, we have these two witnesses, and can easily get hold of the two or three footmen who expressed those particular views. So much for the past six months. Now for last night. The third man who is out there waiting for me to see him is Frederick Power, hall-porter at the Veterans'

Club. The story which he told to our Mr. Travers
is so important in its minutest detail, that I have
decided to question him myself so that I may leave
no possible loophole to doubt or to inaccuracy in the
re-telling. I am going to send for the man now.
You come and sit round here, the other side of my
desk ; from this position you will be able to watch
the man's face, as well as hear what he has got to
say. Now, would you like that ? "

" Right you are, Tom," was Colonel Harris's brief
method of acknowledging his brother-in-law's kindness, in thus breaking a piece of red tape, and setting
aside a very strict official rule. He did as Sir Thomas
directed, and sat down in the recess behind the chief's
desk, in a comfortable arm-chair with his back to
the curtained window.

He would not acknowledge even to himself how
deeply stirred he was by all that he had heard, and
now by the anticipation of what was yet to come.
Emotion—like he was experiencing now—had never
come his way before. He had lost his only son
on the Modder River . . . that had been sorrow of
an acute kind ; he had laid a much-loved wife to rest
in the village churchyard close to his stately home
in Kent, and he had escorted his late beloved sove-
reign to her last resting-place on that never-to-be-
forgotten day close on eight years ago now : those
three events in his life had been the great strains to
which his nerves and sensibilities had been subjected
in the past.

But this was altogether different. The sensations

which the good man experienced were such that he scarcely knew them himself ; he had faced sorrow before, never dishonour—some one else's dishonour, of course, still it touched him very nearly, for, though he might not be a very keen observer, he dearly loved his daughter, and dishonour seemed to be touching her, striking at her through Luke.

CHAPTER XX

AND THAT'S THE TRUTH

FREDERICK POWER was shown in.

I won't have you think that there was anything remarkable about the man, or anything that would— even momentarily—distinguish him from any number of other hall-porters, who wear an uniform and peaked cap, have the air of having seen military service, and wear a couple of medals on a well-developed chest.

He was perfectly respectful, all the more so because Sir Thomas was General Sir Thomas Ryder, K.C.B.—a fact which impressed the ex-soldier far more than any other exalted title, non-military in character, would have done.

He saluted and stood at attention, and as he gave answer to Sir Thomas's preliminary questions his words rang out clear and direct, obviously truthful, as if echoing in the barrack-yard at six o'clock of a frosty spring morning.

"Your name is . . .?"

"Frederick Power, sir."

"You are hall-porter at the Veterans' Club in Shaftesbury Avenue?"

" Yes, sir."

" You were in the lobby of the Club last night as usual ? "

" Yes, sir."

" And Mr. Philip de Mountford, who is a member of the Club, was in the smoking-room at eight o'clock yesterday evening ? "

" Yes, sir."

" He came almost every evening, I understand ? "

" That's right, sir."

" Alone mostly ? "

" Not often, sir. Lord Radclyffe was with him most evenings."

" And Lord Radclyffe and Mr. de Mountford dined together on those occasions in the Club dining-room ? "

" Yes, sir."

" But last night Mr. de Mountford was alone ? "

" Yes, sir   He had some dinner at about half-past seven and then he went to the smoking-room."

" Later on a gentleman called to see him ? "

" That's right, sir. It was about quarter - past eight. The gentleman asked to see Lord Radclyffe, but I said that 'is lordship 'adn't come to the Club this night. Then the gentleman asked if Mr. de Mountford was in, and I said yes."

" And you showed him into the smoking-room ? "

" I told 'im he would find Mr. de Mountford in the smoking-room : yes, sir."

" Isn't that rather against Club rules to allow strangers to walk in and out of the rooms ? "

" Well, sir, the Veterans' is a new Club . . . and the committee ain't very partik'lar."

" I see."

So far the questions and answers had followed on one another in quick succession. Sir Thomas Ryder, with his clever lean head held somewhat on one side, appeared to be reciting a well-learned lesson, so even and placid was the tone of his voice and so indifferent the expression of his furrowed face. One leg was crossed over the other and his tapering hands, white and wrinkled like his face, toyed with a large ivory paper knife hardly whiter in colour than they.

He had not told Frederick Power to sit down, as he might have done in the case of a witness who was a civilian. He preferred to keep the man standing, and at attention, confident that he would thus get clearer and sharper replies.

"Well, then," he resumed after a brief interval, during which he had modified his position somewhat, but had not varied the placid expression of his face, " you told the visitor that he would find Mr. de Mountford in the smoking-room. What happened after that ? "

" The gentleman walked in, sir. And he shut the door, sir, after 'im."

" Did you hear anything that went on inside the room ? "

" No, sir. I didn't pay no attention at first, sir."

" Then afterwards ? After a while, you did pay attention, didn't you ? "

" Yes, sir, I did. The door of the smoking-room

is quite close to the entrance, sir, and presently I heard loud voices like as if the two gentlemen was quarrelling."

" Did you hear what was said ? "

" No, sir, not the words. But the voices they sounded awful. And one other gentleman 'e come along from the dining-room, and asked me what the noise was about. There ain't many members not at the Veterans', sir, and being a foggy night we was partik'lar quiet. But this gentleman 'e was curious about the noise, so 'e just opened the smoking-room door and peeped in, and then I did 'ear a few words."

" What were they ? "

" Abuse, sir, mostly. One gentleman was goin' on awful, but I couldn't rightly say which one it was. I 'eard the words ' beggar ' and ' lazy, idling, good-for-nothing,' but I couldn't rightly say 'oo said 'em."

" How long did this go on ? "

" Oh ! a long time, sir ; I couldn't say for sure. After a bit it got quiet in the smoking-room. And at about nine o'clock or soon after, the visitor come away, and 'e asked me for a light."

" What did he seem like then ? "

" I thought he'd been drinking, sir. His face was queer, and pale and moist-like, and his 'and shook like anything when he lighted 'is cigarette."

" Mr. de Mountford did not come out with him ? "

" No, sir, not just then, but 'e come out of the smoking-room a moment or two later, whilst 'is visitor was still in the 'all. Mr. de Mountford 'e was

quite calm, sir, didn't look at all as if 'e'd been 'aving
a quarrel He'd his cigar between his lips, his hat on,
and 'is overcoat over 'is arm."

"Did he speak to the visitor then ? "

"Not right away, sir. 'E seemed to be 'esitating
like at first, then he came forward and 'e says : ' I am
going back to Grosvenor Square now ; would you
like to see Uncle Rad about this business yourself ?
But I warn you that he is of the same mind as myself.' "

"And what did the other gentleman say ? "

"'E just kind o' laughed and shrugged his shoulders
and said : ' I've no doubt of that.' "

"Then after that did they agree to go to Grosvenor
Square together ? "

"I don't rightly know, sir, if the two gentlemen
said anything about that, but the visitor 'e went out
first, and Mr. de Mountford followed 'im into the outer
lobby. Then 'e turned and spoke to me."

"Who did ? "

"Mr. de Mountford, sir ; the other gentleman wasn't
a yard away from 'im and must 'ave 'eard every word
'e said."

"What did he say ? "

"'E said to me : ' Power, I say, you've no business
to allow people to enter the Club rooms like that.
You must keep them waiting in the hall : one will
get hopelessly pestered by beggars at this rate.'
Them were Mr. de Mountford's very words, sir, I
take my Bible oath to every one of 'em, and the other
gentleman 'e was in the outer lobby, sir, and 'e must

'ave 'eard every syllable. I caught sight of 'is face, and, my word, there was murder in his eye."

" That'll do, Power," admonished Sir Thomas, thus checking the man's flow of excited eloquence.

" Very good, sir," replied the other humbly.

" And after that what happened ? "

" Both gentlemen went off, sir. I tried to look after them, but the fog was that thick one couldn't see one's 'and before one's eyes."

" So you lost sight of them just outside the Club house ? "

" That's right, sir."

" And did you see either of these two gentlemen since then ? "

" No, sir." And the man's voice dropped to a solemn whisper. " Mr. de Mountford was murdered in a taxi-cab, sir . . . must 'ave been soon after 'e left the Club."

" Very soon, I should say. But the other ? "

" I saw the other gentleman this morning, sir."

" Where ? "

" Mr. Travers from the police, sir, 'e called to see me at the Club, and 'e took me in a taxi-cab to Grosvenor Square, and told the shoffer, sir, to pull up by the kerb on the garden side. Then 'e told me to watch a partik'lar 'ouse opposite and see 'oo was goin' in or out. I didn't 'arf like it, sir, because I'm not supposed to absent myself for very long of a morning, though the committee ain't very partik'lar. But Mr. Travers 'e was of the police, sir, so I thought it was right to do as 'e told me."

" Quite right. And what did you see ? "

" Nothing much for close on an hour, sir : a carriage drew up to the door of the house and an elderly gentleman got out. Mr. Travers told me that it was the doctor. 'E rang the bell and went into the 'ouse. Then after a bit 'oo did I see walking down the street and straight up to the front door of the partik'lar 'ouse I'd been told to look at, but Mr. de Mountford's visitor of last night."

" You recognized him ? "

" Couldn't mistake 'im, sir."

" Did you call Mr. Travers' attention to him ? "

" Yes, sir. I told 'im that was the gentleman 'oo'd had an awful quarrel with Mr. Philip de Mountford at the Club last night."

" That's all, Power. I won't trouble you further now."

" No trouble, sir."

" Your position at the Club is a permanent one ? "

" Yes, sir."

" You are always to be found there ? "

" Always, sir, whenever you want me."

" Well ! send a line to the Chief Superintendent at Scotland Yard in case your plans get suddenly modified and you are no longer to be found at the Club."

" Not likely, sir. Thank you, sir. Good morning."

" Good morning."

Sir Thomas touched the electric button in the wal behind him, and a man in dark blue uniform appeared. Frederick Power was dismissed. He saluted both gentlemen, and, turning on his heel in proper military fashion, he marched out of the room, obviously delighted with his own importance and with the adventure which varied so pleasantly the monotonous evenness of his existence.

CHAPTER XXI

"WELL, William, what do you think of it all?"
The two men had sat in silence for quite a
considerable time after Frederick Power had marched
out of the room. Colonel Harris, buried in thought, was
in no hurry to talk things over. Sir Thomas Ryder—
a very busy man—was the more impatient of the two.

"I must tell you," he said, seeing that his brother-
in-law seemed disinclined to speak, "that our man
Travers, as soon as Power had pointed Luke out to
him, went and rang the bell at Radclyffe's house, and
quickly enough established beyond a doubt that the
man who had just entered it was Mr. Luke de Mountford. I tell you this now, so as to disabuse your mind
once and for all in case you should imagine that this
might be a case of mistaken identity. Moreover, you
yourself know and have admitted to me that Luke's
intention was to seek out his uncle and his cousin at
the Veterans' Club, after he parted from you at eight
o'clock last night."

"Yes," said Colonel Harris, "I know that. I was
not thinking of mistaken identity."

"You," rejoined the other, "were thinking of Luke,
and so am I. I have thought little of any one else since

first the crime was reported to me last night. And long before Travers gleaned the outlines of the story which Power has just amplified for us, I vaguely guessed at the broad lines of it. Now that I know it in all its details, I can see the whole scene in the lobby of the Veterans' Club before me. You may believe me or not as you like, but as a matter of fact I know quite a good deal about Luke de Mountford. I have often met him, of course, and though we have never been very intimate—for I am a busy man and have but little time for intimacy with my fellow-men—I have had many opportunities of studying him. He has a very curious power of self-control—almost an abnormal one, I call it, and a morbid hatred of public scenes or scandal. This, of course, he shares with a great many men of his class, and his self-control is all the more remarkable as he is not by any means the impassive young man about town which he pretends to be. Well! that same power, I suppose, stood him in good stead in the lobby of the Veterans' Club. In Power's picturesque parlance ' there was murder in his eye.' Of course, he had been provoked beyond the bounds of endurance, and if he had rushed at Philip de Mountford and strangled him then and there, no one would have been astonished. I should," continued Sir Thomas, with emphasis, " because it would not have been like the Luke whom I had studied. The picture of two gentlemen at fisticuffs like a pair of navvies would not have been an edifying one, and Luke—as I know him—would, above all, wish not to make a spectacle of himself before the hall-porter or before a crowd in the ante-room of a second-rate club. He naturally—for that sort of thing becomes second nature—pulled himself together and walked out into the street."

You must not think for a moment that Sir Thomas Ryder was habitually a talkative man. Englishmen of his class and type are rarely talkative, and Sir Thomas's position and occupation had rendered him less communicative than most. But Colonel Harris and he had been brother officers, friends long before family ties were closely knit by marriage, and he considered the present crisis a very serious one.

He had had enough to do with crime in the past few years since he had obtained the interesting post which he now occupied, but never with a crime which affected him personally as this one did. Luke de Mountford was, of course, nothing to him, except in connection with Louisa Harris. But this was a strong tie. Louisa was his own wife's niece ; she was the daughter of a friend, of a brother officer. No one who is not in some manner or other in touch with military men, can have the slightest idea of how much those two magic words mean : " brother officer " ; what magnetism lies in them ; what appeal they make to all that is most loyal, most willing, most helpful in a man.

Sir Thomas felt that the mud of irretrievable disgrace which was bound to smirch Luke de Mountford would in no small measure redound on Louisa too. Instinctively, too, all his sensibilities recoiled against the idea of a gentleman, one of his own caste, being dragged in this peculiarly loathsome mire. It seemed impossible that that type of man should commit a murder . . . a murder ! just an ordinary, brutal, commonplace murder such as the rough-and-tumble herd of humanity commit when under the stress of vulgar passions : greed, avarice, jealousy. It was this juxtaposition of the mean and sordid against his own class that revolted Sir Thomas Ryder. He was loyal to his brother officer in his endeavour to induce him to keep out of all that mud which would be scattered all round presently, when the papers came out with their sensational headlines, but he was also—perhaps more so—loyal to his caste ; his was the esprit de corps not only of militarism, but of birth and breeding. He would not—if he could—have a gentleman held up to opprobrium, and if this could be avoided by the unfortunate criminal's flight from justice, well ! Sir Thomas was ready and willing to take upon his shoulders the burden of contempt and ridicule which the Press and the general public would presently be hurling at him and at his Department for their hopeless incompetence in allowing a murderer to escape.

Therefore he was putting the case against Luke more clearly and with a greater wealth of detail before his brother-in-law than the conscientious discharge of duty should have allowed. In fact, we see Sir Thomas Ryder—a hard disciplinarian, a hide and tape-bound official—freely transgressing the most elementary rules which duty prescribes. He was sitting in his private office with his brother-in-law, giving away secrets that belonged not to him, but to his Department : conniving, through the words which he spoke, at the fleeing from justice of a criminal who belonged not to him, but to the State.

He was making the case against Luke de Mountford to appear as black as it was in effect, so that Colonel Harris and Louisa might take fright and induce the unfortunate man to realize his danger in time and to shrink from facing the consequences of his own terrible deed.

But Colonel Harris—with the obstinacy of those who throughout life have never led, but have always ruled—would not see the case through his brother-in-law's spectacles. He clung to his own repudiation of the possibility of Luke de Mountford's guilt. He behaved quite unconsciously just as Louisa would have wished him to behave, had she been present here to prompt him.

To Sir Thomas's most convincing exposé of the situation he lent an attentive ear, but the shrug of his shoulders when the other man paused to take breath was in itself a testimony of loyalty to Luke's cause.

"Hang it all, man," he said, "you are not going to sit there and tell me that Luke de Mountford—the man whom I myself would have chosen as a son-in-law had Loo not forestalled me—that Luke would commit a deliberate murder. In the name of common sense, Tom! why it's unthinkable. Do you mean to say that you actually believe that Luke, after he left that God-forsaken Club, joined his cousin again as if nothing had happened; that he got into a taxi-cab with him, and poked him through the neck whilst the man was looking another way?"

" Roughly speaking," assented Sir Thomas, " I believe that that's what happened."

" And you call yourself a shrewd detective ! " exclaimed Colonel Harris hotly ; " and you hold the lives of men practically in the hollow of your hand ! Why, man ! have you forgotten one thing," he continued, his gruff voice assuming a note of triumph, " the most important in all this damnable business ? "

" What have I forgotten, Will ? " asked the other, not at all ruffled by the gallant Colonel's sudden tone of contempt.

" The weapon, Tom ! "

" I haven't forgotten the weapon," rejoined Sir Thomas calmly.

" Oh yes ! you have ! Do you mean to tell me that Luke de Mountford habitually walks about the streets of London with an Italian stiletto in his trousers pocket ? for I am told that it was with a thing of that sort that the murder was committed. Or, according to you, did Luke escort Louisa to a dinner-party with the avowed intention at the back of his mind of committing a murder later on if occasion offered ? Did he bring an Italian stiletto from home when he came to meet his fiancée at the Langham Hotel, or did he buy one on the way to the Veterans' Club ? Which of these cock-and-bull theories do you hold, Tom ? "

" Neither," admitted Sir Thomas, with a placid smile.

" Then," concluded Colonel Harris contemptuously, " you think that Luke was—as I said—in the habit of carrying an Italian stiletto in his trousers pocket ? "

" No," rejoined the other, still unruffled ; " but I know that Luke de Mountford is in the habit of carrying a snake-wood walking-stick, which he once bought years ago—somewhere abroad, and the top of which contains a short pointed dagger which fits into the body of the stick. And what's more, you know that stick too, Will ; you have often seen it. Are you prepared to swear that Luke hadn't it with him last night ? "

" He hadn't it with him."

" You are prepared to swear to that ? " insisted the other earnestly.

Colonel Harris was silent. For the first time since the beginning of this long interview he felt as if all the blood in his body was receding back to his heart, causing it to beat so wildly that he thought it was about to choke him. The colour fled from his cheeks, and the cigar dropped from between nerveless fingers. Swift as lightning a recollection came back to him—a vision of Luke entering the sitting-room of the Langham Hotel, with his coat on and his hat and stick in the left hand.

But he would not give in even now—not on such paltry surmises. Any number of men he knew carried sticks that contained weapons of self-defence. He himself possessed a very murderous-looking sword-stick, which he had once bought in Paris. He fought down this oncoming attack of weakness, and blamed himself severely for it too. It savoured of disloyalty to Louisa and to Luke. He stooped and picked his cigar up, and looked his brother-in-law boldly in the face.

" I wouldn't," he said, " swear either way, whether

Luke had his stick with him last night or not. I know that stick, of course. I have got one very like it myself."

" So have I," rejoined Sir Thomas, with his placid smile.

" And if that's one of the proofs on which you are going to accuse my future son-in-law of having committed a murder, then all I can say is, Tom, that you and I are seeing the last of one another to-day."

But Sir Thomas took this threat, as he had taken Colonel Harris's undisguised expressions of contempt, with perfect equanimity.

" If," he said quietly, " I did accuse Luke de Mountford or any other man of murder on such paltry grounds as that, Will, you would be perfectly justified in turning your back on me, if for no other reason than that I should then be an incompetent ass."

" Well ! what more is there then ? "

" Only this, Will. That the stick which you have so often seen in Luke de Mountford's hand, was found this morning inside the railings of Green Park ; it bears unmistakable signs of the use to which it was put last night."

" You mean . . . that it was stained . . . ? "

How long a time elapsed between the beginning of that query and its last words Colonel Harris could not say. The uttering of the words was a terrible effort. They seemed to choke him ere they reached his lips. A buzzing and singing filled his ears so that he did not hear Sir Thomas's reply ; but through a strange veil which half obscured his vision he saw his brother-in-

N

law's slow nod of affirmation. For the first time in his life, the man who had fought against naked savages in the swamps or sands of Africa, who had heard—unflinching—the news of the death of his only son—felt himself totally unnerved. He heard as in a dream the hum of the busy city in the street below, hansoms and omnibuses rattling along the road, the cries of news-vendors or hawkers, the bustle of humdrum everyday life ; and through it the ticking of his own watch in his waistcoat pocket.

He remembered afterwards how strangely this had impressed him : that he could hear the ticking of his own watch. He had never been conscious before of such an acute sense of hearing. And yet the buzzing and singing in his ears went on. And he was horribly, painfully conscious of silly, trivial things—the ticking of his watch which obsessed him, the irregularity in the design of the wall-paper, the broken top of the inkstand on Sir Thomas's desk.

The great, all-important fact had escaped momentarily from his consciousness. He forgot that Philip de Mountford had been murdered, and that Luke's stick, blood-stained and damning, had been found inside the railings of the Park.

A cycle of time went by—an eternity, or else a few seconds. Sir Thomas Ryder pulled open the long drawer of his monumental desk.

Colonel Harris watched him doing it, and long before Sir Thomas took a certain Something from out the drawer, the Colonel knew what that Something would be.

A familiar thing enough. The Colonel had seen it over and over again in Luke de Mountford's hand. A slender stick of rich-looking, dark wood, only very little thicker at the top than at the base, and with a silver band about six inches from the top. On the band the initials " L. d. M." daintily engraved.

" Put it away, Tom, for God's sake ! " Colonel Harris hardly recognized his own voice ; he had spoken more from a sudden instinct of shrinking from loathsome objects than from any real will of his own. One glance at the stick had been enough. It was thickly coated with mud, and about six inches from the top, there where the silver band showed a deep dark cleft between it and the length of the stick, there were other stains—obvious stains of blood.

Yet Colonel Harris had seen worse sights than this in Zululand, and at Omdurman. But on this stained stick, that discoloured silver band, he felt it impossible to look.

" I have broken it to you, Will, as gently as I could," said Sir Thomas, not quite as placidly as before. He too was not unmoved by the distress of his old friend. " You see that I have no option but to tell you all. You must keep out of all this, old man, and above all you must keep Louisa out of it. Take her abroad, Will, as soon as you can."

" She won't go ! " murmured the father dully.

" Nonsense ! "

" She won't go," he reiterated. " She has given her heart to Luke."

" She'll soon forget him."

" Not she ! "

" And she'll be horrified . . . when she knows."

" She'll not believe it."

" If he is wise, he'll plead guilty. . . . His solicitor will advise him to do that. . . . It is his one chance . . ."

" His one chance ? " queried the other vaguely.

" Of escaping the gallows. . . . If he pleads guilty —many extenuating circumstances will be admitted . . . his own spotless reputation . . . and also intense provocation . . . he'll get a life sentence, or even perhaps . . ."

But with a loud oath, the most forcible one he had ever uttered in his life, Colonel Harris had jumped to his feet and brought a heavy fist crashing down upon the table.

" And by the living God, Tom," he said, " I'll not believe it. No ! not for all your witnesses, and your cross-questionings, and your damnable proofs. No ! I'll not believe it, and I know that my girl will not believe it either . . . not until we hear the word ' guilty ' spoken by Luke's own lips. And we'll not leave London, we'll not go abroad, we'll not desert Luke ; for I swear by God ! that I don't believe that he is an assassin."

Men who have always been accounted weak often have moments of unexpected strength. Colonel Harris now seemed to tower morally and mentally over his brother-in-law. The passion of loyalty was in him and caused his eyes to sparkle and his cheeks to glow. The oath he uttered, he spoke with fervour :

there would be no faltering, no wavering in his defence of Luke.

Sir Thomas waited a minute or two, allowing his old friend to recover his normal self-control as well as his breath, which was coming and going in quick gasps. Then he said quietly—

" As you will, old man. Have another cigar."

CHAPTER XXII

THEN THE MIRACLE WAS WROUGHT

WHEN Colonel Harris once more arrived at the Langham he found Luke and Louisa comfortably installed in front of the fire in the private sitting-room upstairs. She was leaning back against the cushions, her head resting in her hand, he at the foot of the sofa, his hands encircling one knee, gazing now and then into the fire, now and then into her face.

Not troubled creatures these, not man and woman fighting a battle against life, against the world, for honour, for peace and for love, not souls racked by painful memories of the past or grim dread of the future! only two very ordinary human beings, with a life behind them of serene contentment, social duties worthily performed, a smooth lake whereon not a ripple of sorrow or disgrace ever dared to mar the shiny surface.

And the ruling passion, strong in death, was stronger still in face of this new life to be led : the life of to-morrow, full of the unknown, the ugly, the sordid and mean, full of nameless dangers, and of possible disgrace. The puppets were still dancing, moved by the invisible strings held by the hand of the implacable giant called Convention : they danced even as though no gaping or ravenous lions, no Bulls of Bashan were there to see. Even before one another they hid the secret mysteries of their heart, he his overwhelming passion for her, she her dread for his immediate future.

They had not forborne to talk of Philip de Mountford's death, they would not have admitted that there was anything there that could not be discussed with perfect indifference—she, reclining against the cushions, and he in immaculate morning coat, with hair smoothly brushed, and speckless tie and linen, talking of things which meant life or death for them both.

He had told her all he knew: his visit to Philip at the Veterans' Club, his quarrel with him, the hatred which he bore to the man that was dead. He made no secret of the police officer's questionings, nor of Dr. Newington's extraordinary attitude.

" One would think those fellows had a suspicion that I had murdered Philip," he said quite lightly.

And her face never moved whilst she listened to these details, analysing them in her mind, comparing them with those at which the morning papers had hinted, the " clues " and " startling developments," to obtain confirmation of which her father had gone out to seek Sir Thomas Ryder.

Luke de Mountford would no more have dreamed of telling Louisa of the dark suspicions which really threatened him than he would have laid bare before her some hideous wound if he happened to be suffer-

ing from one. The police officer's insolence and the
doctor's easy contempt had sounded a note of warning of what was imminent, but beyond that he
had no fear. Why should he have ? And having
none, why worry Loo with plaints that might agitate
her ?

Remember that he individually was quite convinced
that Philip's murderer would soon be discovered.
He too had read his morning paper, and knew as
well as anybody that for the moment suspicion rested
upon him. " Seek whom the crime will benefit ! "
was a phrase freely used in the Press this morning.
But it was only a question of time ; an unpleasant
phase to be traversed, some mud that presently would
have to be brushed off. No use to worry Louisa with
it. Fortunately she took it lightly too. She was
far too sensible to attach importance to such nonsense.

Nevertheless mud thrown in such boundless pro-
fusion was apt to hurt very considerably. Luke had
to set his teeth this morning when he perused *The
Times*, and even now there was in him a sensation
of having been bruised all over, after his second
interview with Travers, and his talk with Doctor
Newington in the library. Louisa did him good. She
was calm and sensible and a woman of the world.
She never puzzled Luke, nor had she that vague
longing to be misunderstood, the peculiar attribute
of the woman of to-day. In face of her serenity he
almost despised himself for the intensity of his own
passion. She was so pure, so womanly in her tender-

ness, a girl still, she was hardly conscious of passion. But she knew that he was in pain—morally and mentally in pain—and that worse was yet to come, and she, the commonplace, sensible girl, brought forth her full array of calm and of triviality, checking by a placid smile the faintest onrush of passion in him, for passion could but torture him now, when his very soul was troubled and every nerve on the jar.

And thus Colonel Harris found them.

When he entered Louisa was recounting to Luke the menu of last night's dinner.

" And ' Homard à la Danoise ' was a perfect dream," she was saying. " I suppose it would not be etiquette to ask Her Excellency for the recipe."

Luke rose as the Colonel entered and passed his hand across the back of his smooth head, a gesture peculiarly English and peculiarly his own. The older man was undoubtedly the most troubled of the three.

" It's a damnable business this," he said as soon as he had shaken Luke by the hand and thrown off hat and coat.

" Does Sir Thomas Ryder," asked Luke lightly, " also think that I have murdered Philip ? "

He knew where Colonel Harris had been. Louisa had not thought of keeping this from him.

" Tom's a fool ! " retorted the Colonel involuntarily.

It was tantamount to an avowal. Luke never flinched ; he even contrived to smile. Louisa sat up very straight, and with an instinctive movement gave the sofa cushions a nervy shake up. But her eyes were fastened on Luke.

"Don't worry, sir," said Luke very quietly. "I'll get out of it all in good time."

"Of course you will! Damn it all!" ejaculated the other fervently.

"The inquest, you know, is to-morrow."

It was Luke who spoke, and Colonel Harris looked up quickly.

"Then," he said, "surely some light will be thrown on this mysterious business."

"Let's hope so, sir," rejoined Luke dryly.

"Has Uncle Ryder told you anything fresh, father? Anything that we don't yet know?"

Colonel Harris did not reply, and Louisa knew that there was something that Uncle Ryder had said, something awful, which had caused her father to wear the troubled look which had terrified her the moment he came in.

Something awful! . . . which would affect Luke!

"Won't you tell us, father," she said, "what Uncle Ryder told you? Luke ought to know."

"Oh!" rejoined Luke, "there's no hurry, I'm sure. Colonel Harris will tell me presently. Loo, you were coming to the Park this morning. I suppose we can't go to the Temple Garden Show very well."

"Not very well, I think," she replied, "but I'll come for a walk after lunch with pleasure. Father must tell us now what Uncle Ryder said."

Then, as Colonel Harris still seemed to hesitate, she became more insistent, and her voice more firm.

"Father dear," she said, "I must know as well as Luke."

The old man took a turn up and down the room, with hands behind his back. He would not look either at Louisa or at Luke, for it would be easier to tell them everything without meeting their eyes. And he had to tell them everything. To her as well as to him. It was no longer any use trying to avoid the subject, pretending that it was trivial, unworthy of discussion.

Facts had to be faced at last, like the dervishes at Omdurman, and a plan of campaign decided on in the event of momentary defeat.

"Ryder," he began quite abruptly at last, "had the hall-porter of that confounded Club up to his room while I was there, and questioned him before me."

"He could," suggested Luke, "only repeat the story which we all know already. I never denied seeing Philip at the Club or quarrelling with him, for the matter of that. Hang it all! I have often quarrelled with him before."

"Yes," rejoined the Colonel, "they've ferreted out the old servants of your uncle's household, and heard innumerable stories of quarrels."

"Exaggerated, I expect. But what of it?"

"And that hall-porter didn't mince matters either. Damn him."

"Philip," remarked Luke dryly, "shouted pretty loudly. I did not."

"The porter said that when you left the Club you had 'murder in your eye.'"

" Possibly."

" You had overheard Philip's last remark to the porter ? "

" Yes . . . something about pestering beggars. I was ready to make him swallow his words ; but I loathe a scene, before people like those who frequent the Veterans' Club."

" I wish to goodness you had gone for him then and there."

" Why ? "

" This accursed business would not have occurred."

" Oh yes, it would—sooner or later."

" What makes you say that ? "

" Philip must have had an enemy."

" Who murdered him last night, you think ? "

" An enemy," assented Luke, " who evidently lay in wait for him, and murdered him last night. It is bound to come out at the inquest."

" About this enemy ? " queried Colonel Harris vaguely.

" Why, yes," rejoined Luke a little impatiently ; " surely the police have made other investigations. They are not just fastening on me and on no one else."

" Could you," asked Louisa, " help the police in that, Luke ? "

" No," he replied, " I know absolutely nothing about Philip or about his past life."

" Did Lord Radclyffe ? "

" I don't know."

" He has been questioned, has he not ? "

" He is too ill to see any one. Doctor Newington declares that he must not attempt to see any one. His condition is critical. Moreover, he is only partly conscious."

" But . . ."

" There's Philip's lawyer, Davies," said Luke ; " the police ought to be in communication with him. It is positively ridiculous the way they seem to do nothing in the way of proper investigation, but only make up their minds that I have killed my cousin. . . . Why! they don't even seem to trouble about the weapon with which the murder was committed."

" The weapon . . . ? "

The ejaculation, spoken hardly above a whisper, had come from Colonel Harris. Once more the old man felt—as he had done in his brother-in-law's office— that every drop of blood in him had receded back to his heart, and that he would choke if he attempted to utter another word.

" They say," continued Luke quietly, " that Philip was killed by the thrust of a sharp dagger or stiletto, right through the neck. Well, where is that dagger? Have they found it ? or traced it to its owner ? "

Then as Colonel Harris was still silent he reiterated once more—

" Did Sir Thomas tell you if they had found the weapon ? "

And Colonel Harris nodded and murmured—

" Yes."

" Actually found the weapon ? " insisted Luke.

" Yes."

" Where ? "

" Behind the railings. . . . In Green Park. . . .
Close to Hyde Park Corner."

" Was it a stiletto ? Or a dagger ? Or what ? "

" It was a stick with a dagger fitting into it. A
snake-wood stick. It was covered with mud and . . .
other stains,"

There was silence in the room now for the space of
a few, brief seconds. A silence solemn and full of meaning. All through this rapid succession of questions and
answers between Colonel Harris and Luke, Louisa had
kept her eyes fixed upon the younger man's face, had
seen light indifference at possible danger alternating
with impatience at the singular obstinacy of his ac-
cusers. Throughout this time the face she knew so well,
mirrored that perfect calm which she understood and
admired, since it was the reflex of a calm, untroubled
soul,

But now there came a change in the face : or rather
not in the face, but in the soul behind it. The change
came at Colonel Harris's last words ; a change so
subtle, so undetermined that she was quite sure her
father had not perceived it. But movement there was
none ; one mere, almost imperceptible quiver of the
eyelids . . . nothing more. The mouth beneath the
slight fair moustache had not trembled, the brow remained smooth, the breath came and went as evenly
as before.

But the change was there, nevertheless ! the grey
tint just round the eyes, the stony look in the pupils
themselves, a tiny speck of moisture round the wing

of each nostril. Colonel Harris had not looked at Luke, whilst he spoke of the stick. He was staring straight in front of him, hardly conscious of the silence which had cast a strange and mystic spell on these three people standing here in the banal atmosphere of a London hotel,

It was Luke who broke the silence. He said quite quietly, asking the question as if it related to most trivial, most indifferent matter—

"Did Sir Thomas show you the stick ? "

The Colonel nodded in acquiescence.

"It was my stick, I suppose ? "

The query was so sudden, so unexpected, that Colonel Harris instinctively uttered an exclamation of amazement,

"Luke ! By God, man ! Are you mad ? "

Louisa said nothing. She was trying to understand the un-understandable, Luke almost smiled at the other man's bewilderment,

"No, sir," he said ; "not mad, I think. I only want to know how I stand."

"How you stand, man ? " ejaculated Colonel Harris, with uncontrolled vehemence. "Great heavens, don't you realize that here is some damned conspiracy, as mysterious as it is damnable ? and that you will have to look this seriously in the face, if you don't wish to find yourself in the dock before the next four-and-twenty hours ? "

"I am," replied Luke simply, "looking the matter squarely in the face, sir, but I don't quite see how I can avoid standing in the dock, as you say, before the next four-and-twenty hours. You see, I had quarrelled with Philip, and my stick—which contains the dagger —was found in the Park, covered with mud, as you say, and other stains."

" But, hang it all, man ! you did not murder your cousin ! "

This was not a query, but an assertion. Colonel Harris's loyalty had not wavered, but he could not contrive to keep the note of anxiety out of his voice ; nor did he reiterate the assertion when Luke made no answer to it.

Once more the latter passed his hand over the back of his head. You know that gesture. It is so English ! and always denotes a certain measure of perturbation. Then he said, with seeming irrelevance—

" I suppose I had better go now."

His eyes sought Louisa's, trying to read what she thought and felt. Imagíne the awful moment ! for he loved her, as you know, with that intensity of passion of which a nature like his—almost cramped by perpetual self-containment—is alone capable. Then to have to stand before her wondering what the next second would reveal ! hardly daring to exchange fear for certitude, because of what that certitude might be.

He sought her eyes and had no difficulty in finding them. They had never wandered away from his face. To him—the ardent worshipper—those eyes of hers had never seemed so exquisitely luminous. He read her soul then and there as he would a book. A soul full of trust and brimming over with compassion and with love. Colonel Harris was loyal to the core ; he clung to his loyalty, to his belief in Luke as he would to a rock, fearful lest he should flounder in a maze of wonderment, of surmises, God help him ! of suspicions. But in Louisa even loyalty was submerged in a sea of love. She cared nothing about suspicions, about facts, about surmises. She had no room in her heart for staunchness : it was all submerged in love.

There was no question, no wonderment, no puzzle in the eyes which met those of Luke. You see, she was just a very ordinary kind of woman.

All she knew was that she loved Luke ; and all that she conveyed to him by that look, was just Love.

Only Love.

And Love—omnipotent, strange, and capricious Love—wrought a curious miracle then ! For Colonel Harris was present in the room, mind you, a third—if not an altogether indifferent—party, there where at this moment these two should have been alone.

It was Colonel Harris's presence in the room that transformed the next instant into a wonderful miracle : for Luke was down on his knees before his simple-souled Loo. She had yielded her hand to him and he had pressed an aching forehead against the delicately perfumed palm.

In face of that Love which she had given him, he could only worship : and would have been equally ready to worship before the whole world. And therein lay the miracle. Do you not agree, you, who know Englishmen of that class and stamp ? Can you con-ceive one of them falling on his knees ? save at the

o

bidding of omnipotent Love, and by the miracle which makes a man forget the whole world, defy the whole world, give up the whole world, driven to defiance, to forgetfulness, to self-sacrifice for the sake of the torturing, exquisite moments of transcendental happiness.

CHAPTER XXIII

WHY ALL THIS MYSTERY ?

I HAVE often smiled myself at the recollection of Luke de Mountford walking that self-same afternoon with Louisa Harris up and down the long avenue of the Ladies' Mile : the self-same Luke de Mountford who had knelt at his Loo's feet in humble gratitude for the love she gave him—the self-same Luke de Mountford who stood under suspicion of having committed a dastardly and premeditated murder.

The puppets were once more dangling on the string of Convention. They had readjusted their masks and sunk individuality, as well as sentiment, in the whirlpool of their world's opinion.

Louisa had desired that Luke should come with her to the Park, since convention forbade their looking at chrysanthemums in the Temple Gardens on the day that Philip de Mountford lay dead in the mortuary chamber of a London police court ; but everybody belonging to their own world would be in the Park on this fine afternoon. And yet the open air, the fragrance of bare earth in the formal beds would give freedom to the breath ; there would not reign the oppressive atmosphere of tea-table gossip : the dying chrysanthemums bowing their stately heads would suggest aloofness and peace.

And so they went together for a walk in the Park, for she had wished it, and he would have followed her anywhere where she had bidden him to go.

He walked beside her absolutely unconscious of whisperings and gossip which accompanied them at every step.

" I call it bad form," was a very usual phrase enunciated by many a rouged lip curled up in disdain.

This was hurled at Louisa Harris. The woman, in such cases, always contrives to get the lion's share of contempt.

" Showing herself about with that man now! I call it vulgar."

" They say he'll be arrested directly after the inquest to-morrow. I have it on unimpeachable authority."

" Oh! I understand that he has been arrested already," asserted a lady whose information was always a delightful mixture of irresponsible vagueness and firm conviction.

" How do you mean ? "

" Well! you see, he is only out on—what do they call it ? . . . I mean he has had to give his word that he won't run away . . . or something. . . . I heard Herbert say something about that at lunch. . . . Oh! what lovely tulips. I dote on that rich coppery red, don't you ? "

" Then does he go about in Black Maria escorted by a policeman ? "

" Probably."

This somewhat more vaguely, for the surmise was doubtful.

" I can't understand Louisa Harris, can you ? "

" Oh! she thinks it's unconventional to go about with a murderer. She only does it for notoriety."

But the Countess of Flintshire, who wrote novels and plays under the elegant *nom de plume* of Maria Annunziata, was deeply interested in Luke and Louisa, and stopped to talk to them for quite a considerable time. She said she wanted " to draw Luke de Mountford out." So interesting to get the impressions of an actual murderer, you know.

The men felt uncomfortable. Englishmen always do, when the unconventional hovers about in their neatly ordered atmosphere. Common sense—in their case—whispered loudly, insisting that this man in the Sackville Street clothes, member of their own clubs, by Jove ! could not just be a murderer. Hang it all ! Harris would not allow his daughter to go about with a murderer !

So they raised their hats as they passed by Louisa Harris, and said " Hello ! how de do ? " to Luke with quite a genial smile.

But Luke and Louisa allowed all this world to wag on its own irresponsible way. They were not fools— they knew their milieu. They guessed all that was being said around them and all that remained unspoken. They had come here purposely in order to see and to be seen, to be gossiped about, to play their rôle of puppet before their world as long as life lasted, and whilst Chance and Circumstance still chose to hold up the edifice of their own position, of their consideration, mayhap of their honour.

The question of the crime had not been mooted between them again ; after the understanding, the look from her to him, and his humble gratitude on his knees, they had left the mystery severely alone. He had nothing to say, and she would never question, content that she would know in good time, that one day she would understand what was so un-understandable just now.

Colonel Harris alone was prostrated with trouble. Not that he doubted Luke, but, like all sober-sensed Englishmen, he loathed a moral puzzle. Whilst he liked and trusted Luke, he hated the mystery which now met him at every turn, just as much as he hated the so-called problem plays which alien critics try to foist on an unwilling Anglo-Saxon public.

He would have loved to hear Luke's voice saying quite frankly—

" Of course I did not kill my cousin. I give you my word, Colonel, that I am incapable of such a thing."

That was the only grievance which the older man of the world had against the younger one. The want of frankness worried him. Luke was innocent, of course, but, d—n it, why didn't he say so ?

And how came that accursed stick behind the railings of the Park ?

CHAPTER XXIV

A HERD OF CACKLING GEESE

WHEN at ten o'clock the next morning Louisa Harris entered the Victoria Coroner's Court accompanied by her father, the coroner and jury were just returning from the mortuary at the back of the building, whither they had gone in order to look upon the dead.

Already the small room was crowded to its utmost holding capacity. Louisa and Colonel Harris had some difficulty in making their way through the groups of idlers, who filled every corner of the gangway.

The air was hot and heavy, with the smell of the dust of ages which had gathered in the nooks and crannies of this dull and drabby room. It mingled with irritating unpleasantness with the scent of opoponax or heliotrope that emanated from lace handkerchiefs, and with the pungent odours of smelling-salts ostentatiously held to delicate noses.

Louisa, matter-of-fact, commonplace Louisa, looked round at these unaccustomed surroundings with the same air of semi-indifferent interest with which she would have viewed a second-rate local music-hall had she unaccountably drifted into one through curiosity or desire.

She saw a dull, drabby paper on the wall, and dull, drabby hangings to the single window which was set very high, close to the ceiling—the latter once white-washed was now covered with uneven coatings of grime.

In the centre of the room, a long table littered at one end with papers tied up in bundles of varying bulk, with pieces of pink tape, also a blotting-pad, pen, ink, and paper—more paper—the one white note in the uniform harmony of drabby brown ; and in among this litter that encumbered the table a long piece of green baize covering a narrow formless something, which Louisa supposed would be revealed in due course.

On each side of the table half a dozen chairs, of early Victorian design, upholstered in leather that had once been green. To these chairs a dozen men were even now making their way, each taking his seat in solemn silence : men in overcoats and with velvet collars, somewhat worn at the back of the neck . . . it seemed to Louisa as if they were dressed in some kind of uniform, so alike did their clothes appear. She looked at their faces as they filed in . . . haggard faces, rubicund, jolly faces, faces which mirrored suspicion, faces which revealed obstinacy, the whole of middle-class England personified in these typical twelve men all wearing overcoats with shabby velvet collars, who were to decide how and when Philip de Mountford, heir-presumptive to the Earl of Radclyffe, had been done to death.

Louisa and her father were able at last to reach the forefront of the crowd, where chairs had been reserved for them, immediately facing the table at the further end of which the coroner already sat. Louisa recognized Mr. Humphreys, one of Mr. Dobson's clerks, who did his best to make her and Colonel Harris comfortable. Further on sat Mr. Davies, who had been Philip de Mountford's solicitor, when he had first desired an interview with Lord Radclyffe. Louisa knew him by sight—Luke had on one occasion pointed him out to her.

Luke and Mr. Dobson were even now making their way to the same group of seats. They had—like the jury and the coroner—been in the mortuary to have a last look at the murdered man. Louisa thought that Luke looked years older than he had done yesterday. She saw him standing for a moment right against the dull, drabby background of the court-room wall, and it seemed as if something of that drabbiness had descended upon his soul. Youth seemed to have gone out of him. He appeared to be looking out on to a dreary world through windows obscured by grime.

There was a look not so much of dejection as of absolute hopelessness in the face. No fear, or anxiety . . . only a renunciation. But this was only for one moment, the next he had caught sight of her, and the look of blank dejection in his eyes suddenly gave place to one of acute and intolerable pain. The face which usually was so calm and placid in its impassive mask of high-bred indifference, was almost distorted by an expression of agony which obviously had been quite beyond control.

The whole thing was, of course, a mere flash, less

than a quarter of a second perhaps in duration, and already Luke was just as he had always been : a correct well-born English gentleman, perfect in manner, perfect in attitude and bearing, under whatever circumstances Fate might choose to place him.

Mr. Dobson spoke to him, and he at once followed his friend and solicitor across the body of the court-room to the row of reserved chairs in front of the crowd.

A whisper went round the room, and Louisa with cool indifference turned to greet those among the crowd whom she had recognized as acquaintances and friends. Some were sitting, others standing back against the walls in the rear. Lady Ducie was there, excited and over-dressed, with large hat that obstructed the view of a masculine-looking woman who sat immediately behind her, and who seemed quite prepared to do battle against the obstruction.

Further on sat the Countess of Flintshire, novelist and playwright, eager and serious, notebook in hand and a frown between her brows, denoting thought and concentration of purpose. She bowed gravely to Louisa, and contrived to attract Luke's attention, so that he turned towards her and she was able to note carefully in indelible pencil in a tiny notebook that a murderer about to meet his just fate may bestow an infinity of care on the niceties of his own toilette.

(N.B.—The next play written by the Countess of Flintshire, better known to the playgoing public as Maria Annunziata, had an assassin for its principal hero. But the play found no favour with actor-managers, and though it subsequently enjoyed some popularity in the provinces, it was never performed on the London stage.)

Louisa looked on all these people with eyes that dwelt with strange persistency on trivial details : the Countess of Flintshire's notebook, Lady Ducie's hat, the masculine attire of the militant suffragette in the rear. All these minor details impressed themselves upon her memory. In after years she could always recall the vision of the court-room, with its drabby background to a sea of ridiculous faces.

For they all seemed ridiculous to her—all these people—in their obvious eager agitation : they had pushed one another and jostled and fought their way into this small stuffy room, the elegant ladies with their scent-bottles, the men about town with their silk hats and silver-topped canes : they were all ready to endure acute physical discomfort for the sake of witnessing the harrowing sight of one of their own kind being pilloried before the mob—it was just a pinch of spice added to the savourless condiment of everyday life. Then there were the others : those who had come just out of idle curiosity to hear a few unpleasant details, or to read a few unwholesome pages in the book of life of people who lived in a different world to their own.

Ridiculous they seemed, all of them ! Louisa felt a sudden desire to laugh aloud, as she realized how very like a theatre the place was, with its boxes, its stalls, and its galleries. But in this case those who usually sat in stalls or boxes displaying starched shirt-

fronts, bare shoulders, and bad manners, they were
the actors now made to move or dance or sing, to
squirm or to suffer for the delectation of pit and gallery.

On the left a group of young men with keen young
faces, all turned towards Luke and towards Louisa and
her father. Notebooks protruded out of great-coat
pockets, fountain pens and indelible pencils snuggled
close to hand : lucky the lightning artist who could
sketch for the benefit of his journalistic patrons a rough
outline of the gentleman with more than one foot in
the dock. Close by a couple of boys in blue uniform,
with wallet at the side and smart pill-box cap on the
head, stood ready to take messages, fractions of news,
hurried reports to less favoured mortals whose duty or
desire kept them away from this scene of poignant
interest.

Louisa saw them all, as in a vivid dream. Never
afterwards could she believe that it had all been
reality : the coroner, the jury, the group of journalists,
the idle, whispering, pushing crowd, the loud murmurs
which now and again reached her ear—

" Oh ! you may take it from me that to-morrow
he'll stand in the dock."

" Such brazen indifference I've never seen."

" And they've actually found the dagger with which
he murdered the wretched man."

" B-r-r-r ! it makes me feel quite creepy."

" Yes ! he was at your At Home, dear, wasn't he ?
a week ago ? "

" Oh ! one had to ask him for form's sake, you
know."

"Poor Lord Radclyffe, what a terrible blow for him."

"They say he'll never recover his speech or the use of his limbs."

"Silence there!"

The cackling herd of geese stopped its whisperings, astonished at being thus reproved. Louisa again felt that irrepressible desire to laugh ; they were so funny, she thought, so irresponsible ! these people who had come to gape at Luke.

Now they were silent and orderly at the bidding of authority. An old woman, with black bonnet and rusty jacket, was munching sandwiches in a corner seat ; a young man at the further end of the room was sharpening a lead-pencil.

By the door through which a brief while ago coroner and jury, also Luke and Mr. Dobson had filed out— the door which apparently gave in the direction of the mortuary—a small group in shabby clothes had just entered the court-room, escorted by one of the ushers. The latter made his way to the coroner's table and whispered to that gentleman somewhat animatedly. Louisa could not catch what he said, but she saw that the coroner suddenly lost his morose air of habitual ennui, and appeared keen and greatly interested in what he heard.

He gave certain instructions to the usher, who beckoned to the group in the shabby clothes. They advanced with timid, anxious gait, a world of unspoken apologies in their eyes as they surveyed the brilliant company through which they had to pass. The feathers in Lady Ducie's hat attracted the attention of one of them—a young girl with round black eyes and highly decorated headgear : she nudged her companion and pointed to the gargantuan hat, and both the girls giggled almost hysterically.

The man in front led the way. He was pale and cadaverous-looking, with scanty hair and drooping moustache : in shape he was very like a beetle, with limbs markedly bowed and held away from his stooping body. There were five of them altogether, two men and three women. Louisa was interested in them, vaguely wondering who they were.

That they were personages of importance in this case was apparent from the fact that the usher was bringing some chairs for the women and placing them close to those on which sat the solicitors, and Luke and Louisa herself. The men were made to stand close by and remained just where they had been told to stay, tweed cap in hand, miserably conscious of the many pairs of eyes that were fixed upon them.

" Who are these people, do you know ? "

Lady Ducie was leaning forward, and had contrived to catch Luke's ear.

He turned round very politely.

" How do you do, Mr. de Mountford ? " she continued in her shrill treble, which she took no trouble to subdue. " You hadn't seen me, had you ? "

" No, Lady Ducie," he replied, " I had not."

" I don't wonder," she commented placidly ; " you must feel so anxious. Who are those common people over there, do you know ? "

" No, I do not."

" Some of your late cousin's former associates perhaps ? " suggested Lady Flintshire, " Maria Annunziata," who sat close by.

"My dear, how can you suggest such a thing ? " retorted the other ; " they are so common."

" Silence there ! "

And once more the cackling geese were still.

CHAPTER XXV

THE FOG WAS DENSE, I COULDN'T RIGHTLY SEE

THE curtain went up on the first act of the play. It was not, perhaps, so interesting from the outset as the audience would have wished, and the fashionable portion thereof showed its impatience by sundry coughings and whisperings, which had to be peremptorily checked now again by a loud—

"Silence, there ! " and a threat to clear the court.

The medical officer was giving his testimony at great length as to the cause of death. Technical terms were used in plenty, and puzzled the elegant ladies who had come here to be amused. The jury listened attentively, and the coroner—himself a medical man—asked several very pertinent questions.

"The thrust," he asked of Dr. Blair, who was medical officer of the district, " through the neck was effected by means of a long narrow instrument, with two sharp edges, a dagger in fact ? "

" A dagger or a stiletto, or a skewer," replied the doctor, " any sharp two-edged instrument, would cause a wound like the one in the neck of the deceased."

" Was death instantaneous ? "

" Almost so."

He explained at some length the intricacies of the human throat, at the point where the murderer's weapon had entered the neck of his victim. Louisa listened attentively. Every moment she expected to see the coroner's hand wandering to the piece of green baize in front of him, and then drawing it away disclosing a snake-wood stick with silver ferrule stained, and showing the rise of the dagger sheathed within the body of the stick. Every moment she expected to hear the query—

" Is this the instrument which dealt the blow ? "

But this apparently was not to be just yet : the opaque veil of green baize was not to be lifted, that certain long Something was not to be revealed, the Something that would condemn Luke irrevocably, absolutely to disgrace and to death.

Only one of the members of the jury—Louisa understood that he was the foreman—asked a simple question.

" Would," he said, " the witness explain whether in his opinion the . . . the unknown murderer . . . the . . . I mean . . ."

He floundered a little in the phrase, having realized that in his official capacity he must keep an ope mind . . . and in that open mind of an English juryman there could for the present dwell no certainty that a murderer . . . an unknown murderer did exist.

They were all here—he and the others and the

P

coroner—in order to find out if there had been a murder committed or not.

The coroner, one elbow on the table, one large hand holding firmly the somewhat fleshy chin, looked at the juryman somewhat contemptuously.

" You mean . . . ? " he queried, with an obvious effort at patience.

" I mean," resumed the man more firmly, " in this present instance, would a certain medical or anatomical knowledge be necessary in order to strike—er— or to thrust . . . so precisely . . . just on the right spot to cause immediate death ? "

With amiable condescension the coroner put the query to the witness in more concise words.

" No, no," replied the doctor quickly, now that he had understood the question, " the thrust argues no special anatomical knowledge. Most laymen would know that if you pierce the throat from ear to ear, suffocation is bound to ensue. It was easily enough done."

" When the deceased's head was turned away ? " asked the coroner.

" Why, yes . . . to look out on the fog, perhaps ; or at a passer-by. . . . It would be fairly easy if the would-be murderer was quick and determined and the victim unsuspecting."

And Doctor Blair, with long tapering fingers, pointed towards his own throat, giving illustration of how easily the deed might be done.

" Given the requisite weapon of course."

After a few more courteous questions of a technical

kind, the first witness was dismissed . . . only momentarily, for he would be required again . . . when the green baize would be lifted from the hidden Something which lay there ready to hand, and the medical man be asked to pronounce finally whether indeed the dagger stick were the requisite weapon for the deed, which had been so easy of accomplishment.

The chauffeur, who had driven the taxi-cab, was the next witness called : a thick-set man in dark blue Melton coat and peaked cap ; he came forward with that swinging gait which betrayed the ex-coachman.

He gave his evidence well and to the point. He had been hailed on the night in question by two gentlemen in evening dress. It was in Shaftesbury Avenue, just opposite the Lyric Theatre, and a little while after he had heard St. Martin's Church clock strike nine o'clock. "The fog was so dense," he added, "you could not see your hand before your eyes."

He had just put down at the Apollo, and had crossed over to the left going down towards Piccadilly, when the two swells hailed him from the kerb. He couldn't rightly see them, because of the fog, but he noticed that both wore high hats, and the collars of their overcoats were turned up to their ears. He hardly saw their faces, but he noticed that one of them carried a walking-stick.

"Or it might 'ave been a umbrella," he added, after a moment's hesitation, "I couldn't rightly say."

"You must have seen the faces of your fares," argued the coroner, "if you saw that one of them

carried a walking-stick . . . or an umbrella. . . .
You must have seen something of their faces," he
reiterated more emphatically.

"I didn't," retorted the man gruffly. "Was you
out in that there fog, sir ? If you was, you'd know
'ow you couldn't see your 'and before your eyes. . . .
I saw the point of the stick—or the umbrella, I couldn't
rightly say which—only because one of them gents
waved it at me when 'e was 'ailing me . . . that's
'ow I seed the point."

The coroner allowed the question of identification
to drop : clearly nothing would be got out of the man.
The gentlemen, he declared, entered the cab, and then
one of them gave directions to him, putting his head
out of the right-hand window.

"I didn't turn to look at 'im," he said bluntly.
"I could 'ear 'is voice plain enough—so why should
I take a look at 'im ? 'Ow did I know there was
a-goin' to be murder done in my cab, and me wanted
to say what the murderer looked like ? "

He looked round the room defiantly, and as if
expecting applause for this display of sound common
sense, opposed to the coroner's tiresome officialism.

"And what directions," asked the latter, " did the
gentleman give you ? "

"To go along Piccadilly," replied the witness, " till
'e told me to stop."

"And when did he tell you to stop ? "

"By the railings of Green Park, just by 'Yde Park
Corner. One of 'em puts 'is 'ead out of the window
and calls to me to pull up."

" Which you did ? "

" Which I did, and one of 'em gets out, and standin'
on the kerb 'e leans back to the interior of the cab,
and says : ' S'long—see you to-morrow ' ; and then
'e says to me : ' No. 1 Cromwell Gardens,' and dis-
appears in the fog."

" Surely you saw him then ? "

" No. The fog was like pea-soup there, though it
looked clearer on Knightsbridge way. And 'e got
out left side, of course. I was up on my box right-
'and side . . . a long way from 'im. . . . I could see
a man standin' there, but not 'is face. 'Is 'at was
pulled down right over 'is eyes, and 'is coat collar up
to 'is ears."

" Had he his stick . . . or umbrella with him
then ? "

" Yes. With 'is 'ands in 'is pockets, and the tip
pointing upwards, like a soldier's bayonet."

" You saw that and not his face ? " once more insisted the coroner, making a final effort to draw some
more definite statement out of the man. It would
help justice so much if only this witness were less
obstinate . . . no one would believe that he really
saw nothing of the face of the man who had twice
spoken to him. He may not have seen it clearly,
not the upper part of the face, perhaps, but surely
he saw the mouth that had actually framed the
words.

But the chauffeur was obstinate. He was not going
to swear away the life of a man whom he had not
rightly seen, only through a fog as thick as pea-soup :

this was the fortress behind which after a while he entrenched himself.

In vain did the coroner, pleased at having gained this slight advantage, try to draw him further, explaining to him, with the quiet patience of a man moved by official ambition, that far from jeopardizing the life of any man, he might be saving that of an innocent one, falsely accused through circumstantial evidence. In vain did he press and argue, the man was obstinate. After a very long while only, and when the coroner had almost given up arguing and cross-examining, he admitted that he did think that the gentleman who directed him to No. 1 Cromwell Gardens had a moustache.

" But mind ! " he added hurriedly, " I won't swear to it, for I didn't rightly see . . . the fog was that dense in the Park. And 'e wasn't the same as the one 'oo told me to go along Piccadilly until 'e stopped me. The dead man done that."

"How do you know," came as a quick retort from the coroner, " since you declare you could not see the faces ? "

" The first gent 'oo spoke to me," replied the chauffeur somewhat sullenly now, " 'ad no 'air on 'is face ; the second one I think 'ad . . . but I can't rightly say . . . I wouldn't swear to neither. And I won't swear . . ." he reiterated with gruff emphasis.

A sigh went round the room, a tremor of excitement, the palpitation of many hearts, and in-drawing of many breaths. No one spoke. No one framed the thought that was uppermost in the mind of every one of the interested spectators of this strange and un-understandable drama. The dead man who lay in the mortuary chamber was clean-shaved, but Luke de Mountford wore a moustache.

Lady Ducie's feathers nodded in the direction of the literary Countess who went by the name of Maria Annunziata, and the latter made hasty notes in her diminutive book.

But Louisa leaned slightly forward so as to catch fuller sight of Luke, and she encountered his eyes fixed steadily upon her.

After that the driver of the cab concluded his evidence more rapidly. There was little more there than what every one had already learned from the news-papers. The second pulling up in Cromwell Gardens this time : the silent fare, the descent from the box, the discovery of the huddled figure in the far corner of the cab, the call for the police.

People listened with less attention ; thoughts were busy with the contemplation of a picture : two men, one clean-shaved—the dead man of course—and the other wearing a moustache. The first link in the chain of evidence against the assassin had been forged, and was ready to be riveted to the next.

The crowd in the body of the court could only obtain a view of the top of Luke de Mountford's head ; it was smooth and fair, of that English fairness of tint which is golden when the light catches it. And the group of elegantly dressed women who came here to-day in order to experience an altogether novel sensa-tion, shuddered with delightful excitement as they thought of Black Maria and handcuffs, and crowds of police officers in blue : a jumble of impressions ran riot in frivolous and irresponsible minds, foremost amongst which was one that the public was no longer allowed to witness a final scene on the gallows.

CHAPTER XXVI

THE NEXT WITNESS, PLEASE

THE air grew more and more heavy as the morning dragged on. It was now close on twelve o'clock.

Frederick Power, hall-porter of the Veterans' Club, had finished his evidence. With the precision of a soldier he had replied curtly and to the point to every question put to him, and had retold all that had occurred on that foggy night, in the smoking-room and the lobby of the Veterans' Club in Shaftesbury Avenue.

It was but a repetition of what he had told Sir Thomas Ryder in Colonel Harris's presence the day before. Louisa had had it all at full length from her father ; she had drawn the whole story out of him, point by point, just as the man had told it originally. Colonel Harris, reluctant to tell her, was gradually driven to concealing nothing from her. Moreover, since she had made up her mind to attend the inquest, she might as well hear it all from him first, the better to be prepared for the public ordeal.

Though she knew it all, she listened attentively to every word which Frederick Power uttered, lest her father had—in telling her—omitted some important detail. She heard again at full length the account of Luke's visit to the Veterans' Club, his desire to see

Philip de Mountford, the interview in the smoking-room behind closed doors, the angry words of obvious violent quarrelling.

Then Luke's return to the lobby, his departure, the final taunt spoken by Philip, and the look of murder in his eye, sworn to by the hall-porter. She listened to it all, and heard without flinching the last question which the coroner put to the witness—

" Did Mr. de Mountford's visitor carry a stick when he left the Club ? "

" 'E 'ad a stick, sir, when 'e came," was the porter's reply, " and I 'anded it to 'im myself when 'e left."

Louisa had been sitting all this while at the extreme end of the row of chairs, right up against the wall. She sat with her back to the wall, her head leaning against it, her hands hidden within the folds of a monumental sable muff lying idly in her lap. She had her father on her right, and beyond him Mr. Dobson and his clerk ; she saw them all in profile as they looked straight before them at the coroner and at each succeeding witness.

Luke sat further on, and as he was slightly turned towards her she could watch his face, all the while that she listened to the hall-porter's evidence. It was perfectly still, the features as if moulded in wax ; the eyes, which actually were a clear hazel, appeared quite dark and almost as if they had sunk back within their circling lids. He sat with arms folded, and not a muscle in face or body moved. No stone-carved image could have been more calm, none could have been so mysterious.

Louisa tried to understand and could not. She watched him, not caring whether the empty-headed fools who sat all round saw her watching him or not.

When the coroner asked the hall-porter about the stick and the man gave his reply, Luke turned and met Louisa's fixed gaze. The marble-like stillness of his face remained unchanged, only the eyes seemed as if they darkened visibly. At least to her it seemed as if a velvety shadow crept over them, an inscrutable, an un-understandable shadow, and the rims assumed a purple hue.

It was her fancy, of course. But Luke's eyes were naturally bright, of varying tones of grey, blue or green, with never a shadow beneath them. Now they appeared cavernous and dark, and again as he met her gaze, that swift flash of intense misery.

No longer had she the feeling that she was living in a dream, no longer that this was a theatre wherein she and Luke and the dead man were puppets dancing and squirming for the benefit of shallow-hearted dolts. That sense of unreality left her together with the hysterical desire to laugh which had plagued her so in the earlier part of the proceedings. On the contrary, now an overwhelming feeling of intense reality oppressed her, so that she could have screamed with the awful soul-agony which the sight of Luke's misery had caused her.

All her nerves were on the rack, her every faculty concentrated on the one supreme desire to understand and to know.

Love, the omnipotent, had encountered an enemy—

grim, unexplained Mystery—and he sat pondering, almost cowed by this first check to his supreme might. Louisa had sought and compelled Luke's gaze, and Love had gleamed in one great flash out of her eyes. Yesterday, at her glance, he had knelt at her feet, and buried his sorrow with his aching head in the scented palm of the dearly loved hand.

To-day the look of Love brought but a surfeit of misery, an additional load of sorrow. The eyes in response remained tearless and hard, and circled with the dark rings of utter hopelessness.

I'll grant you that if Louisa Harris had been an extraordinary woman, a woman endowed with a wonderfully complex, wonderfully passionate, or wonderfully emotional nature—if, in fact, she had been the true product of this century's morbid modernity, she would, whilst admitting Luke's guilt, have burned with a passion of self-sacrifice, pining to stand beside him pilloried in the dock, and looking forward to a veritable world of idealistic realism in the form of a picturesque suicide after seeing the black flag hoisted over Newgate prison.

But Louisa, though a modern product of an ultra-modern world, was an absolutely ordinary woman— just a commonplace, sensible creature who thought and felt in a straight and essentially wholesome manner. Though she had read Tolstoy and Dostoiewsky and every Scandinavian and Russian crackbrain who has ever tried to make wrong seem right, black appear white, and animalism masquerade as love, yet she had never been led away from her own clean outlook on life.

She loved Luke and would have given—did, in fact, give—her whole life to him ; but she loved him without analysis or thought of self. It never entered her mind at this moment to wonder if he were guilty or not guilty, if he was capable or not of committing a crime to gain his own ends. All that troubled her was his misery which she would have given her very soul to alleviate, and the hopelessness in him which she had given the world to console.

The mystery troubled her, not the sin ; the marble-like rigidity of his face, not the possibility of the crime.

For the moment, however, she was brought back quickly enough to present realities. The coroner—satisfied with Frederick Power's answers—was giving him a moment's breathing space. The grating of fountain pens against paper was heard from that corner of the room where sat the journalists ; the crowd waited silent and expectant, for—unversed though most people there present were in proceedings of this kind—yet instinctively every one felt that one great crucial moment was just about to come, one great, leading question was just about to be put.

The coroner had fingered the papers before him for the space of a few seconds, then he looked up once more at the witness, his elbow resting on the table, his fleshy chin buried in his hand, in an attitude which obviously was habitual to him.

" The visitor," he said, speaking loudly and clearly, " who called the night before last at the Veterans' Club and had an interview with the deceased, you saw him well, of course ? "

" Yes, sir," was the prompt reply.

" You would know him again ? "

" Certainly, sir."

" Looking round this room now, should you say that he was present ? "

The man looked across the room straight at Luke and said, pointing to him—

" Yes, sir, the gentleman sitting there, sir."

As every one had expected the reply, no one seemed astonished. The many pairs of eyes that turned on Luke now expressed a certain measure of horrified compassion, such as might be bestowed on some dangerous animal brought to earth by a well-aimed gun-shot.

The coroner made no comment. He turned to the jury, glancing along either row of solemn faces, on both sides of the long table. Then he said—

" Would any of you gentlemen like to ask this witness a question ? "

Receiving no reply, he added—

" Next witness, please ! "

CHAPTER XXVII

A ND now it was Luke de Mountford's turn at last.
A wave of excitement swept over the crowd,
every neck was craned forward, every eye fixed on
this next witness, as he rose from his seat, and with
courteous words of apology to those whom he disturbed in passing, he made his way to the centre
table.

An absolute embodiment of modern London society !
Luke stood there, facing the crowd, the coroner, and
jury, as he would have faced friends and acquaintances in the grand stand at Ascot, or in the stalls of
a West End theatre. There are hundreds and thousands of young Englishmen who look exactly as Luke
de Mountford looked that morning : dress is almost
an uniform, in cut, style, and degree of tone : hair and
even features are essentially typical. Luke de Mountford, well-born, well-bred, behaved just as Eton and
Oxford had taught him to behave : concealing every
emotion, raising neither voice nor gesture.

An Englishman of that type has alternately been
dubbed hypocritical, and unemotional. He is neither :
he is only conventional. Luke himself, facing the most
abnormal condition of life that could assail any man

223

of his class, was so absolutely drilled into this semblance of placidity, that it cost him no effort to re-
strain himself, and none to face the forest of inquisitive
eyes levelled at him from every side.   And since there
was no effort, the outward calm appeared perfectly
natural ; an actor who has played one part two
hundred times and more, does so night after night,
until the rôle itself becomes reality, and he, in ordinary everyday life, seems even to himself strange
and unnatural.

Now Luke was given the Bible to kiss, and told to
take the oath.   From where he stood, he could see
Louisa and a number of faces turned towards him in
undisguised curiosity : mocking eyes and contemptuous eyes, eyes of indifference and of horror met his
own as with quick glance they swept right over the
crowd.

I don't think that he really saw any one except
Louisa : no living person existed for him at this
moment except Louisa.   Hypocritical or unemotional
nature ? which ? none could say, none would take
the trouble to probe.   All that the crowd saw was a
man to all intents and purposes accused of a horrible
murder, confronted at every turn with undeniable
proofs of his guilt, and yet standing there just as if
he were witnessing the first act of some rather dull
play.

Hypocrisy or effrontery, were the two alternatives
which the idle and the curious weighed, whilst antici-
pating the joy of seeing the mask torn from this
wooden image before them.

The coroner was asking the witness his name, and Luke de Mountford's voice was quite steady as he gave reply.

"You were," continued the coroner, "until quite recently, and are again now, heir-presumptive to the Earl of Radclyffe?"

"It was supposed at one time," replied Luke, "that besides myself, there was no other heir to my uncle's title."

"Deceased, I understand, arrived in England about six months ago?"

"So I understand."

"He made claim to be the only son of Lord Radclyffe's elder brother?"

"That is so."

"And to all appearances was able to substantiate this claim in the eyes of Lord Radclyffe?"

"Apparently."

"So much so, that Lord Radclyffe immediately accorded him that position in his household which you had previously occupied?"

"Lord Radclyffe accorded to the deceased the position which he thought fitting that he should occupy."

"You know that the servants in Lord Radclyffe's household have informed the police, that in consequence of Mr. Philip de Mountford's advent in the house, you and your brother and sister had to leave it?"

"My brother, sister, and I now live at Fairfax Mansions, Exhibition Road," said Luke evasively.

Q

" And the relations between yourself and the deceased have remained of a very strained nature, I understand."

" Of an indifferent nature," corrected Luke.

There was a pause. So far these two—the coroner and the witness—had seemed almost like two antagonists, going through the first passes of a duel with foils. Steel had struck against steel, curt answers had followed brief questions. Now the combatants paused to draw breath. One of them was fighting the preliminary skirmish for his life, against odds that were bound to overwhelm him in the end ; the other was just a paid official, indifferent to the victim, interested only in the issue. The man standing at the foot of the table was certainly interesting ; the coroner had made up his mind that he was the guilty party . . . a gentleman, and yet a cowardly assassin. He amused himself during this brief pause with a quick analysis of the high-bred, impassive face . . . quite Saxon in character, fair, and somewhat heavy of lid . . . in no way remarkable, save for the present total lack of expression : there was neither indifference, nor bravado, neither fear, remorse, nor defiance . . . only a mask made of wood, hiding every line of the mouth, and not allowing even the eyes to show any signs of vitality,

Beyond that the whole appearance was essentially English : the fair hair neatly groomed, with just a suspicion of curl here and there, and a glint of gold in the high lights, the stiff neck encased in its immaculate collar, the perfectly tailored clothes, the hands, large, but well-formed and carefully tended, which, lightly interlaced, hung in marble-like stillness before him.

When a man happens to be out in mid-winter, with a stout stick in his hand, and he comes across a layer of ice on the top of a pool, or a trough of water, he always—or nearly always—is at once a prey to the silly desire to break that layer of ice. The desire is irresistible, and the point of the stick at once goes to work on the smooth surface, chipping it, if not actually succeeding in breaking it.

The same desire exists, in a far stronger degree, when the ice is a moral one—one that covers the real nature of another man : the cold impassiveness that hides the secret orchard to which no one but the owner has access. Then there is an irresistible longing to break that cold barrier, to look within, and to probe that hidden soul ; if not within its innermost depths, at any rate below the ice-bound surface : to chip it, to mark it, and break its invincible crust.

Some such feeling undoubtedly stirred at the back of the coroner's mind ; the hide-bound, red-tape-ridden official was more moved than he would have cared to admit, by a sense of irritation at the placidity of this witness, who was even now almost on his trial. Therefore, he had paused in his questionings, afraid lest that sense of irritation should carry him beyond the proper limits of his own powers.

And now he resumed more quietly, with his voice less trenchant, and his own manner outwardly more indifferent.

" When," he asked, " did you last see the deceased ? "

" In the lobby of the Veterans' Club," replied Luke, " the night before last."

" You had called there to see him ? "

" Yes."

" For what purpose ? "

" To discuss certain family matters."

" You preferred to discuss these family matters at a Club, rather than in your cousin's own home ? "

" Yes."

" Why ? "

" For private reasons of my own."

" It would help this inquiry, if you would state these private reasons."

" They have no bearing on the present issue."

" You refuse to state them ? " insisted the coroner.

" I do."

The coroner was silent for a moment : it almost seemed as if he meant to press the point at first, then thought differently, for after that brief while, he merely said—

" Very well."

Then he resumed—

" Now, Mr. de Mountford, on the night in question, you say, you went to see the deceased at the Veterans' Club. You were, I understand, shown into the smoking-room ? "

" Yes," was the simple answer.

" Your cousin was in the room ? "

" Yes."

" Alone ? "

" Alone."

" And how long did your interview with him last ? "

" About an hour, or less perhaps."

" Was it of an amicable character ? "

This question was identical to the one already put to Luke on the actual night of the crime, by the detective charged to elucidate its mysteries. And Luke's reply was identical to his former one—

" Of an indifferent character," he replied.

" There was no quarrel between you and the deceased gentleman ? "

" Our interview was of a private nature," rejoined Luke with unalterable calm.

" But other witnesses," retorted the coroner sharply, " heard angry voices issuing from the smoking-room."

" That, no doubt, is for those other witnesses to say."

" You deny, then, that you quarrelled with the deceased on the night when he was murdered ? "

" I deny nothing. I am not on my trial, I presume."

Again a pause. The coroner closed his eyes, and stroked his heavy chin. He had not yet succeeded in chipping the smooth surface of the ice.

" At what precise hour, then, did you last see the deceased alive ? " he asked, allowing his voice once more to appear harsh and his manner more peremptory.

" At nine o'clock, or thereabouts, the night before last."

" Where was that ? "

" He was in the lobby of the Veterans' Club, and I just outside."

" He made certain remarks to the hall-porter at that moment which offended you very deeply, I understand."

" Mr. Philip de Mountford was not always guarded in his speech when he spoke to servants."

" And his remarks offended you ? "

" My opinion on this point is of no consequence, I imagine."

" You then left the doorstep of the Veterans' Club, and a moment later the deceased joined you in the street."

" I finally left the Club soon after nine, but I did not again see Mr. Philip de Mountford alive."

" The deceased suggested that you should come with him, then and there, to see Lord Radclyffe at Grosvenor Square ; he hailed a taxi-cab, and you entered it with him," insisted the coroner with sudden slow emphasis.

" I last saw Mr. Philip de Mountford alive in the lobby of the Veterans' Club," reiterated Luke calmly, " soon after nine o'clock."

" He overtook you in the street outside the Club ? "

" It is not true."

" And hailed a cab ? "

" He may have done so, but not in my company."

" You entered the cab with him, and he told the driver to follow along Piccadilly."

" He may have done so," once more reiterated

Luke, in the same calm and even voice, " but not in my company."

" You parted from him in the lobby of the Club ? "

" I have told you so."

" And you never saw him again after that ? "

" Never."

" You were not with him when he came out of the Club ? "

" No."

" When he hailed a taxi-cab ? "

" No."

" You were not with him when he entered the cab and put his head out of the window, telling the driver to go along Piccadilly until he was stopped ? "

" No."

The answers had come clear, sharp, and distinct, quick ripostes of the foils against the violent attack. Now the adversary drew breath—the pause was dramatic in its effect, far-reaching in its significance. The coroner, with eyes steadily fixed on the witness, made a quick movement with his hand. He drew away the long narrow strip of green baize in front of him, revealing a snake-wood stick, with ferrule stained and tarnished.

" Is this your stick ? " he asked curtly.

" It is my stick," replied Luke.

He had not flinched, yet there were many scores of pairs of eyes fixed upon him when that green baize covering was removed. But not one of those who gazed so steadily upon him could boast that he or she had seen the slightest tremor of the lids, or the merest quiver of the mouth. The voice sounded perfectly clear, the cheeks, though pale, had assumed no greyish hue.

" Very well. That will do," said the coroner quietly.

What more was there to say ? The dagger-stick, stained and rusty, told the most graphic tale there was to tell. Yet Luke de Mountford stepped quietly away from the table, looking neither self-conscious nor dazed. He went back to his seat, beside Mr. Dobson, and leaning towards him answered some whispered questions which the solicitor was putting to him, He folded his arms before him, and after a while allowed his head to fall forward a little, closing his eyes as he did so. He seemed a little tired, but otherwise unperturbed, even though the hall-porter was now recalled, and was busy identifying the stick, which lay across the coroner's table, with the one which he himself had handed to Mr. de Mountford's visitor at nine o'clock the night before last.

And the police, too, added its share to this work that was going on, of enmeshing a criminal. There was the constable, who had found the stick inside the railings of Green Park, and had taken it straight away to his chief's at Scotland Yard, before the stains on it had been further disturbed ; and there was, finally, Dr. Blair, the district medical officer, also recalled, who examined the dagger which fitted into that snake-wood stick.

He had been shown it yesterday, it seems, and found how accurately it fitted the wound in the murdered man's throat. To this he swore now in open court, for the *coup de théâtre*, the production of the dagger-stick, had been kept back until now, in order that it should work its fullest and most dramatic effect.

Colonel Harris, sitting near his daughter, would have given worlds to know what she thought. He himself did not know what to think. His simple, unsophisticated mind was in a maze. The question of Luke's possible guilt had suddenly loomed up before him, dissipating the former blind impulse of partisanship and loyalty. Mr. Dobson too looked puzzled, the old family solicitor, who had seen Luke and his brothers and sister grow up, who a few hours, nay, minutes ago, would have sworn to his client's innocence before the entire world, he too now was face to face with a hideous feeling of doubt.

Not one other person in the room either, believe me, who was not convinced of Luke's guilt. Louisa knew that well enough as her aching eyes wandered over the sea of faces, meeting hollow compassion, morbid curiosity, at best a certain sympathetic horror in the glances round. She knew that every one here, the officials, the jury, the police, the public, believed that Luke struck his cousin in the dark, she knew that Mr. Dobson had begun to doubt, and that her father had begun to fear.

And she, with all the fervour of unconquered Love, prayed in her heart that she might understand. She prayed to Love to open the eyes of her mind, for it was her reason which did not understand, which yearned to understand.

Her heart cared nothing, cared for nothing except for the man she loved and the bitter, bitter sorrow which he endured alone, shut away from all, even from her.

There was general stir in the court-room, the coroner had risen, also the jury. The journalists were holding agitated parlance with the boy messengers. Louisa—like one who has received a sharp blow on the head—wondered what all this stir meant.

Was it all over ? Had Luke irretrievably lost himself in that secret orchard of his, into which he was obviously determined that even she should not enter ?

Then she found out that the stir only meant the luncheon hour. All these people were going to eat and to chatter. Heavens above ! how they would chatter !

Her father said something about getting a cab, and trying to find a decent hotel where to have luncheon. But she scarcely heard. She had just seen Luke disappearing through the crowd in company with Mr. Dobson, and he had not even glanced back to look at her.

Every one whispered round her. Lady Ducie's nodding feathers worried her almost to distraction. She allowed her father to lead her away and to make way for her through the crowd.

Presently she found herself sitting near him in a cab. He was silent, and would not look at her. Not that he had begun to think that Luke had killed his cousin : but once she heard him repeating the word " damnable ! " twice under his breath. Thus she knew that his loyalty was at bay.

It seems that they had luncheon somewhere together. She did not take the trouble to inquire where she was : an old-fashioned hotel somewhere in Kensington, with table-cloths that looked as if they had been used for several previous luncheons, and foreign waiters who wore weird-looking shoes, and trousers frayed at the edges.

To please her father she ate a little, though she thought that eating must choke her. But it was wearisome to argue, and he—poor dear—looked so miserable.

Time was precious, and luncheon interminably slow ; it was past two o'clock when Louisa saw Luke again in the court-room.

CHAPTER XXVIII

WHICH TELLS OF AN UNEXPECTED TURN OF EVENTS

IT seems that coroner and jury had not spent quite so much time over luncheon as the more or less interested spectators. When the crowd began to file back again into the seats the coroner had already examined and dismissed one witness, and was questioning another.

The past and present servants of the Grosvenor Square household would all have to pass before the coroner during the course of this long afternoon. It was only two o'clock, and already the gas had to be lighted : two incandescent burners just above the coroner's table. Hard, uncompromising lights, that threw a sickly green tinge on every face, and cast deep black shadows under every eye.

It was this light, no doubt, that made Luke's face seem positively ghastly to Louisa : it looked almost like a death-mask, so deep and cavernous did the eyes appear, and so hollow the cheeks. He was sitting in his usual attitude, with arms folded, between Mr. Dobson and one of the women in seedy black, whose presence here had puzzled every one.

Old Parker, ex-butler to Lord Radclyffe, was giving evidence. He had a tale to tell, how Mr. de Mountford " went on awful " when he—the innocent, well-drilled servant—had thought it his duty to introduce Mr. Philip into his lordship's presence.

"Just think of it, your honour," he exclaimed, " his lordship's rightful heir."

Then he added, with calm effrontery—

"Mr. Luke, 'e give me the sack then and there! He was that wild!"

Just a paltry, silly, meaningless revenge. The death-mask on Luke's face relaxed for a moment, when he looked on the fat creature standing before the jury : vainly trying to look pompous and self-righteous, and only succeeding in being a liar.

The evidence would have been of little worth but for the corroboration from other servants of the Grosvenor Square household. The present two—man and wife—wastrels and drunkards, counted for nothing : they had only entered Lord Radclyffe's service recently, when all visitors had ceased from calling at the inhospitable house, and they had seen little or nothing of Luke ; but the others—those whom Philip's arbitrary temper had driven out of the house— they had many a tale to tell of the dead man's arrogance, his contemptuous treatment of his younger kinsmen, and the bitter words that often flew between the cousins, when doors were closed and eaves-droppers behind the keyholes.

These witnesses—an ex-housekeeper, a footman, a maid—were trying their best, poor things, to " do the right thing by Mr. Luke "—little guessing how ill they succeeded. They had been dragged into this, much against their will. As a class, they hated the police and its doings, even though the cook might occasionally show a preference for the local guardian of peace and order. As for the detective in plain clothes, the man who wore a peaked cap instead of the familiar helmet, him they hated and feared, especially since he seemed to mean mischief for Mr. Luke.

They gave their evidence unwillingly: every admission had to be dragged out of them, once they realized that the revelations of past quarrels between "the gentlemen" would not be to the detriment of the dead, only, perhaps, to the undoing of the living.

The hours wore on wearily. The atmosphere, now surcharged with the heat from the gas brackets, had become intolerably oppressive. Opoponax and white heliotrope waxed faint to the nostrils. Through the badly-fitting window-frame, something of the outward fog had penetrated into the room. It hung about in the air round the gas that burned yellow and dim through it, and obscured the far corners of the place, throwing a veil over the twelve mutes in uniform overcoats, with threadbare velvet collars, over the eager and perspiring journalists, whose fountain pens had scraped the paper incessantly for so long.

Hot, tired, and oppressed humanity made its warm breath felt in the close, ill-ventilated room. Smelling-salts would not dispel the unpleasantly mingling odours of damp clothes and muddy boots, which rose from the plebeian crowd in the rear.

But nobody stirred: no one would have thought of

leaving before the last act of this interesting play.
The chief actor was not on the stage for the moment,
but his presence was felt. It was magnetic in its
appeal to excitement. Every question put by the
coroner, every reply given by the witnesses, had, as it
were, Luke de Mountford for its aim : every word
tended towards him, his undoing, the enmeshing of
his denials in the close web of circumstantial evidence.

Then a diversion occurred.

The man in the shabby clothes, who looked like a
beetle, and who had marshalled his companions into
the court-room early in the day, was called upon by
the usher to come forward. His strange poorly-clad
figure detached itself from the groups immediately
round him : his long, loose limbs seeming to swing
themselves forward.

His four companions—the three women and the
other man—were seized apparently with great agitation, and whispered eagerly among themselves. No
one in the crowd could guess why these people had
been called. They seemed so completely out of the
picture, which had its invisible frame in Grosvenor
Square.

" Go on, Jim ! " whispered one of the young women,
" they can't do nothing to ye."

And the beetle-like creature shambled forward,
with arms dangling beside him, a humble apologetic
look on his care-worn face. He might have been any
age from thirty to sixty : time, and a perpetual
struggle for existence, had wiped away all traces of
actual age. The cheeks were hollow, and eyes, mouth,

and moustache had a droop which added to the settled melancholy of the face.

He was obviously very nervous, and looked across at his own friends, who strove to encourage him by signs and whispers.

He nearly dropped the Bible when it was handed to him, and no one could really hear the oath, which he repeated mechanically at the usher's bidding.

At last, he mustered up a sufficient amount of courage to state his name and address.

" James Baker," he said, in answer to the coroner's question. " Bricklayer by trade."

" And where do you live ? "

" At 147 Clapham Junction Road, sir," replied the man, scarcely above a whisper.

" Speak up, please," admonished the coroner, " the jury can't hear you. You came here, I understand, prepared to make a statement ? "

" Yes, sir."

" Of what nature ? "

The man shifted his position from one leg to the other. Heavy beads of perspiration stood out on his pallid forehead.

" Go on, Jim, don't be afeeard," came from the body of the court.

" Silence, there ! " commanded the usher.

" I wish to say, sir," resumed the man, trying to steady his voice, " that the deceased, whom I saw lying in the coffin yonder, is my own son, Paul Baker, sir."

" Your son ! "

" My son, sir," asserted the man, somewhat more

steadily, " my son, and 'is mother's, as is sitting over there. My son, Paul Baker, as left 'ome two year ago come next Christmas. We all come 'ere, sir, to-day, me and 'is mother and sister, an' Smith and Jane—we all come 'ere to swear to 'im."

" Your son ! "

The exclamation once more came from the coroner, but had any one else dared, that exclamation would have been echoed and re-echoed by every mouth in the court-room, coupled with emphatic ejaculations of incredulity.

It was as if in a new Castle of some grim Sleeping Monster a magic wand had touched every somnolent spirit. Smelling-salts and scented handkerchiefs were forgotten : the jurymen leaned forward, half across the table, oblivious of their own dignity, in their endeavour to obtain a fuller view of this wielder of the magic wand : the beetle-like creature with the sad eyes and pale hollow cheeks. Even the reporters—accustomed to sensational events—gave up scribbling, in order to stare open-mouthed at the shabby figure standing by the table.

At first, of course, the predominant sensation was one of sweeping incredulity. Coroner and jury had met here to-day in this stuffy room in order to conduct an inquiry on the death of Philip de Mountford, heir-presumptive to the Earldom of Radclyffe. The crowd of fashionable and idle gapers had pushed and jostled, in order to hear the ugly story of how wealth and position are fought for, and intrigued for, even at the cost of crime.

R

And now, to think that the man who lay dead was just a bricklayer's son ! It was absolutely incredible. Not till a few moments later did the spectators realize that if the seedy man at the table spoke truly, then they were witnessing a drama even more poignant than that of the original murder ; a drama of deception and of fraud, and a mystery far deeper than that which had originally confronted the sensation-mongers.

Strangely enough, incredulity died down, and died down very quickly. A subtle wave filled the murky atmosphere, compelling every mind to belief, long before the man's assertions were proved to be correct. The most indifferent became conscious of an overwhelming conviction that the witness was speaking the truth.

This conviction was absolutely paramount in the minds of the chief actors in the play. To them all : to Colonel Harris and to Louisa, to Mr. Dobson and the solicitors, the truth of the statement was never in question. An unerring instinct forced them to believe : and such beliefs are as unconquerable as they are overwhelming. Truth that is an absolute, unquestionable truth, finds its way to the mind, when the latter is attuned to subtle or psychic impressions.

And as the truth was borne in upon these people, so did they realize the fullness of its meaning : the deep significance of its portent.

To some of them it seemed as if in a brilliantly illuminated world, all the lights had suddenly been extinguished ; to others, as if in a dark and intricate

cavern, full of black impenetrable shadows, dazzling
lights had been suddenly switched on.

Louisa, looking across at Luke, saw that to him
it meant the latter, and that some of the new dazzling
light had illumined the darkness of his soul.

Something of the tense rigidity of his attitude had
gone from him : not the sorrow, perhaps, but the
blank hopelessness of a misery that flounders in a sea
of the Unknown.

CHAPTER XXIX

THE WORLD IS SO LARGE

AS for the man who had made the extraordinary assertion, he seemed quite unconscious of the effect which it had produced : as if the fact that the supposed heir to an earldom, being actually the son of a Clapham bricklayer, was one that found its natural place in everyday life.

He had his cap in his hand—a shabby grey tweed cap—and he was twirling it between his fingers round and round with an irritatingly nervous gesture. His eyes, now and again, were furtively raised at the coroner, as if he were wondering anxiously what punishment would be meted out to him for having created so much commotion, and then with equal furtiveness he dropped them again. His shoulders were bowed, and his knees parted company from one another : thus giving him more than ever the appearance of a beetle.

Of course, the coroner had to recover his official manner as quickly as possible. But even to him the statement had come as a surprise. He had only known very vaguely that a witness had come forward at the eleventh hour, having only just had time to communicate with the police before the opening of the inquest.

In view of the importance of the evidence, the witness was called as soon as possible : what he had to say
would materially affect the whole trend of the inquiry. He had, it seems, brought others with him—
members of his own family among them—in order
that they might corroborate the truth of what he
said.

Quite a minute or so had elapsed in the meanwhile :
then, at last, was the coroner able to resume with at
least a semblance of official indifference.

" Now," he said, " let the jury understand a little
more clearly what you said just now."

" What I said ? " rejoined the man vaguely.

" Yes : what you said. Let us understand it clearly.
You went to the mortuary this morning, and saw the
body of the deceased ? "

" Yes, sir."

" And you state here, on oath, that in the deceased
you recognized your own son ? "

" I'll swear to 'im ! " replied the witness simply.
" Ask 'is mother there ! "

And with long, thin finger, generously edged with
grime, he pointed to the woman in seedy black hat
and shabby tweed jacket, who sat quite close to
Luke de Mountford.

" Never mind about his mother just now," admonished the coroner. " We want your statement
first. You realize that you are on oath ? "

" Yes, sir. I've sworn my Bible oath."

" And you understand the importance of an oath ? "

" Yes, sir."

"And you swear that the body of the murdered man, whom you saw in the mortuary chamber this morning, is that of your son ? "

"I swear to that, sir."

I believe that had coroner and jury, and practically every man there present, dared to put their thoughts into words at that moment, the ejaculation : "Well ! I am blowed ! " or " I'm d—d ! " as the case might be, would have been generally heard throughout the room. The women, on the other hand, were far too excited even to think.

"Now," resumed the coroner, " tell the jury, please, when you first identified the deceased as your son."

"This morning, sir."

" In the mortuary chamber ? "

"Yes, sir."

"You had not seen the body before ? "

"No, sir."

"Did you know that other witnesses have sworn that the body is that of a gentleman called Philip de Mountford ? "

"Yes, sir. I knew that."

"Then do you mean to assert that those other witnesses have sworn false oaths ? "

"Oh, no, sir," rejoined James Baker, with an apologetic smile of self-deprecation, " I wouldn't say such a thing, sir."

"Well then ? "

"They was mistaken, sir, that's all. Paul was that clever, sir ; ask 'is mother there ! "

And once more the lean and grimy finger pointed

to the seedy-looking matron, who nodded a melancholy head, half in pride, half in regret.

"Clever, did you say?" asked the coroner, more briskly now. At last he held a thread in this extraordinary tangled skein. "Then do you mean to assert that your son—Paul Baker—went about the world calling himself Philip de Mountford?"

"That must 'ave been it, sir, I think."

"Deceiving people?"

"Aye! 'e was ever a bit o' no good."

"You think he imposed upon his lordship the Earl of Radclyffe?"

"'E must 'ave done, sir, mustn't 'e now? seein' as 'ow 'is lordship must 'ave been took in."

"You helped him in the deception, I suppose?"

"Me, sir? Lor' bless ye, no! Me an' 'is mother ain't clever enough for such things! We knew nothin' of Paul's doin's, and 'e allus went 'is own way, sir."

"But at least you knew that this fraud was going on?"

"Not exactly, sir."

"How do you mean, 'not exactly'?" retorted the coroner sharply. "You seem to be unconscious of the fact that this story which you are telling the jury is a very serious matter indeed. If it is true, you are not only making a grave accusation against your dead son, but with this accusation you may be involving yourself, or some other member of your family, in an exceedingly serious charge of fraud: the penalty for which, if proved, would be very severe indeed. On the other hand, if the story you tell is nothing but a cock-and-bull tale, which further evidence would presently demolish, then you lay yourself open to a charge of perjury, and of conspiracy to defeat the ends of justice. I have thought best to give you this word of warning—the last which you will get from me—because really you do not seem to be fully conscious of the extreme gravity of your position."

The bricklayer from Clapham had listened to this admonition, delivered with solemn emphasis and no small measure of severity, with a kind of stolid indifference. He retained his humble, apologetic attitude, but clearly the coroner's threats did not affect his simple equanimity.

"I thank you, sir, kindly," he said, when the coroner had ceased speaking, "but I can't 'elp it. Paul would go on 'is own way. Ask 'is mother there. 'E never would be spoken to, wouldn't Paul. And me and 'is mother allus said 'e'd come to mischief some day."

"Did you know anything at all of this fraud ? "

"No, sir. We knew nothin' of it really. You see, Paul left 'ome nearly two year ago come Christmas. 'E didn't tell us nothing."

"Then you last saw your son alive two years ago ? "

"Yes, sir. That's the last me and 'is mother seed of 'im. Christmas Day, sir, 'twas two year ago nearly. Paul, 'e said then 'e'd 'ad enough of knockin' about in London. 'E was goin' abroad, 'e was, that's what 'e said. And 'e left 'ome, sir, the next day—Bank 'Oliday, 'twere—and that's the last me and 'is mother seed of 'im."

He had told this with all the simple fatalism peculiar to his class. The son went "abroad"; and "abroad" to a Clapham labourer is a very vague term indeed. It means so many things: geographically it means any place beyond a twelve-mile radius from home; the Antipodes are "abroad," but so is Yorkshire. Domestically it means that the traveller passes out of the existence of those that are left behind, as surely as if he had stepped into the grave. Financially it means a mouth less to feed, seeing that the intending traveller is nearly always a wastrel at home. In any event, the proposed journey "abroad" is taken with quiet philosophy by family and friends. The traveller starts for "abroad" as easily, as simply as he would for the nearest public-house. He has no impedimenta, nothing to burden him or to cause him regret. Strangely enough, no one ever has any idea where the money comes from that pays for the journey "abroad." The traveller, being a wastrel, never has any himself, and the family is invariably too poor to provide it. But the wastrel goes, nevertheless.

And life within the narrow precincts of the family circle goes on just as it had done before. Sometimes, news comes from the traveller—a picture post card from "abroad," usually a request for pecuniary assistance—seldom does good news arrive; still more seldom does the traveller come back home.

But it is all very simple. Nothing to make a fuss about.

"Then," said the coroner, "he didn't tell you where he meant to go?"

" No, sir," replied Jim Baker, " he just was going abroad."

" Do you know where he went ? "

" No, sir."

" Did you ever try to find out ? "

" No, sir. Where 'ad been the use ? "

Where indeed ? The world is so large ! and the Baker family so insignificant !

" He didn't write to you ? "

" No, sir."

" Nor communicate with you in any way ? "

" No, sir."

" You had no idea what had become of him ? "

" Not until last summer, sir."

" What happened then ? "

" His sister, sir, our Emily, she was out walkin' with Harry Smith—young Smith, from next door to us, sir—and she was down in the West End o' London with 'im one day, and 'oo should they meet, sir, but Paul."

" Did they speak to him ? "

" Yes, sir. They says : ' 'Ello, Paul, we didn't know as 'ow you was 'ome ' ; and 'e seemed upset like at first, and pretended 'e didn't know 'em, and that they'd made a mistake. But they chaffed 'im and went on talkin', so I suppose Paul, 'e thought it best to make a clean breast of it all."

" Do you mean to say that he told his sister and his friend that he was carrying on a criminal fraud against the Earl of Radclyffe ? "

" Oh no, sir, not all that. 'E only told 'em that 'e

was in for a good thing. A gentleman's gentleman, 'e told 'em 'e was, and doin' well for hisself. 'E said 'e would come and see the family—'e meant me and 'is mother, sir—some day soon. But 'e never come."

" Did he say where he was living ? "

" Yes, sir. 'E gave 'is address to Emily. Up 'Ampstead way, it were. A long way, sir. Me and 'is mother never seemed to 'ave the time to go and look 'im up ; but Emily, she went with young Smith one Sunday, but they never found the street : not where Paul said 'e was livin'. There weren't no such street in 'Ampstead, sir."

" And you never thought of making further inquiries ? "

" No, sir." This again with that quiet philosophy, the stolid fatalism peculiar to those who live from day to day, from hand to mouth : who have neither leisure nor desire to peer outside the very circumscribed limits of their own hearths.

" You never made any effort to know more about what your son was doing, or how he was living ? " suggested the coroner ; who, though accustomed to this same quiet philosophy in men and women of that class, was nevertheless strangely moved in this instance by the expression of a fatalism that carried in its train such extraordinary consequences.

But Jim Baker, mildly astonished at the coroner's insistence over so obvious a matter, explained meekly—

" We knew that Paul was doin' well, you see, sir. 'E was that splendidly dressed when Emily and young

Smith seed 'im, they was quite respectful like to 'im.
So we knew 'e was all right."

" And you never troubled any further about your
son ? "

" We didn't want to interfere with 'im, sir. Gentlemen don't allus like their servants to be 'aving visitors,
or to 'obnob with poor people like us."

More calm philosophy, not unmixed with a delicate
sense of pride this time, and a sublime, if unconscious,
vein of selflessness.

" Well ! " rejoined the coroner, not unkindly this
time : the man, who looked so like a beetle, who was
so humble and apologetic, compelled quite a certain
amount of regard, " we'll leave that matter for a
moment, Mr. Baker. Now will you tell the jury what
made you come to this court to-day ? What led you
to think that the man who had been murdered in a
cab the night before last, and of whom all the newspapers spoke as Mr. Philip de Mountford, what made
you think that he was your son ? "

Jim Baker, by way of a reply, plunged one of his thin
hands in the pocket of his shabby coat, and drew out
a portion of very grimy newspaper, carefully folded
up quite small. He undid the folds, until his eyes
lighted on that which they sought. Then he held the
paper out towards the coroner, and pointed to a
picture sandwiched in among the letterpress.

" I saw this," he said, " in the *Daily Graphic* yesterday. ' It's the picture of Paul,' I says to myself."

The coroner took the paper from the witness and
laid it down on the table, glancing at it casually.

There had been innumerable portraits of the murdered man published, both in the morning and the evening papers of yesterday.

"It's Paul to the life," insisted Jim Baker. "I was at my work, you understand, when I seed the paper in one o' the other chaps' 'ands. I couldn't give up my work then. I 'ad to wait till evenin' to speak to my missus. Then we talked it all over : and young Smith, 'e took a day off and me too, and Mrs. Baker and Emily and Jane Smith, they all come along."

"And you looked on the face of the dead man, and you swear that it is your son ? "

"I take my oath, sir. Ask 'is mother there. She knows 'er own son. She'll tell you just what vaccination marks 'e 'ad on 'is arm, and about the scar on 'is leg, and all. The ladies, sir, they are that sharp . . ."

Jim Baker—feeling, no doubt, that his ordeal was nearly over—was losing his nervousness, or perhaps it took a new form : that of jocularity. The coroner thought it best to check his efforts at humour in the bud.

"That will do," he said curtly.

And the Clapham bricklayer at once retired within his shell of humble self-deprecation. He answered a few more questions that the coroner put to him, but clearly his own circle of vision was so circumscribed, that—willing as he undoubtedly was—he could throw no light whatever on the unknown events which led up to the extraordinary fraud practised on the Earl of Radclyffe, and which culminated in the mysterious murder in the taxi-cab.

The father of the strangely enigmatic personality, who indeed had taken many a secret with him to the grave, was far too indifferent, too fatalistic to put forth any theory as to his son's motives, or the inducements and temptations which had first given birth to the astoundingly clever deception.

Wearied and impatient at last, the coroner gave up his questionings ; he turned to the jury with the accustomed formula—

" Would any of you gentlemen like to ask this witness any questions ? "

The foreman of the jury wanted to know if the witness's son had any birth-marks on him, or other palpable means of identificaton.

" Yes, sir," replied Jim Baker, " but 'is mother'll tell you better'n me . . . she knows best . . . about the vaccination marks and all."

The foreman then asked the coroner whether the jury would be allowed to identify the marks. On being assured by the coroner that after adjournment this very day every means would be taken to corroborate Jim Baker's statement, the jury seemed satisfied.

And the coroner called the next witness.

CHAPTER XXX

AND THEN EVERY ONE WENT HOME

THOUGH the hour was getting late, no one among the crowd thought of leaving the court. Even the desire for tea, so peculiarly insistent at a certain hour of the day in the whole of the British race, was smothered beneath the wave of intense excitement which swept right over every one.

Although the next witnesses—who each in their turn came forward to the foot of the table—swore to tell the truth, and faced the coroner with more or less assurance, they could but repeat the assertions of the head of the family. Nevertheless, the public seemed ready to listen with untiring patience to the story which went to prove that the man, whom everybody believed to be the heir of one of the oldest titles and richest rent rolls in England, was the son of a Clapham bricklayer : a master of audacity and of fraud.

The mother—a worthy and simple soul—was the first to explain that Paul, her only son, had always been something of a gentleman. He had done very well at school, and never done a stroke of work like 'is father. When he was fifteen, he was quite stage-

struck. " Always play-acting," as the mother put it,
" and could recite poetry beautiful ! "

Mrs. Baker seemed distinctly proud of her son's
deeply-rooted horror of work. She thought that all
the instincts of a gentleman were really in him. When
he was a grown lad, he went as footman in a gentleman's family, somewhere in the Midlands. The
mother loftily supposed that it was there that Paul
learned his good manners.

" He was a perfect gentleman, sir," she reiterated
complacently.

It appeared, too, that the wastrel had had a period
in his career, when the call of the stage proved quite
irresistible : for he seemed to have left the gentleman's
family in the Midlands somewhat abruptly, and
walked on as super for a time in the various melo-
dramas produced at the Grand Theatre, Nottingham,
whenever a crowd was required on the stage. There
seems also to have existed a legend in the heart of
the fond mother and of the doting sister, that Paul
had once really played a big part in a serious play.
But this statement was distinctly wanting in corroboration.

What was obviously an established fact was, that
the man had a certain spirit of adventure in him,
and that he had been a regular rolling stone : a
regular idle, good-for-nothing wastrel, possessing a
certain charm of manner which delighted his family,
and which was readily mistaken by the simple folk
for that of a gentleman.

They were all called in turn : the sister, and young

Smith "from next door," and the latter's sister. Not one of them swerved for a moment from the original story told by Jim Baker. Emily and young Smith told of the meeting, which occurred on a fine summer's afternoon, between themselves and Paul. By the strange caprice of wanton coincidence, the meeting occurred inside Green Park. Paul seemed a little worried, thinking that the passers-by would see him talking to " poor people like us," as Emily Baker had it, " although,"·she added proudly, " I 'ad me new 'at on, with the pink roses." Otherwise he was quite pleasant, and not at all " off-'and."

The account of this interview was fully corroborated by young Smith "from next door." Jane Smith, who at one time had considered herself engaged to Paul Baker, had a few tender reminiscences to recount. She had seen the prodigal once on the boards of the Queen's ·Theatre, Lewisham, and she declared that he looked " a perfect gentleman."

The day wore on, or rather the commencement of evening. The evil-smelling fog from outside had made its home inside the dismal room. People there only saw one another through a misty veil : the corners of the room were wrapped in gloom. Exciting as was the story which had been unfolded this afternoon, one or two among the audience had given way to sleep. Lady Ducie's feathers nodded ominously, and the old dame who had munched sandwiches was inclined to give forth an occasional snore.

Louisa's eyes were aching. Constant watching had tired them ; they even ceased to see clearly. Her

s

brain, too, had become somnolent. She was tired of
hearing these people talk. From the moment that
Jim Baker had stated that the murdered man was his
own son, Louisa had known that he had spoken the
truth. Instinct was guiding her towards the truth :
showing her the truth, wherever possible. She listened
at first—deeply interested—to the scrappy evidence,
which told of Paul Baker's early life ; but the family
from Clapham Junction Road had marvellously
little to relate. They no more understood their
adventurous-spirited son than they would have been
capable of aiding and abetting the fraud which he
concocted.

They themselves were far too simple, and too stupid,
to be dangerously criminal. And so the evidence
quickly lost its interest for Louisa. She herself—with
the fragmentary statements which she heard—could
more easily surmise the life history of Paul Baker
than could the doting mother, who retailed complacently every mark on the skin and on the body of
her son, and knew nothing whatever—less than
nothing—of his thoughts, his schemes : of the evil
that was in him, and the ambition which led to his
end.

And now the last of the Baker contingent was dismissed. Jane Smith—the sweetheart of the murdered
man—was the last to leave the coroner's table. She
did so in a flood of tears, in which the others promptly
and incontinently joined.

The coroner—somewhat impatient with them all,
for their vague notions on the most important bearings

of the case had severely tried him—adjourned the inquiry until the morrow.

He ordered the jury to be present at a quarter before ten, and gave the signal for general withdrawal.

After which every one went home.

CHAPTER XXXI

AND THERE ARE PEOPLE WHO DO NOT CARE

FOR the first time, I think, in the whole course of her life Louisa Harris felt that convention must be flouted, and social duties could not be fulfilled.

When the coroner—rising from his seat—gave the signal for general exodus, she had felt her father's firm hand grasping her arm and leading her out of the fog-ridden, stuffy room into the cold, grey passages outside.

The herd of cackling geese were crowding round her. Heavens above ! how they cackled and gossiped ! It seemed as if the very floodgates of a noisy, bubbling stream had been torn asunder, and a whirlpool of chattering women been let loose upon the earth.

Convention, grim and untractable, tried to pull the strings to make all puppets dance. But for once Louisa Harris rebelled. She closed her ears to insinuating calls from her friends, responding with a mere curt nod to the most gushing : " Oh, Miss Harris, how are you ? " which greeted her from every side.

She turned her back resolutely on convention. The slave for once rebelled against the taskmaster : the puppet refused to dance to the ever-wearying monotonous tune.

She had lost sight of Luke the moment the court rose. She supposed that his solicitor, Mr. Dobson, knowing the ropes, had got him away from the reach of cackling geese, by leading him through some other more private way. But she was far too dazed, too numb, either to wonder or to be disappointed at this. She felt as if she had pitched head foremost down a long flight of stairs, and had only just had sufficient strength to pick herself up, and not to let other people see quite how severely she had been bruised.

Mentally, morally, even physically she felt bruised from head to foot.

Colonel Harris contrived to steer her through the crowd; at the gate outside, even the smoke-laden atmosphere seemed pure and invigorating in comparison with that stuffy pen, wherein the herd of cackling geese had found its happy hunting-ground. Louisa drew in a long breath, filling her lungs with fog, but feeling a little freer, less choked in spite of the grime which she inhaled.

" I think," said Colonel Harris now, " that you'd better go straight back to the Langham and get some tea. You'll feel better when you've had your tea."

" I feel all right, dear," she said, trying to smile.

" So much the better," he retorted, with an equal effort at cheerfulness. " I'll come along as soon as I can."

" Where are you off to, dear ? " she asked.

" I'll just go and have a talk to Tom," he replied.

" I'll come with you. I can wait in the cab. I don't suppose that you'll be long."

He tried to protest, but obviously she had made up her mind. Perhaps she did not like the idea of going back to the hotel alone. So he hailed a passing cab, and told the man to drive to Scotland Yard.

He had deliberately—and despite former prejudices —selected a taxi-cab. He wanted to see Tom as soon as possible.

Louisa leaned back in the corner of the vehicle silent and motionless. Father and daughter did not exchange a single. word whilst the cab rattled through the crowded streets of London. Hansoms, omnibuses, innumerable other taxis, rattled along the self-same way, just as they had always done before this, just as they would go on doing to the end of time. People walked along, busy and indifferent. Many went past the shrieking news-vendors without even stopping to buy a paper.

Luke stood accused, almost self-convicted of a horrible crime, and there were thousands—nay, millions—of people who didn't even care !

The taxi-cab flew past the railings of the Green Park, there where another taxi-cab had drawn up a couple of evenings ago, and where a snake-wood stick stained with tell-tale stains had been found clumsily buried in the mud. Louisa peered out of the window of the cab. People walked past that spot, indifferent and busy. Two girls were standing close to the railings, chatting and giggling.

And Luke to-morrow—or perhaps to-night—would be under arrest—charged with murder . . . horrible, cruel, brutal murder . . . a vulgar, cowardly crime !

The snake-wood stick had told a tale which he had not attempted to refute.

Presently the cab drew up and Colonel Harris jumped down.

" I won't be longer than I can help," he said. " Will you be all right ? "

" Yes, father dear," she replied ; " I'll be all right. Don't hurry."

She saw her father disappearing through the wide-open door, above which a globe of light shone yellow through the fog. She remained huddled up in her furs —for she felt very cold. Her feet were like ice, and the fog seemed to have penetrated to her very marrow. Few people were to be seen in the narrow roadway, and only an occasional cab rattled past.

From the Embankment close by came the cry of news-vendors, rushing along with the late editions of the evening papers.

A church clock not far away slowly struck six. But she held no count of time. A kind of drowsiness was upon her, and the foggy atmosphere, coupled with intense, damp cold, acted as a kind of soporific.

She may have waited years, or only a few minutes, she did not know, but presently her father came back. His presence there under the lintel of the door seemed to have roused her from her torpor, as if with a swift telegraphic current. As he stood for a moment beneath the electric light, adjusting the collar of his coat, she saw his face quite distinctly : its expression told her everything. Luke's arrest was imminent. It was but a question of a few hours, moments perhaps.

"I am going to Exhibition Road at once," he said, speaking quickly, like a man deeply troubled.

And without waiting for her assent, which was a foregone conclusion, he gave the chauffeur the address : "Fairfax Mansions, Exhibition Road," and added, "Drive as fast as you can ! "

Then he jumped in beside Louisa. The taxi-cab moaned and groaned whilst it manœuvred for turning, then it rattled off once more at prohibited speed.

"It is," she said simply, "only a question of time, I suppose ? "

"The warrant is out," he replied curtly. "Any moment now the police may be at his door."

"Uncle Ryder is convinced of Luke's guilt ? "

"Absolutely."

"Beyond that what does he say ? "

"That unless Luke chooses to make a bolt of it, he had better plead guilty and intense provocation. But he thinks Luke would be wise to catch the night boat for Calais."

"They'd get him back on extradition."

"Tom says they won't try very hard. And if Luke keeps his wits about him, and has a sufficiency of money, he'll be able to get right through to Spain and from thence to Tangiers. With money and influence much can be done ; and Tom says that if Luke will only get away to-night he himself is prepared to take all the blame and all the responsibility of having allowed a criminal to escape. It's very decent of Tom," added the Colonel thoughtfully, "for he risks his entire future."

But the sorely troubled father did not tell his daughter all that Sir Thomas Ryder had told him in the course of the brief interview.

In effect, the chief of the Criminal Investigation Department had given a brief alternative by way of advice.

" A ticket to anywhere via Calais at once . . . or a revolver."

And he had added dryly—

" I see nothing else for it. The man has practically confessed."

But this Colonel Harris would not admit, and so the two men parted. Louisa's father, thinking a great deal of his friend, but still more of his daughter, wanted, above all things, to have a final talk with Luke.

Louisa, in the meanwhile, sat silent in the corner of the cab.

She was trying to visualize this new picture : Luke— a fugitive from justice !

The taxi-cab was making a slight detour as Whitehall and the Mall were closed for road repairs. The chauffeur was driving round by St. Martin's Lane. At one of the theatres there, a popular play was filling the house night after night with enthusiastic crowds. It was only half-past six now, and in a long queue, extending over two hundred yards away from the pit and gallery doors of the lucky playhouse, patient crowds waited for the evening's pleasure.

People were going to theatres—they laughed at farces, and wept at tragedies. Was there ever such a

tragedy enacted inside a theatre, as now took place in
the life of a commonplace man and woman ?

Luke !—a fugitive from justice ! Money and influence could do much ! they could enable a wealthy
criminal to escape the consequences of his own crime !
They could enable him to catch express trains unmolested, to fly across land and sea under cover of the
night, to become—Cain-like—a wanderer on the face
of the earth without rest and without peace.

Could they prevent him from seeing ever present at
his elbow the grim Angel of Remorse, holding in one
hand the glass wherein relentlessly flowed the sands
of time, and in the other the invisible sword of a re-
tarded but none the less sure vengeance ? Could they
prevent his hearing the one word : Nemesis ?

Luke !—a fugitive from justice ! accused of a crime
which he did not commit, self-convicted, almost self-
accused, and fleeing from its consequences as he would
from Remorse.

And people went to theatres, and laughed and cried.
People ate and danced and sang. News-vendors
shrieked their wares : the latest sensational news : the
gentleman-criminal who had money and influence and
with their help evaded the grip of justice.

CHAPTER XXXII

A MAN MUST ACT AS HE THINKS BEST

LOUISA knew the flat in Exhibition Road very well. She had helped Edie to furnish it, and to make it pretty and cosy; for Edie's passion was for dogs and for golf; drawing-room chairs and saucepans were not much in her line. So Louisa had chosen practically everything: the piano, as well as the coal-scuttles, and every stick of furniture in Luke's room.

To-night she went up the well-known stairs very slowly: she ached so in every limb that she could scarcely walk. She seemed to have aged twenty years in two days.

Edie was sitting alone in the pretty drawing-room, buried in a capacious arm-chair, her hands folded before her. The room was in darkness, save for the glow of the firelight. She jumped up, when Colonel Harris and Louisa were announced, and the neat servant in black dress and smart cap and apron switched on the electric light.

"Oh!" said poor little Edie impetuously, "I am so thankful you've come."

She ran up to Louisa and put her arms round her, kissing her.

"Do come and sit with me," she continued, loth to relinquish Colonel Harris's hand after she had shaken it. "I feel that in this solitude I shall go dotty."

Whilst she spoke, she detached with nervous, febrile movements Louisa's fur from round her neck, and dragged the older woman nearer to herself and to the fire. Then she threw herself down on the hearthrug : squatting there in front of the fire, with nervy fingers picking at the fringe of the rug. Her cheeks were red and blotchy, with traces of recent tears ; her hair, touzled and damp, clung to her moist temples. Suddenly she burst into a torrent of weeping.

"Oh, Loo, what does it all mean ? " she exclaimed between heavy sighs, " what does it all mean ? They say Luke has murdered that odious Philip ! and I have been cooped up here for two days now, not daring to go out ! ashamed to face any one ! and Luke . . . Luke . . . oh ! "

The outburst was almost hysterical. The young girl was obviously fearfully overwrought, and had endured a severe nerve-strain, by not having the means for giving vent to her feelings. Colonel Harris, with all an Englishman's horror of feminine scenes, was clearing his throat, looking supremely uncomfortable all the time.

"Sh ! . . . sh ! " admonished Louisa impatiently, " be quiet, Edie, you mustn't go on like that ! be

quiet now ! " she added more severely, seeing that
the girl made no effort to control herself; "what will
your servants think ? "

"Do you suppose," retorted Edie, "that I care
what they think ? They can't think more, can they ?
when they all talk of Luke as if he were a murderer."

"Do for God's sake be silent, Edie. This is too
awful."

And Louisa—almost roughly—dragged herself away
from the girl's hysterical embrace. She had tried so
hard for two days and two nights to keep herself
together and her nerves in check. All day to-day
had been one long, continuous battle against the
danger of "breaking down," that bugbear of the
conventional woman of the world.

Now this danger—backed up by this poor child's
grief—loomed greater than ever . . . now . . . that
"breaking down" would become a positive sin : the
most abject form of cowardice. But Edie's bewilderment, her loneliness, were intensely pathetic. Louisa
had tried to be severe, and insisted on checking the
access of hysteria ; but her heart went out to the
child, and to her puzzlement in face of this awful,
un-understandable riddle.

"Look here, Edie," she said gently, putting her
own kind arms round the quaking shoulders of the
younger girl, "you are just going to show father and
me how brave you can be. You are Luke's nearest
and dearest one on earth : you must not add to his
troubles by this exaggerated show of grief. We'll all
have to be brave . . . all of us . . . but Luke will

have to be the bravest of us all ; and so we must all do our best to keep up our courage, and help his own."

She was not accustomed to making such long speeches, nor yet to preach and to admonish. Life, before now, had never placed her in the necessity of admonishing others : everybody round her—the people with whom she came in contact—always behaved very much as they should : in the proper, conventional, worldly manner. People she had hitherto to do with did not give way to hysterical tears, nor had they occasion to display fortitude in the face of an overwhelming moral shock.

Therefore, Louisa was not sure if her words would carry weight, or if they would produce the effect she desired. She gazed anxiously at Edie whilst she spoke : looking with hopeful, yet fearful eyes in the poor girl's face, wondering if she had succeeded in calming the hysterical outburst.

Edie hung her head, wilfully veiling her eyes beneath the drooping lids. She twirled her gossamer handkerchief into a tight wet ball, and toyed with it nervously.

" It's not much good," she said at last, in very low tones, so that Louisa had some difficulty in hearing what she said, " my trying to be brave . . . when Luke is such a coward ! "

" Be quiet, Edie," retorted Louisa, all her kindness and sympathy gone, and pushing the girl roughly away from her. " You have no right to talk like that."

"Well, Colonel Harris," rejoined Edie, turning to the man in her distress, "I ask you, if it isn't just cowardice to run away now, and leaving me and Jim to face the whole thing alone?"

"To run away? What do you mean?" demanded Louisa, placing her hand on the girl's shoulder, forcing her to turn round and to face her.

"Who's running away?" queried Colonel Harris with a frown.

"Luke," said Edie hotly, "is running away. He came home just now, and calmly told me that he was going off abroad to-night; and since then he has been shut up in his room, packing his things. I have been all alone here all day. Jim won't be home till late to-night. Poor old Jim! what a fearful home-coming it will be for him. . . ."

But to this renewal of Edie's lamentations, Louisa had not listened, only to the words: "Luke said that he was going abroad to-night!"

Luke: fugitive from justice! The monstrous, unbelievable picture, which she had tried to visualize just now, had become a mirror, reflecting awful, hideous reality.

"Where's Luke?" asked the Colonel. "I'd better see him."

"No, father," interposed Louisa quickly. "I'd sooner speak to Luke. Can I go to him, Edie?"

"Yes, I think so," replied the other. "I don't suppose that he has locked his door."

"Louisa," said her father gently, "I don't think

you'll be doing any good, dear. A man must act as he thinks best."

"I'm not," she replied, "going to interfere with Luke's plans. I only want to speak to him. Don't bother, Edie. I know my way."

CHAPTER XXXIII

L UKE was sitting at a desk, writing, when Louisa entered his room. Only one lamp, shaded with yellow silk, hung above the desk, throwing golden light on paper and blotting-pad, and on the hand which held the pen.

When Luke turned at sound of the opening door, his face remained in deep shadow. He could not, of course, see her distinctly, as her figure was silhouetted against the light in the passage behind her ; that was no doubt the reason why he did not rise to greet her when she entered, but remained seated at his desk.

"May I come in, Luke ? " she asked.

"Certainly," he replied. "I was just writing to you."

"Then give me your unfinished letter, and tell me what else you were going to write."

"Oh ! I had only got as far as your name," he said, pointing to the empty page before him.

"Was it so difficult then," she asked, "to tell me everything ? "

She had come forward into the room, and stood beside his desk, one hand resting upon it, her face

T   273

looking down at the letter which he had not yet begun to write. He still made no attempt to rise : for now her face was in full golden light, and he could see its every feature.

"It is so difficult," he said, "not to write drivel when one is saying good-bye."

"You are going away ? " she asked.

"Yes."

"To-night ? "

"In half an hour."

"You are going abroad ? "

"Certainly."

"Why ? "

This last question came abruptly, in harsh, trenchant tones, altogether different to those of her smooth contralto voice. He turned his eye away from her face, and looked down at his own hands, which were clasped in front of him.

"Because," he replied, without the slightest hesitation, "I cannot face what lies before me if I remain."

"Why not ? "

"For many reasons. There's Uncle Rad to consider first and foremost, then Edie and Jim and Frank."

"What have they to do with it ? "

"Everything. After the evidence at the inquest to-day, a warrant will be out for my arrest within the next few hours."

"What of it ? "

"The evidence against me is overwhelming. I should be tried, perhaps hanged for murder : at best sent to penal servitude for life. I cannot chance that.

I must think of Uncle Rad, of Edie, of Jim, and of Frank."

"You have yourself to think of first and foremost."

"Well," he retorted simply, "I have thought of myself, and I do not see how, with my own dagger-stick brought up in evidence against me, and my ill-feeling towards , . . towards the dead man so well-known, I can possibly escape condemnation."

He spoke in such even and perfectly natural tones, that just for a moment—it was a mere flash—Louisa wondered if he were absolutely sane. It seemed impossible that any man could preserve such calm, in face of the most appalling fate that ever threatened human being. She too—like the indifferent hidebound official this afternoon—was seized with an irrepressible desire to break through that surface of ice. The outer covering must be very thin, she thought, her presence must have melted all the coldness that lay immediately below the surface. Without saying another word, quietly and simply, she came down on her knees. Her skirts had not swished as she did so : not a sound from her revealed the movement. When he looked up again, her face was on a level with his, and her eyes—those great luminous eyes that shed no tears at moments such as this—looked straight into his own.

"For pity's sake, Loo," he said, "don't make a drivelling coward of me now."

And he rose, pushing his chair aside, leaving her there, kneeling beside the desk, humbled and helpless. And he retreated within the shadow of the room.

"Luke," she said, imploring him, "you are going to tell me all that troubles you."

"Nothing," he replied curtly, "troubles me. You are wasting your sympathy, you know. And I have a train to catch."

"You are not going, Luke?"

"Indeed I am."

"You condemn yourself for a crime which you have not committed."

"I am already as good as condemned. But I do not choose to hang for the murder of the Clapham bricklayer's son."

He laughed—it almost sounded like a natural laugh—would have done so, no doubt, to all ears except hers. Then he added dryly—

"Such a purposeless crime too. Fancy, being hanged for killing Paul Baker."

"Luke," she said simply, "you don't seem to realize how you are hurting me!"

One ejaculation : "My God!" escaped him then. He stood quite still, in the shadow, and presently his hand wandered with the old familiar gesture down the smooth back of his head. She remained on her knees, and after a while he came back to her, and sat down on the chair beside the desk, his eyes on a level with hers.

"Look here, Loo," he said quietly, "I have got to go, and that's all about it. I have got to, do you understand? The consequences of this crime cannot be faced . . . not by any one . . . not by me. . . . There's Uncle Rad to think of first. . . . He is broken

and ill . . . he has more than one foot in the grave.
. . . The trial and the scandal couldn't be kept from
him ; it would be bound to leak out sooner or later.
. . . It would be too big a scandal ! . . . and it would
kill him outright. . . . Then ! you see, Loo, it would
never do ! . . . I should be Earl of Radclyffe and a
felon . . . it wouldn't do, now would it ? Who has
ever heard of a peer undergoing a life sentence . . .
or being hanged ? . . . it wouldn't do . . . you know
it wouldn't do. . . ."

He reiterated this several times, with quaint insistence : as if he were discussing with her the possibility, or impossibility, of attending a race-meeting,
or a ball in Lent—she proving obstinate.

She did not reply, leaving him to ramble on in his
somewhat wild speech, hoping that if she let him
talk on uninterruptedly he would sooner or later
betray something of that enigma which lay hidden
behind the wooden mask which he still so persistently
wore.

"Besides," he continued, still arguing, "there's
Frank to think of . . . the next heir to the title. . . .
I believe that people in penal servitude live an uncon-
scionable time . . . especially if they are wanted to
die. . . . Think of poor old Frank waiting to come
into his own . . . into an old title held by a felon. . . .
It is all much too much of a muddle, Loo . . . it is
simpler that I should go. . . ."

"But," she said, really trying now to speak as
simply, as calmly, as he did himself, "all these
arguments, which you are using now, Luke, will

equally apply if you make yourself a fugitive from justice."

"Oh! I shouldn't be that for very long!" he said lightly.

"You are thinking of suicide?"

"No," he replied simply, "I am not. Only of the chances of a wandering life."

"You seem to look at every chance, Luke, except one."

"Which one is that?"

"That though you might be arrested, though you might be accused, and even tried for the murder of . . . of that man . . . truth might come out, and your innocence proved."

"That would be impossible, Loo," he said quietly.

"Why? . . . in Heaven's name, Luke," she exclaimed passionately—" why?"

"My dagger-stick was found inside the railings of the Park . . . and the stains on it are irrefutable proofs."

"That's only circumstantial evidence," she argued; "you can demolish it, if you choose."

"I cannot," he replied. "I should plead guilty. . . . Mr. Dobson says that if I plead guilty, counsel can plead extenuating circumstances . . . intense provocation and so forth . . . and I might get a more lenient sentence."

"Luke," she said, looking him straight in the face, compelling his eyes to meet hers, for in their clear depths she meant to read the truth, to compel the truth at last. He had never lied in his life. If he lied now she would know it, she would read it in his face. "Luke! you are shielding some one by taking the crime on your own shoulders."

But his eyes remained perfectly clear and steady as they gazed straight into hers. There was not a shadow in them, not a quiver, as he replied quietly—

"No, Loo, I am shielding no one."

"It was you who killed that man . . . Philip de Mountford . . . or Paul Baker . . . whoever he may be ? "

And he answered her firmly, looking steadily into her face—

"It was I."

She said nothing more then, but rose to her feet, and went quite close up to him. With a gesture that had no thought of passion in it, only sublime, motherly love, she took Luke's head in both her hands, and pressed it to her heart.

"My poor old Luke! " she murmured.

She smoothed his hair, as a mother does to an afflicted child : the motherly instinct was up in arms now, even fighting the womanly, the passionate instinct of a less selfish love. She bent down and kissed his forehead.

"Luke," she said gently, "it would do you such a lot of good if you would only let yourself go."

He had contrived to get hold of her hands : those hands which he loved so dearly, with their soft, rose-tinted palms and the scent of sweet peas which clung to them. His own hot fingers closed on those small hands. She stood before him, tall, elegant . . . not

beautiful ! . . . Louisa Harris had never been beautiful, nor yet a fairy princess of romance . . . only a
commonplace woman ! a woman of the world, over
whose graceful form—her personality even—convention invariably threw her mantle ! . . . but a woman
for all that ! . . . with passion burning beneath the
crust of worldly sang-froid—with heart attuned to feel
every quiver, every sensation of joy and of pain. . . .
A woman who loved with every fibre in her—who had
the supreme gift of merging self in Love—of giving all,
her soul, her heart, her mind and every thought . . .
a woman who roused every chord of passion in a man's
heart . . . the woman whom men adore !

And now as Luke de Mountford held her hands, and
she stood close beside him, her breath coming and
going in quick gasps, with the suppressed excitement
of latent self-sacrifice, her eyes glowing and tearless,
he half slid from the chair on which he was sitting,
and one knee was on the ground, and his face turned
up to hers.

He almost smiled, as she repeated, with a little sigh—

" If you would only let yourself go ! "

" If I would let myself dwindle down to the level
of drivelling fools," he said. " God knows, Loo, it
would be easy enough now, when I hold those lovely
little hands of yours ; and the scent of sweet peas which
comes from your dear self reminds me of summer, of
old-fashioned gardens, of enduring peace. Loo ! I
dare not even kiss your hands, and yet my whole body
aches with the longing to press my lips on them. You
see how easily I drift into being a drivelling fool ?

Would to God I could lie on the ground here before you, and feel the soles of your feet on my neck. How lucky slaves were in olden days, weren't they ? They could kneel before their mistress and she would place her naked foot upon their neck. I am a drivelling fool, you see. . . . I talk and talk and let the moments slip by. . . . I am going, Loo, and this is the vision which I am taking with me, the last impression which will dwell in my memory, when memory itself will seem only a dream. You, Loo, standing just here, so close to me that your sweet breath fans my cheeks, your dear hands in mine, the scent of sweet peas in my nostrils. The light of this lamp throws a golden radiance over you, your lips are quivering . . . oh ! ever so slightly, and your eyes reveal to me the exquisiteness of your soul. Loo ! I am a lucky mortal to have such a vision on which to let my memory dwell ! "

She listened in silence, enjoying the delight of hearing him unburdening his soul at last. His love for her ! never had it seemed so great and so pure, now that he spoke of parting ! and there was a quaint joy in hearing him thus rambling on—he, the reserved man of the world. Convention had so often sealed his lips, and restrained his passion when he was still wandering happily with her on the smooth paths of Love. Now Fate had hurled stone upon stone down that path. The way was rugged and difficult, parting too was close at hand : all the restraint of past months tore at the barrier of convention. Luke, about to lose the mortal presence of his love, allowed his lips to say that which he had hidden in his heart for so long. The man of the world lost himself in the man who loved.

When he had ceased speaking, she said quietly—

" You talk, Luke, as if we were going to part."

" To-night, Loo. I must catch the night boat to Calais."

" My luggage can be sent on," she rejoined simply. " I am quite ready to start."

" To start ? " he repeated vaguely.

" Why, yes, Luke," she replied, with a smile ; " if you go to-night, or at any time, I go with you."

" You cannot, Loo ! " he stammered, almost stupidly, feeling quite bewildered, for he had been forcibly dragged back from a happy dreamlike state to one of impossible reality.

" Why not ? "

" You have said it yourself, Loo. I shall be a fugitive from justice . . . a man with whom no decent woman would care to link her fate."

" Let us admit then," she said, almost gaily, " that I am not a decent woman, for my fate is irretrievably linked with yours."

" This is preposterous . . ." he began.

But already she had interrupted him, speaking quietly in that even, contralto voice of hers which he loved to hear.

" Luke," she said, " you must try and understand. You must . . . because I have so fully made up my mind, that nothing that you could say would make me change it, unless you told me that you no longer loved me. And this," she added, with the ghost of a

smile, " you cannot now pretend, Luke, after all that
you said just now. It is not that my mind wanted
making up. My mind has very little to do with it all.
It knows just as my heart does that I could not now
live without you. I'm not talking nonsense, Luke,
and I seem to be too old for mere sentimental twaddle ;
therefore, when I say that I could not now live parted
from you, I say it from the innermost conviction of my
heart. Sh . . . sh . . . dear," she whispered, seeing
that he wished to interrupt her, " don't try and say
anything just yet—not just yet—until I have told you
everything. I want you to remember, Luke, that I
am no longer very young, and that ever since I can
remember anything, I have loved you. . . . I must
have loved you, even though I did not know it. But
if you had never spoken of love to me, if you had never
written that letter which I received in Brussels, I
probably would have been satisfied to go on with my
humdrum life to the end of time ;—who knows ? I
might have found contentment if not happiness, by and
by, with some other man. We women are meant to
marry. Men are fond of telling us that our only mission
on earth is to marry. But all this possible, quiet content one letter has dissipated. I could never be happy
now, never, save in continuing to love you. Life to me
would be unspeakably hideous without you and your
love. Therefore I say, Luke, that you have no longer
any right to keep me at arm's length. You have no
right, having once come into my life, having once given
substance and vitality to my love, to withdraw yourself away from me. Love, dear, is a bond, a mutual

bond, as sacred, as binding as any that are contracted on this earth. You—when you wrote that letter, when first you spoke to me of love—entered into a bond with me. You have no right to force me to break it."

The mellow tones of her contralto voice died down in the heavy atmosphere of the room. They echoed and re-echoed in the heart of the man, who was now kneeling before Louisa, as he would before the Madonna, dumb with the intensity of emotion which her simple words, the sublime selflessness of her sacrifice, had brought to almost maddening pitch. She stood there near him, so devoted, so noble, and so pure, do you wonder or will you smile, when you see him with fair, young head bowed to the ground pressing his lips on the point of her shoe ?

"Luke ! don't," she cried, in passionate sympathy. She understood him so well, you see !

"Kiss your feet, dear ? " he asked. " I would lie down in the dust for your dear feet to walk over me. I only wonder why God should love me so that he gave you for this one beautiful moment to me. Loo, my dearest saint, I cannot accept your sacrifice. Dear heart ! dear, dear heart ! do try and believe me, when I say that I cannot accept it. As for imagining that I don't understand it and appreciate it, why, as soon think that to-morrow's sun will never rise. I worship you, my saint ! and I worship your love : the purest, most tender sentiment that ever glorified this ugly world. But its sacrifice I cannot accept. I cannot. I would sooner do that most cowardly of all deeds, end my life here and now, than be tempted for one single instant into the cowardice of accepting it. But the memory of it, dear, that I will take with me. Do not think of me in future as being unhappy. No man can be unhappy whose heart is fed on such a memory!"

He had her two hands imprisoned in his, the scent of sweet peas floating gently to his nostrils. As he buried his lips in their fragrant soft palms he was entirely happy. The world had floated away from him. He was in a land of magic with her ; in a land where the air was filled with the fragrance of sweet peas, a land of phantasmagoria, the land of Fata Morgana, which none can enter save those who love. Time sped on, and both had forgotten the world. The fire crackled in the hearth, the clock alone recorded the passing of time. The noise of the great city—so cruel to those who suffer—came but as a faint echo through the closely drawn curtains.

There was a discreet knock at the door, and as no reply came from within, it was repeated more insistently.

Luke jumped to his feet, and Louisa retreated into the shadow.

"Come in!" said Luke.

The door was opened, quite softly, from outside, and the well-drilled servant said—

"Two gentlemen to see you, sir."

"Where are they, Mary ?" he asked.

"In the hall, sir."

"Did they give their names ? "

"No, sir."

"Where's Miss Edie, Mary ? "

" In the drawing-room, sir, with Colonel Harris."

" Very well. Then show the two gentlemen into the dining-room. I'll come in a moment."

" Very good, sir."

And the discreet little maid retired, closing the door after her.

CHAPTER XXXIV

WHICH ONLY SPEAKS OF FAREWELLS

THE door had scarcely closed, and already she was near him.

"Luke ! " she whispered, and her voice was hoarse now and choked, " the police ! "

"That's about it," he said ; " I thought that they meant to let me get away."

"So father understood from Sir Thomas Ryder. What will you do, Luke ? "

"I can't do anything, I am afraid. I wanted to get away. . . ."

"And I have kept you . . . and now it is too late."

A very little while ago, she had hated the idea of his going. Luke—a fugitive from justice—was a picture on which it was intolerable to look. But now the womanly instinct rose up in revolt : at the very thought that he should be arrested, tried and condemned ! What mattered if he were a fugitive, if he were ostracized and despised ? What mattered anything, so long as he lived and she could be near him ? A very little while ago she would have done anything to keep him from going : she almost longed for his arrest and the publicity of the trial. She was so sure that truth would surely come out, that his innocence would of necessity be proved.

But now, womanlike, she only longed for his safety, and forgetting all the traditions of her past life, all the old lessons of self-restraint : forgetting everything, except his immediate danger, she clung to him with all the true passion in her, which she no longer tried to keep in check.

"No, Luke," she murmured in quick jerky tones, "it is not too late . . . not at all too late. . . . You stay in here quietly, and I'll ask father to go and speak to them. . . . He'll tell them that you haven't come home yet, and that he is waiting here for you himself. . . . Father is well known . . . they won't suspect him of shielding you . . . and in the meanwhile, you can slip out easily . . . we'll send your luggage on . . . you can write and let us know where you are . . . it is quite easy . . . and not too late. . . ."

Whilst she spoke, she was gradually edging towards the door. Her voice had sunk to a hoarse whisper, for maddening terror almost deprived her of speech. With insistent strength she would not allow him to detain her ; and he, whilst trying to hold her back, was afraid of hurting her. But at the last, when she had almost reached the door, he contrived to forestall her, and before she could guess his purpose, he had pressed a finger on the button of the electric bell.

She heard the distinct tinkle of the bell, and this made her pause.

"What is it, Luke?" she asked. "Why did you ring?"

"For your father, dear," he replied simply.

"Then you will do what I want you to?" she rejoined eagerly. "You will go away?"

He gave no immediate answer, for already the maid's footstep was heard along the passage. The next moment she was knocking at the door. Luke went up to it, gently forcing Louisa back into the shadow behind him.

"Mary," he said, with his hand on the latch of the door, holding it slightly ajar, "just ask Colonel Harris to come here, will you?"

"Yes, sir."

The girl was heard turning away, and walking away briskly along the passage. Then Luke faced Louisa once again.

He went up to her, and without a word took her in his arms. It was a supreme farewell, and she knew it. She felt it in the quiver of agony which went right through him as he pressed her so close—so close that her breath nearly left her body, and her heart seemed to stand still. She felt it in the sweet, sad pain of the burning kisses with which he covered her face, her eyes, her hair, her mouth. It was the final passionate embrace : the irrevocable linking of soul, and heart, and mind : the parting of earthly bodies, the union of immortal souls. It was the end of all things earthly, the beginning of things eternal.

She understood, and her resistance vanished. All that had been dark to her became suddenly trans-

U

figured and illumined. With the merging of earthly passion into that Love which is God's breath, she— the pure and selfless woman, God's most perfect work on earth—became as God, and knew what was good, and what had been evil.

Neither of them spoke ; the word "farewell" was not uttered between them. His final kiss was upon her eyes, and she closed them after that ; the better to imprint on her memory the vision of his face, lit up with the divine fire of an unconquerable passion.

The entrance of Colonel Harris brought them both back to present reality. He, poor man, looked severely troubled, and distinctly older than he usually did.

"Did you want me, Luke ? " he asked.

"Yes, sir," replied the latter, " the police is here, and I thought that perhaps you and Louisa would be so kind as to take Edie along with you. Jim is going to sleep in barracks to-night, and Edie ought not to stay here alone."

"Yes. We'll take Edie," said the Colonel curtly ; " she'll be all right with us. Are you ready, Loo ? "

"Yes, dear," she replied.

And she passed out of the door without another word, or another look.

The supreme farewell had been spoken. Further words—even another kiss—would have almost desecrated its undying memory.

The two men remained alone, and Colonel Harris, without any hesitation, held out his hand to Luke de Mountford.

"The police is here, sir," said Luke, without taking the hand that was offered him.

"I know they are," muttered the other, "that's no reason why you should refuse an old friend's hand."

Then as Luke—hesitating no longer—placed his burning hand in that of his friend, Colonel Harris said quietly, almost entreatingly—

"It's only a temporary trouble, eh, my boy? You can easily refute this abominable charge, and prove your innocence?"

"I think not, sir," replied Luke. "I cannot refute the charge, and my innocence will be difficult to prove."

"But you are mad, man!" retorted the older man hotly. "You are mad! and are breaking a woman's heart!"

"Heaven forgive me for that, sir. It is the greatest crime."

Colonel Harris smothered a powerful oath. Luke's attitude puzzled him more and more. And his loyalty had received such a succession of shocks to-day, that it would have been small wonder if it had begun to totter at last.

He turned away without another word. But at the door he paused once more—in obvious hesitation.

"There's nothing else I can do for you?" he asked.

"Nothing, sir. Thank you."

"You . . . you were not thinking . . . of . . . ?"

"Of what, sir?" asked Luke.

Then, as he saw the other man's eyes wandering to the drawer of the desk, he said simply—

"Of suicide, you mean, sir ? "

Colonel Harris nodded.

"Oh no," rejoined Luke. And he added, after a slight pause : "Not at present."

"What do you mean by that ? "

"I mean that I shouldn't exactly hang for the murder of the Clapham bricklayer. I shouldn't let it come to that. I am sorry I did not manage to get away to-night. I thought they meant to let me."

"I think they did mean to. Some blunder, I suppose, on the part of the subordinates."

"I suppose so."

"Well, Luke," said Colonel Harris with a deep sigh, "I have known you ever since you were a child, but by G—d, man ! I confess that I don't understand you."

"That's very kindly put, sir," rejoined Luke, with the semblance of a smile; "you have every right to call me a confounded blackguard."

"I shall only do that after your trial, my boy," said the other, "when I have heard you confess with your own lips that you killed that d—d scoundrel in a moment of intense provocation."

"I had better not keep the police waiting any longer, sir, had I ? "

"No ! no ! that's all right. I'll take my poor Loo away at once, and we'll see after Edie, and Jim . . . we'll look after them . . . and Frank too when he comes home."

"Thank you, sir."

"S'long, my boy."

And Colonel Harris—puzzled, worried, and miserable—finally went out of the room. On the threshold he turned, moved by the simple and primitive instinct of wishing to take a last look at a friend.

He saw Luke standing there in the full light of the electric lamp, calm, quite serene, correct to the last in attitude and bearing. The face was just a mask—marble-like and impassive—jealously guarding the secrets of the soul within. Just a good-looking, well-bred young Englishman in fact, who looked in his elegant attire ready to start off for some social function.

Not a single trace either on his person or in his neat, orderly surroundings of the appalling tragedy which would have broken the spirit of any human creature less well-schooled in self-restraint.

Convention was triumphant to the end.

The man of the world—the English gentleman—hypocritical or unemotional ? which ?—was here ready to face abject humiliation and hopeless disgrace as impassively as he would have received the welcome of a hostess at a dinner-party.

CHAPTER XXXV

WHICH TELLS OF PICTURES IN THE FIRE

IT did not take poor little Edie very long to get her things on and to make ready to go away with Colonel Harris and with Louisa. Something of the truth had to be told to her, and we must do her the justice to state that when she understood the full strength of the calamity which had befallen her and Luke, something of her brother's calm dignity showed itself in her own demeanour.

She pulled herself together with remarkable vigour, and before Mary—the maid—she contrived to behave just as if nothing of great importance had occurred.

" I am going to dine out to-night, Mary," she said, quite calmly, " and I mayn't be home until sometime to-morrow. So don't sit up for me."

" No, miss," replied Mary demurely, who kept her own counsel, like the well-drilled good-class servant that she was.

" And tell cook that Mr. de Mountford won't be in either, nor Mr. Jim. I'll see her to-morrow and let her know when we all come back."

" Very good, miss."

Louisa gave ungrudging admiration, and whispered praise to the young girl. She was proud of Edie's behaviour, and grateful to her too. This atmosphere of reserve did her good. She could not have endured a scene of weeping and keep her own nerves in check all the while.

It was close upon eight o'clock when at last they reached the Langham Hotel. Colonel Harris ordered the dinner to be served in the private sitting-room. Of course, none of them could eat anything. Their inward thoughts were following Luke de Mountford along that weary Calvary which he had set himself to mount.

Soon after dinner Edie elected to go to bed. The poor child had a vague desire to be alone, and also a vague, unhappy feeling that she was in the way. She was quite woman enough now to understand how much more acutely Louisa Harris must be suffering than she did herself, and since she—the sister—longed for solitude, how much keener must be that longing in the heart of the woman who loved and had lost Luke.

So she went quietly off to bed. Louisa kissed her with real affection. Edie seemed like something of Luke : like a tender bequest made by a dying man.

After that she herself said " good night " to her father. Colonel Harris was obviously in such acute distress that Louisa felt that, above all things, he must have the companionship of those of his own sex. The atmosphere of woman's sorrow was essentially bad for him. He was not a young man, and the last two days had tried him very severely. Louisa hoped that if she pretended to go to bed early, he would perhaps be induced to go to his Club for an hour.

If he only sat there for an hour, reading the papers, and nodding to his many friends, it would take him out of himself.

"I am very tired, dear," she said, after she had seen Edie safely tucked up amongst the blankets; "I think I'll follow Edie's good example. It's no use sitting here, staring into the fire. Is it, dear?"

"Not a bit of use, Loo. And I suppose you would like to be alone?"

"I shan't go to bed, dear, unless you go to the Club."

"Very well, Loo. It seems the right thing to do, doesn't it? You go to bed, and I'll go to the Club for an hour. As you say, it's no use sitting staring into the fire."

Her room gave on one side of the sitting-room, and her father's on the other. She waited until Colonel Harris went away, having helped him on with his overcoat. After he left she felt a little twinge of remorse. The night was cold and raw, and he really had not wanted to go out. He would have been quite willing to sit in front of the fire, smoking and reading. He had only gone because his own innate kindliness and tact had suggested to him that Louisa wished to remain alone.

He too, like Edie, felt a little in the way. His daughter's grief was of a nature that a father's love cannot soothe. The greatest solace for it now would be solitude. So, in spite of the fog, in spite of the unpleasantness that met Colonel Harris on every page of every newspaper, he sallied out of the hotel and got into a hansom, with the avowed intention of spending a couple of hours at his Club.

Louisa, left alone in the sitting-room, in front of the cheery fire, sat down for a moment on the sofa and rested her head against the cushions. There was memory even in that, for when she closed her eyes, she could imagine that Luke was sitting at the foot of the sofa ; she could see him almost, with his eyes turned ever towards her, and that quaint gesture of his when he passed his hand over the back of his neatly groomed head.

The memory was intolerable now. She rose—restless and feverish—and stood by the fire, one hand on the high mantelshelf, her forehead resting against that hand, one foot on the fender, and her aching eyes gazing into the red-hot glow.

It was one of those big red fires, partly made up of coke and partly of coal, wherein only here and there tiny blue flames flit waywardly, and in the building of which hotel servants are usually past-masters. The glowing coal heaped up high in the old-fashioned grate presented a wonderful picture of mysterious architecture : streets and lanes of crimson incandescence, palaces and towers of molten heat, and the little blue flames dancing, and peeping out from the fiery depths, mocking and wayward, twirling and twisting as with the joy of life.

Louisa gazed into this city of brilliant crimson and gold, the streets, the palaces, and the towers. And as she gazed—with eyes almost seared—these same streets of fire assumed different shapes, they became stately

and wide, with rows of trees forming an avenue along
the middle, and tall houses on either side. One or two
people were walking along the pavement, but quickly,
as if they had business to transact and did not care to
loiter. One figure, that of a woman, in neat ulster and
serviceable hat, was walking briskly between the rows
of trees.

The blue flames danced, and disclosed a few vehicles
hurrying past swiftly in the night, huge tramcars
lumbering along, and one or two flying motor-cabs.
And far ahead—right in the heart of the glow—the
distant lights of a more busy thoroughfare. Now the
wide street was more dark and lonely than before; only
the solitary female figure appeared in the fiery picture,
walking among the trees. The last of the lumbering
tramcars had been merged in the distant lights : only
from afar came flying on the blue flames, a taxi-cab at
lightning speed.

It came along, its headlights burning more and more
brightly ; it rattled past the solitary female pedestrian.
Then it stopped in the dark angle made by a huge piece
of coal : the blue flames gave a hiss and from every
corner of the grate crowds of people came rushing to
the spot where the taxi-cab had halted. The solitary
female pedestrian also hurried to the spot. She stopped
on the outskirts of the crowd, and yet she saw everything that went on in and around the motor—the
horror-stricken driver, the bustling gendarmes, the
huddled-up mass in the darkest corner of the vehicle.

Then the coal, consumed by its own power, fell
together in a formless heap, and the picture vanished.

Louisa closed her eyes, for the heat in them was intolerable. But only for a moment, for now her mind was made up.

Ever since she had parted from Luke, one thought had been dominant in her mind, one memory had obtruded itself beyond all others, taking definite shape in the visions conjured up by the glowing embers of the fire : that night in Brussels !—the great, unforgetable night, on which her whole life's history seemed to find its birth-time.

One great resolve, too, had now taken definite shape.

Louisa rang for her maid, and asked for hat and cloak. The maid, somewhat horrified that her mistress should think of going out alone at so late an hour, was too well drilled to offer advice or make comment. She brought a warm wrap and a closely fitting, simple hat, and respectfully wished to know when she should expect her mistress home.

" In about an hour's time," said Louisa. " Come down into the hall with me, and tell the porter to call me a cab."

Then she went down, accompanied by her maid. A cab was called, and she directed the driver to 56 Chester Terrace.

The address was that of Lady Ryder's town house. The maid—feeling more satisfied—went upstairs again.

CHAPTER XXXVI

PEOPLE DON'T DO THAT SORT OF THING

LADY RYDER was out of town. She was staying at a country house in the Midlands, chaperoning her nieces—Louisa's twin sisters—but Sir Thomas Ryder was at home.

It was for him that Louisa had asked when the butler opened the door in answer to her ring.

"Sir Thomas is in the library, miss," said the man. "Will you come into the drawing-room? and I'll tell Sir Thomas you are here, miss."

"No!" she said, "don't announce me. I'll go to the library."

Sir Thomas put down the paper, which he had been reading, when his niece entered. He did not seem at all astonished to see her. No doubt the exercise of his profession had taught him never to be surprised at anything in life. He rose, when he recognized who it was, and carefully folded his eyeglasses, and slipped them into their case and into his waistcoat pocket. Then he said—

"My dear Louisa! this is quite unexpected! Is your father with you?"

"No!" she replied. "I came alone. May I sit down?"

"Certainly, my dear child," he said genially, and himself wheeled a capacious arm-chair round to the fire.

"I am not disturbing you, Uncle Ryder?"

"No! no! take off your cloak, won't you? I was only looking at the evening paper, preparatory to turning in early."

She glanced at the paper on the table : that page was uppermost that bore the startling headline, in unusually large type : "The Murder in the Taxi-cab. Sensational Developments." The chief of the Criminal Investigation Department studied the accounts in the newspapers, the opinion of pressmen and reporters. Everything interested him : he weighed everything in his mind, no silly advice, no empty tittle-tattle, was ever dismissed by him without its due meed of consideration.

Uncle and niece now sat opposite each other, facing the hearth. He looked straight into the fire, knowing that she would not wish him to see the misery in her face.

"Will you have something, Loo?" he asked kindly. "A cup of tea, or something?"

"No, thank you, uncle. We had dinner, and father has gone to the Club. I came to see you about Luke."

"Yes?" he said.

"All along," she continued, "ever since father saw you yesterday, I wanted to speak to you. Silly conventionality kept me back."

"It certainly is not usual . . ." he began.

"No," she broke in quickly, "I know it is not. But

this is an unusual case, far too serious for silly ideas of tact or convention to creep in. The man whom I love best in all the world is falsely accused of a most abominable crime. He was arrested—by your orders, I suppose—about an hour ago."

He put up his hand in gentle deprecation.

"Stop a moment, my dear," he said quite kindly, but very decisively. "If you have any idea at the back of your head that I, personally, have any influence at my command, with regard to Luke de Mountford's fate, then the sooner you get that idea out of your head the better. If you came here to-night with the notion that by pleading with me you could save Luke from the consequences of his crime, then get that notion out of your head, my dear, and save us both from a very painful interview. Luke de Mountford was not arrested by my orders : I am only an automaton of the law, which takes its own course, without any personal interference on my part. Officially, I—as an automaton—did just as duty and the law of this country direct. Personally, I sent through your father some sound advice to Luke de Mountford."

She listened, impassive and silent, to his reproof, and then said simply—

"I beg your pardon, Uncle Ryder : I must have expressed myself badly. I knew quite well that you, personally, bear no animosity against Luke : why indeed should you ? I had no intention whatever, in coming to see you to-night, of making a scene of lamentation and supplication. On the contrary, I knew quite well that—acting from the best of motives

—you advised Luke to fly from justice : since in your opinion his condemnation is a foregone conclusion. Father hadn't the chance of passing your advice on to Luke ; because, when he got to Fairfax Mansions, Edie told us that he was packing up his things, meaning to catch the night boat to Calais."

" Then why the dickens did he miss his train ? " exclaimed Sir Thomas gruffly.

" It was not altogether his fault," she replied. " Our arrival delayed him a little ; but he would have had plenty of time even then, only the police came, you see, and it was too late."

" I know. It was silly, officious blundering on the part of one of my subs. I meant de Mountford to have plenty of time to get away ; and I could have managed it somehow, to leave him unmolested, if he kept some distance away from England. The whole thing has been most unfortunate."

" I don't think so, uncle," she said quietly. " I am glad, very glad, that Luke has been arrested."

" Are you ? " he retorted dryly. "The outlook for him is not pleasant."

" I know that. But at any rate, now there is a chance that he can prove his innocence."

Sir Thomas Ryder gave a quick sigh of impatience.

" My dear child," he said gently, " do try and be reasonable about that. You only lay up for yourself further stores of misery and of disappointment. De Mountford is guilty, I tell you. He practically confessed at the inquest, and he practically confessed to our fellows after his arrest."

"Practically," she said with strong emphasis, "but not really. Luke has never confessed that he has committed a murder."

"Well! he admits that the stick with which the murder was done was his stick, that he had it in his hand the night that the murder was committed, that he went out with it in his hand five minutes before the other man was murdered."

"I know all that," she rejoined, "but let me tell you this, Uncle Ryder. Luke has admitted all that, as you say ; but he has never admitted that he killed Philip de Mountford—or Paul Baker—whoever he may be. Luke, Uncle Ryder, is allowing the awful accusation to rest upon him, because he wishes to shield the real perpetrator of the crime."

"Nonsense ! " broke in Sir Thomas curtly.

"Why nonsense ? "

"Because, my dear Loo," he said slowly and firmly, "people don't do that sort of thing. The consequences of having taken another person's life—otherwise a murder—are so terrible that no one will bear them for the sake of any one else on earth."

"Yet I tell you, uncle," she reiterated with firmness, at least equal to his own, "that Luke never killed that man, and that he pleads guilty of the crime in order to shield some one else."

"Whom ? " he retorted.

"That I do not know . . . as yet. But that is the reason why I came here to-night, uncle : because you must help me to find out."

Sir Thomas abruptly rose from his chair, and took his

stand on the hearthrug, with legs apart, and slender hands buried in the pockets of his trousers, in the attitude dear to every Englishman.

His eyes, in their framework of innumerable wrinkles, looked down, not unkindly, at the pale, serious face of the girl before him.

He, who was accustomed to give every scrap of advice, every senseless piece of tittle-tattle, its just meed of attention, was not likely to leave unheeded the calm assertions of a woman for whom he had great regard, and who was the daughter of a brother officer and one of his best friends. Of course, the girl was in love with de Mountford, so her judgment on him was not likely to be wholly unbiassed. At the same time, Sir Thomas—like all men who have knocked about the world a great deal, and seen much of its seamy side—had a great belief in woman's instinct, as apart from her judgment, and he was the last man in the world to hold the sex in contempt.

" Look here, my dear," he said after a little while, during which he had tried to read the lines in the interesting face turned up towards him, " I honour you for your sense of loyalty to de Mountford, just the same as I honour your father for the like reason. And in order to prove to you that I, individually, would be only too happy to see the man's innocence established beyond a doubt, I am going to argue this soberly and sensibly with you. You hold the theory that Luke de Mountford is shielding some one from the consequences of an awful crime by taking the burden on himself. Now, my dear, as I told you before, people don't do that sort

x

of thing nowadays. In olden times, the consequences
of a crime—especially where the aristocracy was concerned—were quite picturesque : the Tower, the block,
and all that sort of thing. But to-day the paraphernalia of vengeful justice is very sordid, very mean, and
anything but glorious. It means the lengthy inquiry
before a police magistrate, then the trial, the past
dragged up to the light, the most private secrets thrown
to the morbid curiosity of the million. In order to face
that sort of thing, my dear, a man must be either guilty
—then he cannot help it ; or wrongfully accused—then
he hopes for the establishment of his innocence. But
a man does not prepare himself to face all that out of
Quixotic motives alone, knowing himself to be innocent, and because he desires that another should be
spared those awful humiliations and the chance of a
disgusting and shameful death."

"What do you mean by all that, Uncle Ryder ? "
she asked.

"I mean that if we are going to admit this Quixotic
motive in de Mountford's attitude now, there can only
be one mainspring for it."

"What is that ? "

"It is perhaps a little difficult . . ." he said somewhat hesitatingly.

"You mean," she interposed quietly, "that if Luke
is taking this awful crime upon himself for the sake of
another, that other can only be a woman whom he loves."

"Well ! " retorted Sir Thomas, "it is not you, my dear,
I presume, who killed this bricklayer from Clapham."

She did not reply immediately ; but her lips almost

framed themselves into a smile. Luke, and another woman! To Sir Thomas Ryder that seemed, indeed, a very simple explanation. Men have been known to do strange things, to endure much and to sacrifice everything for the sake of a woman! But then, Sir Thomas knew nothing of Luke, nothing more than what the latter chose to show of his inward self to the world. The memory of those few moments in the room in Fairfax Mansions laughed the other man's suggestion to scorn. Louisa shook her head and said simply—

"No, Uncle Ryder, I did not kill the Clapham bricklayer in the cab."

"And you won't admit that Luke may be shielding another woman?" said Sir Thomas, with just the faintest semblance of a sneer.

"I won't say that," she replied gravely. "You see, I don't really know. I would take a dying oath at this moment—if I were on the point of death—that Luke never committed that abominable crime. I won't even say that he is incapable of it. I'll only swear that he did not do it. And yet he is silent when he is accused. Then, to me, the only possible, the only logical conclusion is that he is shielding some one else."

"Have you questioned him?"

"Yes."

"Put the question directly to him, I mean?"

"Yes."

"And what did he say?"

"That his own stick condemns him, and that he would plead guilty at his trial."

"He never told you directly or indirectly that he killed the man ? "

For the space of one second only did Louisa hesitate. She had asked Luke the direct question : " Was it you who killed that man ? " and he had replied : " It was I." She had asked it then, determined to know the truth, convinced that she would know the truth when he gave reply. And she did learn the truth then and there, not as Luke hoped that she would interpret it, but as it really was. He had never really lied to her, for she had never been deceived. Now, she did not wish to hide anything from Sir Thomas Ryder, the only man in the whole world who could help her to prove Luke's innocence in spite of himself, therefore when her uncle reiterated his question somewhat sharply, she replied quite frankly, looking straight up at him—

"He told me directly that it was he who had killed the man."

"And even then you did not believe him ? "

"I knew that he tried to lie."

"You firmly believe that de Mountford knows who killed that Paul Baker—or whoever he was ? "

"I do."

"And that he means to go through his trial, and to plead guilty to a charge of murder, so that the real criminal should escape ? "

"Yes ! "

"And that he is prepared to hang—to hang, mind you ! " reiterated Sir Thomas, with almost cruel bluntness, "if he is condemned, in order to allow the real criminal to escape ? "

" Yes."

" And you yourself have no notion as to who this person may be ? "

" No."

" Is there anybody, do you think, who is likely to know more about Luke de Mountford's past and present life than you do yourself ? "

" Yes," she said, " Lord Radclyffe."

" Old Radclyffe ! " he ejaculated.

" Why, yes. Lord Radclyffe adored Luke before this awful man came between them. He had him with him ever since Luke was a tiny boy. There's no one in the world for whom he cared as he cared for Luke, and the affection was fully reciprocated; My belief is that Lord Radclyffe knows more about Luke than any one else in the world."

" But old Rad is very ill just now, unfortunately."

" It would kill him," she retorted, " if anything happened to Luke, whilst he was being coddled up as an invalid, almost as a prisoner, and no news allowed to reach him."

Sir Thomas was silent for a moment, obviously buried in thought. That he was still incredulous was certainly apparent to Louisa's supersensitive perceptions ; but that he meant to be of help to her, in spite of this incredulity, was equally certain. Therefore she waited patiently until he had collected his thoughts.

" Well, my dear," he said at last, " I'll tell you what I will do. To-morrow morning I'll go and see if I can have a talk with old Rad . . ."

"To-morrow morning," she broke in gravely, "Luke will be dragged before the magistrate . . . the first stage of that awful series of humiliations which you yourself say, Uncle Ryder, that no man who is innocent can possibly endure ! "

"I know, my dear," he said almost apologetically, "but I don't see now how that can be avoided."

"We could see Lord Radclyffe to-night ! "

"To-night ? " he exclaimed. "Why ! it's nearly ten o'clock."

"In matters of this sort, time does not count."

"But old Rad is an invalid ! "

"He may be a dead man to-morrow, if he hears that Luke—Luke, who was the apple of his eye, who is the heir to his name and title—is being dragged in open court before a police magistrate, charged with an abominable crime."

"But the doctor, I understand, has forbidden him to see any one."

"I think that the matter has passed the bounds of a doctor's orders. I would go and force my way into his presence without the slightest scruple. I know that any news that he may glean about Luke, within the next few days, will be far more fatal to him than the few questions which I want to ask him to-night."

"That may be, my dear," rejoined Sir Thomas dryly, "but this does not apply to me. Old Rad is a very old friend of mine, but if I went with you on this errand to-night, I should be going not as a friend, but in an official capacity, and as such I cannot do it without the doctor's permission."

"Very well, then," she said quietly, "we'll ask Dr. Newington's permission."

For a little while yet Sir Thomas Ryder seemed to hesitate. Clearly the girl's arguments, her simple conviction, and her latent energy had made a marked impression upon him. He was no longer the sceptical hide-bound official : the man, the gentleman was tearing away at the fetters of red tape. All the old instincts of chivalry, which at times might be dormant in the heart of an English gentleman—but which are always there nevertheless, hidden away by the mantle of convention—had been aroused by Louisa's attitude towards the man she loved, and also by the remembrance of Luke's bearing throughout this miserable business.

After all, what the girl asked was not so very difficult of execution. There are undoubtedly cases where the usual conventional formulas of etiquette must give way to serious exigencies. And there was unanswerable logic in Louisa's arguments : at any time in the near future that old Rad—either through his own obstinacy, or the stupidity or ill-will of a servant—got hold of a newspaper, the suddenness of the blow which he would receive by learning the terrible news without due preparation would inevitably prove fatal to him. Sir Thomas Ryder prided himself on being a diplomatist of the first water ; he did believe that he could so put the necessary questions to Lord Radclyffe, with regard to Luke, that the old man would not suspect the truth for a moment. The latter had, of course, known of the murder before he had been stricken with illness ; he had at the time answered the questions put to him by the police officer, without seeming to be greatly shocked at the awful occurrence, and it was not likely that he would be greatly upset at a professional visit from an old friend, who at the same time had the unravelling of the murder mystery at heart.

All these thoughts mirrored themselves on Sir Thomas's wrinkled face. He was taking no trouble to conceal them from Louisa. Soon she saw that she had won her first victory, for her uncle now said with sudden determination—

" Well, my dear ! you have certainly got on the right side of me. Your aunt always said you had a very persuasive way with you. I'll tell you what we will do. It is now a quarter to ten—late enough, by jingo ! We'll get into one of those confounded taxis, and drive to Dr. Newington's. I'll see him. You shall stay in the cab ; and if I.can get his permission, we'll go and have a talk with old Rad—or rather I'll talk first and you shall pretend that our joint visit is only a coincidence. As a matter of fact he knew all about the murder before he got ill, and he won't think it at all unnatural that I have obtained special medical permission to question him myself on the subject. Then you must work in your questions about Luke as best you can afterwards. Is that agreed now ? "

" Indeed it is, Uncle Ryder," said Louisa, as she rose from her chair, with a deep sigh of infinite contentment. " Thank you," she added gently, and placed her neatly gloved hand upon his arm.

With a kind, fatherly gesture, he gave that little hand an encouraging pat. Then he rang the bell.

"A taxi—quickly!" he said to his man. "My fur coat and my hat. I am going out."

Louisa had gained her first victory. She had put forward neither violence nor passion in support of her arguments. Yet she had conquered because she believed.

A few moments later she and Sir Thomas Ryder were on their way to Dr. Newington's in Hertford Street.

CHAPTER XXXVII

ONCE more Louisa was sitting in the dark corner of a cab, seeing London by night, as the motor flew past lighted thoroughfares, dark, narrow streets, stately mansions and mean houses. The same endless monotony of bricks and mortar, of pillars and railings ; the same endless monotony of everyday life, whilst some hearts were breaking and others suffered misery to which cruel, elusive death refused its supreme solace.

She waited in the cab whilst Sir Thomas Ryder went in to see the doctor. Fortunately the latter was at home, and able to see Sir Thomas.

At first he was obdurate. Nothing that the high officer of police could say would move his medical dictum. Lord Radclyffe was too ill to see any one. He was hardly conscious. His brain was working very feebly. He had not spoken for two days, for speech was difficult.

" If," said Dr. Newington, in his habitual pompous manner, " he had the least inkling now, that that favourite nephew of his was guilty of this awful murder, why, my dear sir, I wouldn't answer for the consequences. I believe the feeble bit of life in him would go out like a candle that's been blown upon."

" Who talks," retorted Sir Thomas somewhat impatiently, and assuming a manner at least as pompous as that of the fashionable physician, " of letting Lord Radclyffe know anything about his nephew's position ? I don't. I have no such intention. But de Mountford's plight is a very serious one. There are one or two points about his former life that Lord Radclyffe could elucidate if he will. I want your permission to ask him two or three questions. Hang it all, man, de Mountford's life is in danger ! I don't think that you have the right to oppose me in this. You take a most awful responsibility upon your shoulders."

" A medical man," said Dr. Newington vaguely, " has to take upon himself certain grave responsibilities sometimes."

" Yes. But not such a grave one as this. You must at least give me the chance of interrogating Lord Radclyffe. Supposing he knows something that may throw light on this awful affair, something that may go to prove de Mountford's innocence or guilt—either way—and suppose that owing to your prohibitions, all knowledge of his nephew's fate is kept from him until it is too late, until de Mountford is hanged—for he risks hanging, doctor, let me tell you that !—suppose that you have stood in the way, when some simple explanation from your patient might have saved him ! What then ? "

" But the patient is too ill, I tell you. He wouldn't understand you, probably. I am sure he couldn't answer your questions."

The doctor's original pompous manner had left him

somewhat. He was now more like an obstinate man, arguing, than like a medical man whose pronouncements must be final. Sir Thomas Ryder—one of the keenest men to note such subtle changes in another—saw that he had gained an advantage. He was quick enough to press it home.

" Let me try, at all events," he said. " The whole matter is of such enormous importance !—after all, doctor, it is a question of one human life against the other. With regard to de Mountford, let me tell you that unless we can get some very definite proof as to his innocence, it is bound to go hard with him. Say that a few weeks hence Lord Radclyffe, recovering from this severe illness, is confronted with the news that his nephew is being tried for murder, or that he has been condemned—I won't even mention the final awful possibility—do you think that you or any one will save the old man's life then, or his reason perhaps ? "

Dr. Newington was silent for a while. Clearly he was ready to give way. Like most men who outwardly are very pompous and dictatorial, his blustering was only veneer. The strong will-power of a more determined intellect very soon reduced him to compliance. And all that Sir Thomas Ryder said was logical. It carried a great deal of conviction.

" Very well," said the doctor at last, " I'll give you permission to interview my patient. But on two conditions."

" What are they ? "

" That the interview takes place in my presence,

and that at the first word from me, you cease questioning my patient, and leave his room."

"Very well," assented Sir Thomas, without any hesitation, content that he had gained his point, and quite satisfied that the two conditions were perfectly reasonable and such that the doctor was really compelled to impose. "I must tell you that I came to see you to-night at the instance of my niece, Louisa Harris, who was fiancée to de Mountford before this unfortunate business. It was she who adduced certain arguments which she placed before me, and which led to my strong desire to question Lord Radclyffe to-night, before de Mountford is brought up before the magistrate to-morrow. She is down below in the cab, waiting for me."

"I cannot allow her to see my patient also," protested the doctor quickly.

"No, no. She shall not see him, unless you give permission."

"Why don't you send her home right away, then ? "

"Because," retorted Sir Thomas tartly, " you might give that permission, you see."

The argument between the two men had lasted close on half an hour. It was long past ten o'clock when at last Louisa saw them emerging through the lighted doorway. The next moment they were seated in the cab with her, Sir Thomas having given the chauffeur the address of Lord Radclyffe's house in Grosvenor Square.

The doctor tried to be bland and polite, but he was not over-successful in this. He did not like being opposed, nor hearing his pronouncements combated. In this case he had been forced to give way, somewhat against his better judgment, and all the way in the cab he was comforting himself with the thought that at any rate he would keep women away from his patient, and that he would in any case cut the interview very short, and demand its abrupt cessation very peremptorily. He would then be backed up by two nurses; and we must do him the justice to say that he was honestly anxious about his patient.

Louisa took no notice of the fashionable doctor's efforts at conversation. She preferred to remain quite silent for those few minutes which elapsed between the departure from Hertford Street and the arrival at the east side of Grosvenor Square. When she saw her uncle coming down the steps of the doctor's house in company with the doctor himself, she knew that the second victory had been won to-night: that Sir Thomas Ryder would be allowed to interview Lord Radclyffe. She had, of course, no suspicion of Dr. Newington's conditions to the interview, but the victory gained was an important one, and for the moment she was content.

CHAPTER XXXVIII

A RESPECTABLE-LOOKING butler opened the door in answer to Dr. Newington's pull at the bell.

Luke had had time—on the day preceding the inquest—to put some semblance of order in his uncle's household. The doctor had sent in the nurses, and he had seen to a nice capable housekeeper being installed in the house. She took the further management at once in her own hands. She dismissed the drunken couple summarily, and engaged a couple of decent servants—a butler and a cook.

The house, though no less gloomy, looked certainly less lonely and neglected.

Mr. Warren, who had been Lord Radclyffe's secretary for years, but who had been speedily given his *congé* when the impostor took up his permanent abode in the house, was installed once more in the library, replying to the innumerable letters and telegrams of inquiry which poured in with every post.

Louisa and Sir Thomas were shown into the room where the young man was sitting. He rose at once, offering chairs, and pushing his own work aside. In the meanwhile the doctor had gone upstairs.

Several minutes elapsed. No one spoke. Mr. Warren, who had always been deeply attached to Luke de Mountford, was longing to ask questions, which, however, he was too shy to formulate. At last there was a knock at the door, and one of the nurses came in to say that Lord Radclyffe would be pleased to see Sir Thomas Ryder upstairs.

Louisa rose at the same time as her uncle, but the latter detained her with a gesture full of kind sympathy

" Not just yet, my dear," he said, " I'll call you as soon as possible."

" But," she asked anxiously, " I shall be allowed to see him, shan't I ? "

" I think so," he replied evasively. " But even if you do not see him, you can trust to me. Oh yes, you can ! " he added insistently, seeing the deeply troubled look that had crept into her face at his words. " I am going to do to-night what I often have to do in the course of my work. I am going to borrow your soul and your mind, and allow them to speak through my lips. When I go upstairs, I shall only outwardly be the police officer, searching for proofs of a crime : inwardly I shall be a noble-hearted woman trying to discover proofs of her fiancé's innocence. That will be right, dear, won't it ? "

She nodded acquiescence, trying to appear content. Then she pleaded once again, dry-eyed and broken-voiced—

" You will try and get permission for me to see Lord Radclyffe, won't you ? "

" I give you my word," he said solemnly.

Then he went upstairs.

Mr. Warren, quiet and sympathetic, persuaded Louisa to sit down again by the hearth. He took her muff and fur stole from her, and threw a log on the fire. The flames spurted off, giving a cheerful crackle. But Louisa saw no pictures in this fire : her mind was upstairs in Lord Radclyffe's room, wondering what was happening.

Mr. Warren spoke of the murdered man. He had not been present at the inquest, and the news that the tyrant, who had ruled over Lord Radclyffe for so long, was nothing but an impostor, came as a fearful shock to him.

There was the pitifulness of the whole thing ! the utter purposelessness of a hideous crime. So many lives wrecked ; such awful calamity ; such appalling humiliation ; such ignominy ! And all just for nothing ! A very little trouble, almost superficial inquiry, would have revealed the imposture, and saved all that sorrow, all the dire humiliation, and prevented the crime, for which the law of man decrees that there shall be no pardon.

The man who lay ill upstairs—and he who was lying in the public mortuary, surrounded by all the pomp and luxury which he had filched by his lies—alone could tell the secret of the extraordinary success of the imposture. Lord Radclyffe had accepted the bricklayer's son almost as his own, with that same obstinate reserve with which he had at first flouted the very thought of the man's pretensions. Who could tell what persuasion was used ? what arguments ? what threats ?

And the man was an impostor after all ! and he had been murdered, when one word, perhaps, would have effaced him from the world as completely, and less majestically, than had been done by death.

Mr. Warren talked of it all, and Louisa listened with half an ear, even whilst every sense of hearing in her was concentrated on the floor above, in a vain endeavour to get a faint inkling of what went on in Lord Radclyffe's room. She had heard her uncle's step on the landing, the few hurried sentences exchanged with the doctor before entering the sick chamber, the opening and shutting of a door. Then again the lighter footsteps of the nurses, who had evidently been sent out of the room when Sir Thomas went in. Louisa heard the faint hum of their voices as they descended the stairs, even a suppressed giggle now and then : they were happy, no doubt, at the few moments of respite from constant watching which had apparently been accorded them.

They ran quickly down the last flight of stairs, and across the hall towards the servants' quarters. Their chattering was heard faintly echoing through the baize doors. Then nothing more.

Less than a quarter of an hour went by, and again she heard the opening and shutting of a door, and men's footsteps on the landing.

Louisa could not believe either her eyes, which were gazing on the clock, or her ears, which heard now quite distinctly the voice of Sir Thomas descending the stairs, and Dr. Newington's more pompous tones in reply.

"The interview," remarked Mr. Warren, "did not last very long."

But already she had risen from her chair, desperately anxious, wondering what the meaning could be of the shortness of the interview. She was not kept long in suspense : for a moment or two later Sir Thomas Ryder came in, followed by Dr. Newington. One glance at her uncle's face told her the whole disappointing truth even before he spoke.

"It was useless, my dear," he said, "and Dr. New-ington was quite right. Lord Radclyffe, I am sorry to say, is hardly conscious. He is evidently unable to understand what is said, and certainly quite in-capable of making any effort to reply."

"I was afraid so," added Dr. Newington in his usual conventional tones. "The patient, you see, is hardly conscious. His mind is dormant. He just knows me and his nurses, but he did not recognize Sir Thomas."

Louisa said nothing : the blank, hopeless disap-pointment, following on the excitement of the past two hours, was exceedingly difficult to bear. The ruling passion—strong even in the midst of despair—the pride that was in her, alone kept her from an utter breakdown. She was grateful to her uncle, who very tactfully interposed his tall figure between her and the indifferent eyes of the doctor. Mr. Warren looked more sympathetic than ever, and that was just as trying to bear as the pompousness of Dr. Newington.

As a matter of fact, Louisa had absolutely ceased

to think. The whole future from this moment appeared as an absolute blank. She had not begun to envisage the possibility of going back to the hotel, having utterly failed in accomplishing that which she had set heart and mind to do : the throwing of the first feeble ray of light on the impenetrable darkness of Luke's supposed guilt. She certainly had not envisaged the going to bed to-night, the getting up to-morrow, the beginning of another day, with its thousand and one trivial tasks and incidents, all the while that she had failed in doing that which alone could prevent the awful catastrophe of to-morrow !

Luke standing in the dock, like a common criminal !

" I'll just see about getting a cab, dear," said her uncle kindly.

The first of those thousand and one trivialities, which would go on and on from now onwards, in endless monotony, whilst Luke mounted, step by step and alone, that terrible Calvary which meant his trial and his condemnation—and on the summit of which there awaited him already an awful and shameful death.

It was indeed unthinkable. No wonder that her mind rebelled at the task : refusing all thoughts, remaining like a grey, blank slate, from which every impression of past and future has been wiped out.

Sir Thomas Ryder went out of the room, and Mr. Warren went with him. They left the door ajar, so that she could hear them talking in the hall. Mr. Warren said—

" Don't go out, Sir Thomas. It's a horrid night. Fletcher will get you a cab."

And Sir Thomas replied : " Thank you."

" Won't you," said the younger man, " wait in the library ? "

He had apparently rung a bell, for the man-servant came into the hall, and was duly told off to whistle for a cab.

" I'd rather go into another room, for a moment, Mr. Warren, if I may," said Sir Thomas. " There are just one or two little questions I would like to put to you."

" Certainly, Sir Thomas," replied Mr. Warren with alacrity.

The two men went together into the dining-room. Louisa, by shutting her eyes, could almost see them, sitting there in the stately and gloomy room which she knew so well. She could call to mind the last occasion on which she had lunched there, with Lord Radclyffe and Luke, and Edie and Jim. It was the day on which the impostor first forced his way into the house. Louisa had a clear vision of him even now, just as she had seen him standing that day in the hall, before his interview with Lord Radclyffe. Parker was helping him with his coat, and Louisa had seen his face : the bricklayer's son, who had come forward with his marvellous array of lies, and who had been so implicitly believed, that he himself had to pay for his lies with a most horrible death.

For that death now—and because of the impenetrable mystery which the impostor had taken with him to his humble grave—Luke stood in danger of being punished with death that was even more horrible than that caused by a stab in the neck under cover of darkness and of fog.˜

The one chance that there had been of finding a clue to the mystery had been dissipated by the silence of the sick man upstairs. The hand of death was upon him too. He also would take the secret of the bricklayer's son silently with him to the grave.

Louisa's eyes, vacant and tearless, wandered aimlessly round the room. Dr. Newington was sitting at the desk, writing either a letter or a prescription, which apparently required a considerable amount of thought. He seemed deeply absorbed in what he wrote, and from time to time referred to a small note-book which he took out of his pocket.

The scratching of his stylo against the paper was the only sound that struck Louisa's ear, the rest of the house seemed lonely and still. Only from far away came the shrill screeching of the cab-whistle.

Louisa rose and went to the door, peeping out into the hall. It was deserted, and the dining-room door was shut. She slipped out into the hall. Dr. Newington apparently did not trouble himself about her. Very softly she closed the library door behind her.

Then she ran swiftly upstairs.

CHAPTER XXXIX

A MERE WOMAN FIGHTING FOR THE THING SHE LOVED

LOUISA reached the landing slightly out of breath. She knew her way about the old house very well. Two doors now were opposite to her. One of these had been left ajar—intentionally, no doubt—it was the one that gave on a smaller morning-room, where, in the olden days, Lord Radclyffe used to have his breakfast and write his private letters, the library being given over to Mr. Warren and to official correspondence.

From this side of the house, and right through the silence that hung over it, Louisa could hear very faintly rising from the servants' quarters below the sound of women's voices chattering and giggling. The nurses, then, had not returned to their post. With the indifference born of long usage, they were enjoying every minute of the brief respite accorded them, content to wait for the doctor's call if the patient had immediate need of them.

Through the chink of the door the red glow of a shaded lamp came as a sharp crimson streak cutting the surrounding gloom.

Louisa pushed open the door that was ajar, and tiptoed softly in.

The little room had been transformed for present

emergencies. The desk had been pushed aside, and a small iron bedstead fitted up for the night nurse. A woman's paraphernalia were scattered about on the massive early Victorian furniture : a comb and brush, a cap and apron neatly folded, a couple of long pins littered the table which used to look so severe with its heavy inkstand and firm blotting-pad. The piano had been relegated into a corner, and the portrait of Luke which always hung over the mantelpiece had been removed.

The door into the bedroom was wide open, and without any hesitation Louisa went in. The bed was immediately in front of her, and between it and the hanging lamp beyond, a screen had been placed, so that the upper part of the sick man's figure was invisible at first in the gloom, and the light lay like a red patch right across the quilt at the foot.

Louisa advanced noiselessly, and then halted beside the bed. The room was pleasantly warm, and the smell of disinfectants, of medicines, and of lavender-water hung in the air—the air of a sick-room oppressive and enervating.

Gradually Louisa's eyes became accustomed to the semi-darkness. She fixed them on the sick man, who lay quite still against the pillows, his face no less white than the linen against which it rested. Louisa had no idea that any man could alter so in such a brief while. It almost seemed difficult to recognize in the white emaciated figure that lay there with the stillness of death, the vigorous man of a few months ago.

The face had the appearance of wax, deep lines from

the nostrils to the corners of the mouth accentuating
its hollow appearance ; the hair was almost snow-white
now and clung matted and damp to the forehead and
sunken temples.

Lord Radclyffe seemed unconscious of Louisa's
presence in the room ; but his eyes were wide open
and fixed on a spot high up on the wall immediately
opposite to the bed. Louisa looked to see on what
those eyes were gazing so intently, and turning she
saw the splendid portrait of Luke de Mountford
—painted by the greatest living master of portraiture
—which we all admired in the rooms of the Royal
Academy a few years ago. It had been taken away
from the boudoir, and brought in here so that the sick
man might have the semblance now that he was parted
from the reality.

Only a feeble breath escaped Lord Radclyffe's parted
lips : there was no distortion in the face, and the
hands lay still—waxen-white against the quilt. Louisa
looked down on the sick man without, at first, at-
tempting to speak. She looked down on this the last
chord of hope's broken lute, the frail thread on which
hung Luke's one chance of safety : this feeble life
almost ended, this weak breath which alone could
convey words of hope ! For the moment Louisa's
heart almost misgave her, when she thought of what
she meant to do : to bring, namely, this wandering
spirit back to earth, in order to make it conscious of
such misery as no heart of man could endure and
not break. It seemed like purposeless, inhuman
cruelty !

Even if she could call that enfeebled mind back to the hideous realities of to-day, what chance was there that the few words which this dying man could utter would be those that could save Luke from the gallows ?

Was it not better to let the broken heart sink to rest in peace, the weakened mind go back to the land of shadows, unconscious of further sorrow ?

Uncertain now and vaguely fearful, she looked up at the portrait of Luke. The eyes in the magnificently painted picture seemed endowed with amazing vitality. To the loving, heart-broken woman it seemed as if they made a direct appeal to her. Yet, what appeal did they make ?

To let the old man—" Uncle Rad "—die in peace, ignorant of the awful fate which must inevitably befall the man whom he loved with such strange, such enduring affection ?

Or did those eyes ask for help there, where no other human being could lend assistance now ?

" Lord Radclyffe ! "

The words escaped her suddenly, almost frightening her, though all along she knew that she had meant to speak.

" Do you know me, Lord Radclyffe ? " she said again. " It is Louisa Harris."

No reply. The great eyes with the shadow of death over them were gazing on the face, on which they had always loved to dwell.

" Lord Radclyffe," she reiterated, and the deep notes of her contralto voice quivered with the poignancy of her emotion, " Luke is in very great danger, the gravest possible danger that can befall any man. Do you understand me ? "

Again no reply. But the great eyes—sunken and glassy—slowly fell from the picture to her face.

" Luke," she repeated, dwelling on the word, " I must speak to you about Luke."

And the lips, stiff and cold, opened slightly, and from between them escaped the word, feebly, like the breath of a dying man—

" Luke ! "

" He is in grave danger, Lord Radclyffe," she said slowly, " in danger of death."

And this time the faded lips framed the words distinctly—

" Luke . . . in danger of death ! "

The hands which had lain on the quilt up to now, still and waxen as those of a lifeless image, began to tremble visibly, and the eyes—those great, hollow eyes—had a searching anxious expression in them now.

" Philip de Mountford has been murdered," said Louisa. " You knew that, did you not ? "

The sick man nodded. Life and consciousness were slowly returning, and with them understanding and the capacity for suffering.

" And Luke is accused of having murdered him."

The trembling of the hands ceased. With a quick, jerky movement they were drawn back against the figure, then used as a leverage. With a sudden accession of strength, the sick man slowly but steadily drew himself up, away from the pillows, until he was almost sitting up in bed. There was understanding in the eyes now, understanding and an awful look of horror.

" It is not true ! " he murmured.

" It is true," she said. " Luke was known to have quarrelled with Philip de Mountford, and the dagger-stick with which the crime was committed was found in the Park—stained with blood—the dagger-stick which belonged to Luke."

" Luke didn't do it," murmured the sick man.

" I know that he didn't," she replied firmly ; " but he pleads guilty. He owns that the stick was his, and will give no denial, no explanation. He is taking upon himself the crime of another . . ."

" It is not true ! " once more murmured the sick man.

Then he fell back exhausted against the pillows.

There he lay once more, with that awful stillness of death : the hands rested on the quilt as if modelled in wax. The eyes were closed, and from between the pale, parted lips not the faintest breath seemed to escape. Helpless and anxious Louisa looked round her. On a table close by stood an array of bottles. She went up to it, trying to read the labels, wondering if there was anything there that was a powerful restorative. She found a small bottle labelled " Brandy," and took it up in her hand ; but as she looked up again she saw Dr. Newington standing in the doorway of the boudoir. One of the nurses was with him, and he was armed with his most pompous and most professional manner.

" What are you doing here ? " he asked sternly.

" I think," she replied, trying to master her excitement, " that Lord Radclyffe has fainted. I did not know what to do."

" I should think not indeed," he said. " And why did you not ring for the nurse ? and why are you here ? "

" I wished to see Lord Radclyffe myself," she replied.

" Without my permission ? "

" You would have refused it."

" Certainly I should. And I must request you to leave the sick-room at once."

Baffled and miserable, she stood for a moment hesitating, vaguely wondering if she could rebel. Indeed, she had no option but to obey. The doctor was well within his rights : she utterly in the wrong.

She turned towards the door ready to go ; but in order to reach it from where she stood, she had to go past the foot of the bed.

The nurse was busy administering restoratives, and Dr. Newington had taken up the attitude dear to every Englishman : his stand upon the hearthrug, and his hands buried in the pockets of his trousers. He was treating Louisa like a disobedient child, and she had no one to appeal to in this moment of complete helplessness.

One moment only did she debate with herself. The nurse just then had gone to a side table to fetch some brandy. The patient, so Louisa heard her tell the doctor, had not actually fainted ; he was merely in a state of exhaustion.

Swift and furtive, like some small animal in danger

of its life, Louisa slipped in between the screen and the bed, and before the doctor or nurse could prevent her she had bent right over the sick man and whispered close to his ear—

" Lord Radclyffe, unless you make an effort now, to-morrow Luke will be standing in the dock—branded as a felon. Make an effort for Luke's sake ! "

And the spirit which had gone wandering in the land of shadows came back to earth at sound of that one name.

" Luke ! " he whispered, " Luke, my boy. I am strong. I can help you."

" Miss Harris . . ." interposed the doctor sternly.

But the sick man's words had put new strength into her. She was ready to fight the doctor now. The conventional woman of the world was transformed into just a mere woman fighting for the thing she loved— child, lover, or husband ! it is all the same when that womanly instinct of combat is aroused.

Dr. Newington would have had to take Louisa Harris by the shoulders now if he meant to eject her ; for until the patient spoke, here she meant to remain.

" Doctor," she said quietly, " you have another duty to perform than that of watching over your patient. An innocent man is accused of a terrible crime. Lord Radclyffe, though very weak, is fully conscious. If he can save his nephew by a word, that word must be spoken to-night."

" Send for Tom Ryder," murmured the sick man, " he'll understand."

The words came in gasps, but otherwise fairly distinctly. Dr. Newington, in all his professional experience, had never been placed in such an extraordinary dilemma. He was not quite so obstinate about the whole thing as he had originally been, and a kind of hopeless bewilderment showed itself upon his face.

"Will you send for Sir Thomas, doctor ? " asked Louisa. " You see that Lord Radclyffe wishes it."

The doctor shrugged his shoulders. The responsibility was getting all too heavy for him. Besides being a fashionable physician, he was also a man, and as such not altogether inhuman. He had seen much acute suffering, both mental and physical, throughout the length of his career, but never had he been brought face to face with such an acute psychological problem, and—frankly !—he did not know how to deal with it.

So he sent the nurse to ask Sir Thomas Ryder once more to step upstairs, whilst he himself went up to his patient, and with the mechanical movement born of life-long habit, he placed his white, podgy fingers on the feebly fluttering pulse.

"God only knows what will be the issue," he said almost inaudibly. " I don't."

The sick man, on the other hand, seemed to be husbanding his strength. He had most obediently taken the brandy which had been given him, and now he lay back quietly among the pillows, with eyes closed and lips slightly parted. The hands wandered somewhat restlessly along the smooth surface of the quilt, otherwise Lord Radclyffe lay perfectly still. It even seemed—to Louisa's supersensitive gaze—as if an ex-

pression of content had settled over the pale face. Once
the sick man opened his eyes and looked up at the
portrait ; the lips murmured the one word—" Luke ! "
and slowly, very slowly two tears formed in the sunken
eyes and trickled down the wan cheeks.

" You had better," said the doctor curtly, " leave
the patient to me and to Sir Thomas."

" Certainly," she replied. " I'll wait in the next
room."

" Sir Thomas will call you, no doubt, if your presence
is desirable."

She was ready enough to obey now : her uncle's
footstep was heard on the landing outside. Quietly
she relinquished her place beside the bed, and as she
did so she bent down and kissed the poor old hand that
wandered so restlessly along the folds of the quilt.

As Sir Thomas entered the room she was just
leaving it. They met under the lintel of the door.

" He seems stronger," she whispered, pointing to
the sick man. " I think that he will make an effort—
for Luke's sake."

She waited a moment in the doorway, until she saw
Sir Thomas Ryder installed on one side of the bed,
and the doctor on the other side, with his finger on the
patient's pulse. Then she retreated into the morning-
room, and moved by some unaccountable impulse she
went to the piano, and opening it, she sat down, and
with exquisite softness began to play the opening bars
of one of her favourite songs.

She sang hardly above a whisper ; the velvety tones
of her voice sounded like the murmur of ghosts through

the heavy tapestries of the room. Whenever her voice died away in the intervals of the song she could hear the hum of men's voices, her uncle's low and clear, now and then a word from the doctor, and through it all the voice of the sick man, feeble and distinct, speaking the words that would mean life to Luke.

CHAPTER XL

HALF an hour had gone by. The fountain pen dropped from Sir Thomas's cramped fingers.

He had been writing, slowly but incessantly, ever since he sat down beside the sick man, and put his first question to him. Lord Radclyffe, with the tenacity peculiar to a strong nature, had clung to his own strength and will-power, and had spoken clearly, so that Sir Thomas could not only understand, but could write down what he heard, word for word— not omitting a phrase—accurately and succinctly.

Once or twice Dr. Newington had to interfere. The patient was in danger of exhaustion, and brandy had again to be administered. Lord Radclyffe took it eagerly : what will-power he had left was concentrated on the desire to keep up his strength.

From the boudoir came the gentle murmur of a tender song, whispered by Louisa's appealing contralto voice. The sick man seemed to enjoy it : it seemed to soothe him too, for every now and again he lay quite still, and listened attentively ; and when he did so his eyes always sought the portrait of Luke.

When all was finished, and the last word written, Sir Thomas rose and grasped his old friend's emaciated hand.

" You'll feel better to-morrow," he whispered cheerily, " when you have your nephew with you. The doctor here must allow you to see him, if you see no one else."

" Lord Radclyffe must have rest now," said the doctor impatiently.

" Certainly, my dear sir," rejoined Sir Thomas. " I need not trouble you any more. I can but hope that your patient will be none the worse for the effort."

The doctor did not reply. The patient, after the great effort, was in a dangerous state of collapse, and required every attention.

Sir Thomas Ryder took his leave, and, going through the smaller room, he beckoned to Louisa to follow him.

A moment later the doctor was heard ringing for the nurses. Sir Thomas in the hall was struggling with his coat, whilst Louisa stood by, quite still and patient. She knew that her hour would come, and she was grateful to her uncle for taking her away from here so quickly.

She had not asked a single question, and Sir Thomas had not volunteered any information. But she was content to wait, until the time when he told her everything.

The cab, which had been called all that long while ago, was still waiting at the door. It was now past eleven o'clock. Silently Sir Thomas and Louisa Harris stepped into the cab, Mr. Warren, sympathetic and attentive to the last, giving the address to the chauffeur on their behalf.

Less than five minutes later they had arrived at the

Langham Hotel, but they had not exchanged a single word during that time.

Colonel Harris was in the sitting-room waiting for his daughter's return. The maid had told him that her mistress had gone to Sir Thomas Ryder's, and had promised to be home again in about an hour; so he was not really anxious, only very worried about her. Personally, he saw no issue to the terrible tangle, and his heart ached for her as much as it did for Luke.

He found himself quite unable to sit at the Club. Luke de Mountford's name was in every man's mouth. The obsession was unendurable; the countless arguments, adduced by indifferent lips, were positively nerve-racking. Colonel Harris, after half an hour, had enough of it, and went back to the Langham.

He did not greet his brother-in-law very warmly; he did not feel very well-disposed towards him, as he had a vague idea that Sir Thomas Ryder was in a measure responsible for Luke's terrible fate.

"Loo, dear, it's very late," he said with gentle reproach, when she came in.

"You'll have to forgive her, Will," interposed Sir Thomas. "She came over to have a talk with me, and we went on to try and see old Rad, who is dying, I am afraid, poor chap.

"Now, my dear," he added, turning to Louisa whilst he dived into his breast-pocket, from which he extracted a notebook, "go to your own room and read this through very quietly, while I talk to your father."

He gave her the book, which she took without a word.

"It won't," he added, "take you very long to read. When you have finished, bring me the notes back I want them to-night."

She kissed her father before she went out of the room. He and she had both guessed—by that unexplainable subtle intuition born of sympathy—what the pages of that notebook contained.

CHAPTER XLI

LOUISA sat beside the fire and read. The notes were written in Sir Thomas's clear caligraphy : in short, jerky sentences, just as the sick man had spoken them, usually in reply to questions put to him.

As Louisa read on she could almost hear Lord Radclyffe's whispered words, whilst she herself sang Tosti's melancholy song : " Good-bye ! "

" I was not altogether ignorant of my brother Arthur's marriage over in Martinique, but he had always given me to understand that the marriage was not a strictly legal one, and that his son Philip had no right whatever to claim any possible succession to our family title and estates. Even on his death-bed Arthur assured me of this, and said to me most emphatically : ' Luke is your heir ! my son Philip has no legal claim ! '

" I never made the slightest effort to communicate with Arthur's widow or with his child ; for Arthur had assured me that they were well provided for, and quite happy amongst their own kindred. After the catastrophe of St. Pierre I completely lost sight of them.

" Then came a letter addressed to me from St.

Vincent, the first inkling which I had that not only did
Arthur's son know of his father's position in life, but
that he had full and justifiable reasons for believing
that he himself was heir-presumptive to the family
title and estates which would have been his father's,
had the latter outlived the present holder.

" This letter was followed by several others, about
which neither Luke nor Mr. Warren knew anything ;
for I told them nothing. At last there came one from
Brussels. By this time I had searched carefully through
some letters which my brother Arthur had desired
that I should destroy after his death, but which I had
always kept by me, meaning one day to comply with
his wish.

" I had more than a suspicion then that my brother's
marriage was a perfectly legal one, and that his son
was the only true heir-presumptive to the title and
estates, which I had always fondly thought could only
devolve upon Luke. I went over to Brussels determined to see this Philip, before he set foot in England.
The thought that he would supersede Luke was more
than I could bear.

" I arrived in Brussels early one morning, having
crossed over in the night. At once I drove to the
mean hotel where he was lodging. He was sharing a
room with a man with whom he had picked up
a casual acquaintanceship on the sea voyage between
the West Indies and Antwerp. The two men had
come over together in the Belgian boat. They
looked a pair of young blackguards, but it did
not take me very long to be convinced that for

some reason best known to himself my brother Arthur had deceived me, and that his son Philip was indeed the legitimate and rightful heir to the title which I hold. The papers were authentic and undisputable. This much I knew, and that Luke whom I loved best in all the world, more than any father has ever loved his son, would never be Earl of Radclyffe, so long as Philip de Mountford lived.

"Men will say that I am an abandoned criminal, and indeed it may be so. May God forgive me hereafter, for I killed my brother's son. I pretended to rejoice at his home-coming, and in half an hour had gained his confidence. In the afternoon we went out together, and after a short walk we picked up a taxicab. Philip gave the driver the address of a restaurant at which I had asked him to dine with me. I kept carefully in the shadow, so that the man shouldn't see me. Then, on the way in the cab, I killed him. When his head was turned away from me I plunged an old Italian stiletto, which I had carried about with me ever since I had had letters from Philip, straight into his neck.

"He died instantly without a groan, and I was sick to death; but I managed to sit quietly beside him until the cab pulled up. Then I jumped out and told the chauffeur to drive my friend on to some remote place on the boulevards.

"I watched the cab until it was out of sight, then I hailed another, and drove straight to the Gare du Nord, and crossed back to England that night. I threw the stiletto overboard into the sea. I had spent twelve hours in Brussels, and I had killed Philip de Mountford, and made sure that Luke would be Earl of Radclyffe after me.

" It was not likely that, in their search for the missing criminal who had stabbed an unknown stranger in a cab, the Belgian police would suspect an English peer. The mystery of that crime has remained impenetrable, because nothing was ever known of the stranger who was murdered. At the mean hotel where he lodged no one knew anything about him. Only one person knew, and he was silent for purposes of his own.

" Before the police searched the unknown stranger's room, the room which he shared with the chance friend whom he had picked up on the Belgian boat, the latter already had found and concealed the papers, which would have revealed the identity of the murdered man, if not that of his murderer.

" I, at home in England, wondered how it was that the Belgian police had never discovered that the murdered man was named Philip de Mountford, and that he claimed to be the heir to the Earldom of Radclyffe. I expected paragraphs in the paper, some unpleasantness even, but none came.

" I could not understand it, for I had forgotten the existence of the chance friend.

" And then one day last April I understood. Once more I had letters from abroad, from a man who claimed to be my brother's son. At first I thought the whole thing a silly imposture, until the day when a man confronted me in my own house, armed with every

proof that I had killed Philip de Mountford in Brussels.
He had the latter's passports, his birth and marriage
certificates, his letters of identification : all, all the
papers that he had filched from among the dead
man's things, and which he now flaunted before me,
daring me to prove him an impostor. ' If I am not
Philip de Mountford,' he said to me, ' then where is
Philip de Mountford ? ' And from that hour, I was
as wax in his hands. He held me, and he knew it.
I might have proved him an impostor, and he could
prove me a murderer.

  " Heaven alone knows how I did not lose my reason
then ! I floundered in a sea of wild conjectures, wild
projects, wild hopes of escape. But my tyrant held
me, and I dared not rebel.

  " And once more I was obsessed with the awful
certitude that Luke would never be Earl of Radclyffe
after me, while this man lived.

  " He had so taken upon himself the personality
of Philip, the evidences which went to prove his identity with the late Arthur de Mountford's son were
so strangely circumstantial, that short of my pro-
claiming loudly that I had killed my brother's son with
my own hand, nothing could prevent the impostor
from succeeding in filching Luke's inheritance.

  " And even if I had confessed then, it seemed to me
that this man would still succeed in proving that I had
murdered an unknown stranger—a chance friend,
who was an English bricklayer's son—and that he and
he only was Philip de Mountford, the late Arthur's son.

  " When did I first dream of killing him, as I killed

the other ? I could not tell you that. But it was some time ago, and I watched my opportunity with patience and perseverance. Then at last the opportunity came, following on terrible provocation. That dark, foggy November night, that you all remember so well! I was to meet my tyrant at the Veterans' Club at nine o'clock. I drove up there, and as I stepped out of the cab I came face to face with Luke. Something in the boy's manner told me what had happened. He didn't tell me, but I guessed. The two men had quarrelled, and Luke had had to endure the other's arrogance.

" The news upset me. I felt faint and choked with the fog. Luke didn't like to leave me, and seeing how I tottered he gave me his stick to lean upon. We walked together for a little while up and down, and I felt stronger and better. I begged Luke to leave me. Presently—as the impostor came out at the Club door—Luke obeyed at last, and said ' good night ' to me.

" Paul Baker—I knew that that was his name— wanted me to drive straight back to Grosvenor Square, but asked me to drop him first near the railings of Green Park. He often walked about there in the evenings—it was a curious fad which he had. We called a cab, and he told the driver where to pull up. When I was sitting next to him, I realized that I had a stick in my hand. I really had forgotten that it was Luke's. Whilst I toyed with it, I noticed that the top came out, and that a sharp dagger was concealed inside the body of the stick.

"Paul Baker was looking out of the window at the fog, and inside the cab it was very dark, so he did not know what I was doing. I killed him, just as I had killed Arthur's son, with a dagger-thrust through the neck. This time I did not feel sick, because I hated this man so. When the driver pulled up near Green Park, I jumped out quite coolly and told the man to take my friend to some distant address in Kensington.

"I threw the stick away behind the railings in the Park. I had forgotten that the stick was Luke's: I knew that it was not mine, and that therefore they could not trace it to me.

"I did not imagine for a moment that Luke could be accused of a crime which he had not committed. I did not think that justice could be so blind.

"All I wanted was to be rid of my tyrant, and that Luke's inheritance should not be filched from him."

CHAPTER XLII

WHICH TELLS ONCE MORE OF COMMONPLACE INCIDENTS

THE notebook fell out of Louisa's hands on to her lap.

How simple the tragedy seemed, now that she knew.

How understandable was the mystery of Luke's silence. He knew that Uncle Rad was guilty. There lay the awful difficulty!

"Uncle Rad has been father, mother, brother, sister to us all! Bless him!" That was Luke's feeling with regard to Uncle Rad.

The un-understandable was so simple after all!

Louisa went back to the sitting-room. The two men were sitting, smoking in silence. Colonel Harris, too, understood the mystery at last. His loyalty was crowned with the halo of justification.

The public never knew, I think, that Luke de Mountford had actually been arrested for the murder of the Clapham Road bricklayer. The police the next day applied for a remand, and then Luke was brought quietly before the magistrate, and equally quietly dismissed.

He was free to go and see Uncle Rad.

Louisa did not see him the whole of that day ; for he sat by the bedside of the sick man, whose strange and perturbed spirit was slowly sinking to rest. Uncle Rad was at peace, for he held the hand and looked into the face of the man on whom he had lavished the storehouse of an affection that had known no bounds.

The two men understood one another perfectly. He who had committed a crime, and he who was ready to bear its burden—both had done their share for the other's sake.

It was only after the magnificent obsequies of the Earl of Radclyffe that the truth about the murder of the bricklayer's son was made known to the public at large.

It had to be done for Luke's sake. Colonel Harris insisted upon it with all the weight of his fatherly authority. Sir Thomas Ryder did likewise.

For Louisa's sake too it had to be. But twenty-four hours before the publication of the confession in the newspapers, Luke and Louisa had been quietly married by special licence, and had gone abroad.

Once more we must think of them as the commonplace, conventional man and woman of the world, who outwardly behaved just like thousands of English men and women of their class behave.

When they came back from their honeymoon—which lasted one year abroad, and all the rest of their lives after that—there was not a trace in them, in their appearance, their manner, their mode of life, of the terrible tragedy which had threatened to annihilate honour, life, and love.

" Ah ! those English ! " murmured the foreign Excellencies who graced the English court. " They have no heart, no sentiment ! Lord and Lady Radclyffe ! they behave just as if he had never been accused of murder ! as if his uncle had never been the awful criminal that he was ! They are hypocrites, these English, and they have no heart ! "

Convention was once more the master ! Its giant hands held the strings which made the puppets dance.

But at times his grip would relax : when Luke and Louisa were all alone, no prying eyes to watch, no indifferent gaze to see the unburdening of their hearts. Then Luke would lie at Louisa's feet : for his love was worship, and his passion uncontrolled. His arms would encircle the perfect form that he loved with such intensity that at times the happiness of loving had in it an exquisite sense of pain. The tragedy of the past was never quite absent from them then : the ghost of a great crime, and the shadow of a still greater renunciation, threw a mystic halo over their love for one another. And at those times—like Paolo and Francesca—they read no more.

But these English, they have no heart, you know !

THE END

PRINTED BY
WILLIAM BRENDON AND SON, LTD.
PLYMOUTH

34, 35 & 36, Paternoster Row,
London, March, 1911.

Messrs. Hutchinson & Co.'s

ANNOUNCEMENTS

❧ For the Spring of 1911 ❧

Madame Roland

By I. A. TAYLOR

Author of "Queen Hortense and Her Times," "Queen Cristina of Sweden,"
"Lady Jane Grey and Her Times."

In demy 8vo, cloth gilt and gilt top, **12s. 6d.** *net, with 13 Illustrations,
including a photogravure frontispiece.*

As one of the most prominent members of the Girondist
party and a representative of the spirit by which its most
enthusiastic and disinterested adherents were animated,
Madame Roland has attracted, for more than a hundred
years, an amount of attention only less than that accorded
to the foremost leaders of the French Revolution.

The Girondists were the idealists of its opening phase,
and she shared to the full their hopes, their illusions, their
devotion and their doom. Men loved or hated her; they
were rarely indifferent to her, and her power and influence
were recognized by all. Her memoirs and letters, as well
as the testimony of contemporaries, afford ample material
for forming a just conception of her character and aims,
and in the present volume an attempt is made to give a
fair and impartial account of her brilliant and tragic
career.

John Opie and his Circle

By ADA EARLAND

Author of " Ruskin and his Circle "

In 1 *large handsome vol. with* 32 *full page collotype illustrations,* 21s. *net.*

The lives of painters do not, as a rule, afford the biographer much interesting material, but there are a few notable exceptions, and among them one of the most remarkable is that of John Opie. The son of a poor Cornish labourer, his extraordinary gifts received recognition at an early age. He came to London in the company, if not in the care, of the notorious Dr. John Wolcot, who is better known by his pen-name, " Peter Pindar." Although his *protégé* was far from unintelligent, Wolcot preferred to let him be known as the " Cornish wonder," a creature reputed to be uncouth both in body and mind, and he dressed him in the character. But Opie's work won the admiration and subsequent support of Sir Joshua Reynolds, and the King himself was one of the earliest patrons of the young Cornish genius. Opie's fame was soon carried abroad, and he steadily rose in popularity until he became one of the most sought-after portrait painters of the day. He did not enjoy an uninterrupted term of prosperity, but when he died at a comparatively early age he was still receiving the favours of the public. Opie's first marriage was unfortunate, and hitherto little or nothing has been written about it. His second wife was the beautiful Amelia Alderson, who in her day was a popular novelist and poet. Until the present work the story of John Opie has never been told properly. The author has collected much new material, and many pictures are reproduced in the book for the first time. A valuable list of Opie's pictures form a copious appendix to the book.

Second Edition.

"No book is more likely to be read and discussed during the present season, and none will more amply repay both study and discussion."—*Daily Telegraph.*

A Diplomatist's Wife in Many Lands

By MRS. HUGH FRASER

Author of "A Diplomatist's Wife in Japan," etc.

In 2 vols., demy 8vo, cloth gilt and gilt top, 24s. *net, with 2 photogravures and* 16 *other illustrations*

It is now some years since, as a diplomatist's wife, Mrs. Hugh Fraser delighted two continents with one of the most charming books that has ever appeared on Japan. Since the publication of that book Mrs. Fraser has won a reputation in another department of literature as the author of several works of fiction. It is not surprising therefore that the publication of her reminiscences has been received with so much interest. As the daughter of Mr. Crawford, the eminent American sculptor, and sister of Mr. Marion Crawford, Mrs. Fraser spent her childhood in Italy, and her earliest recollections are of life and society in Rome, and the splendour of the Papal Court during the fifties, under Gregory XVI. and Pius IX.

The first volume contains reminiscences of such notabilities as the King and Queen of Naples, the Empress of Austria, Cavour, Garibaldi, King Edward as Prince of Wales, the Emperor Frederick as Crown Prince of Prussia, the unfortunate Emperor Maximilian and the Empress Charlotte, and the King of the Belgians—also some of the great painters and writers of the Victorian Era, such as W. W. Story, the Brownings, the Sargents, Hans Andersen, Motley, Prescott, Lowell, Agassiz, Bayard Taylor and Longfellow; while the second volume describes Mrs. Fraser's experiences in China and Vienna, as the wife of a British Minister. It is no exaggeration to say that it is many years since a work has appeared of so varied an interest and written with such a graceful pen.

A NEW WORK BY
OLIVE CHRISTIAN MALVERY
(Mrs. Archibald Mackirdy).

A Year and a Day

By the Author of "The Soul Market."

(NOW IN ITS 9th EDITION).

With illustrations on art paper.   In cr. 8vo. cloth gilt, **6/-**

In this new book Miss Malvery tells the story of her life and work. She has already related her experiences among the London working people in her widely read book "The Soul Market," but that volume did not treat of her life story as a whole. Miss Malvery's life has been unusually busy and varied, but among other matters she tells of the beginning, working and completion of the great Night Shelter Scheme for women and girls in London. There are interesting letters and chapters on travels in unhackneyed places in Europe, and some funny lecturing experiences in various countries. Descriptions of some great and picturesque industrial concerns, her work in Hoxton and her experiences of Spiritualism and Christian Science.

———A STANDARD BOOK FOR EVERY HOME.———

To be completed in 28 Fortnightly parts.   Price 7d. each.

The Wonders of the World

The Marvels of Nature and Man as they Exist to-day.

To contain, when complete, about

1000 Beautiful Illustrations reproduced from Photographs and many Coloured Plates.

The work comprises an absolutely original and almost priceless collection of Photographs of the Marvels of the World. All the World's most wonderful sights as seen by the most eminent travellers, many of whom have supplied the descriptive text.

The World's Greatest Wonders without leaving your Fireside.

The Contributors include—

SIR HARRY JOHNSON, G.C.M.G., K.C.B.

EARL OF RONALDSHAY, M.P.   **ALAN BURGOYNE, M.P.**

PERCEVAL LANDON.   CAPT. C. G. RAWLING, C.I.E., F.R.G.S.

B. L. PUTNAM WEALE.   PHILIP W. SERGEANT.

HERBERT G. PONTING, F.R.G.S.   And many others.

PRINTED THROUGHOUT ON ART PAPER.

In 2 large handsome vols., demy 4to, cloth gilt and gilt top, 12/6 each net. Vol. 1 is nearly ready. Binding cases may be had.

Somaliland

By ANGUS HAMILTON

Author of " Korea," " Problems of the Middle East," etc.

In 1 vol., demy 8vo, cloth gilt and gilt top, **12s. 6d.** *net.*
With 25 illustrations and a map.

This important book on Somaliland should prove most opportune, as the threatened evacuation of that country is likely to keep its affairs prominently before the public for some time to come. Mr. Angus Hamilton, who is the author of a standard book on Korea, as well as of other valuable works on the Far East, is especially well qualified for the present task. For nearly two years he acted as Reuter's Special War-Correspondent in Somaliland, and as he was practically the only war-correspondent present, he alone among writing men can tell the whole story of the four expeditions from start to finish. It was, as he says, " a wild time of danger and night attacks, long ambuscaded marches over the desert in the moonlight, and an occasional ' stand-up sit-down, ding-dong fight.' " Of these expeditions the public knows practically nothing, when troops lost their way in the bush, got strung up for water, and were raided by lions and hyænas. Mr. Hamilton necessarily has something to say respecting the future of Somaliland, and of the far-reaching effects which may result from our evacuation of that country.

Parodies Old and New

By STANLEY L. ADAM

In 1 vol., large crown 8vo, cloth gilt and gilt top, **6s.** *net.*

The present volume comprises the most extensive collection · of poetical parodies available. The only other book of a comprehensive character is a voluminous work, long out of print, in which the verses are ill-arranged and carelessly selected. Mr. Adam, who has spent several years in making this collection, has exercised the greatest care in the choice of his material, which comprises a good proportion of copyright matter.

W. H. Hudson's Works

NEW CHEAPER EDITIONS.

LAND'S END

In demy 8vo, cloth gilt, 6s. net., with illustrations by
A. L. Collins.

" This book on the West of Cornwall should be read by thousands who love nature in all its varied aspects. They will be fascinated with it, and will not be content with reading it only once. Mr. Hudson has an eye for all beautiful things, and a heart to understand something of their meaning. And as we read his beautiful clear English, we share his pleasure and interest in the things he has seen and describes so perfectly."—*Daily Mail.*

AFOOT IN ENGLAND

In demy 8vo, cloth gilt, 6s. net.

" Afoot in England " has thrown open to us human and natural beauty, mixed and separate, as no other writer's books could do. Nor are we under-rating the style in saying this. . . . We perceive that our own words can give no right and full impression of the strength and tenderness, the nobleness of the human spirit in this book, or the freedom and loveliness of Nature which it reveals."—*Daily Chronicle.*

New and Cheaper Edition. Revised.

TAYLOR ON GOLF

Impressions, Comments, and Hints.

By J. H. TAYLOR. Three times Open Champion.

New Edition with latest St. Andrews' Rules and Club Directory.

In large crown 8vo, cloth gilt, gilt top, with 48 illustrations on art paper from photographs, 3s. 6d. net.

" We have read this book from cover to cover without finding a dull page. The book is altogether fascinating—a book no golfer should be without."—*Golf Illustrated.*

" The book is not only fully illustrated, it is edited and sub-edited in a practical workmanlike way, and is furnished with the rules of the game, lists of championship winners, and a club directory. Every devotee of golf will give a place in his library to the really excellent treatise which Taylor has produced."—*Newcastle Leader.*

Sixty Years

Travel and Adventure
In the Far East

By JOHN DILL ROSS

*In 2 vols., demy 8vo, cloth gilt and gilt top, 24s. net,
with photogravure plates and other illustrations.*

The present work, which is the life history of a father and son, covers a period of sixty years. Both for the variety and character of the adventures described, the record will undoubtedly rank as one of the most romantic that has ever seen the light of print. The father was one of the old-fashioned merchant captains, who sailed his own ships on trading voyages between the islands of the Far East, in the brave days when fortunes were easily made, and when fighting at close quarters, with pirates was part of the business.

Born at Singapore, the son, heir to ample means, embarked on a career of commerce, and, like his father, has enjoyed one of singular variety. It was his fortune to engage in pioneering expeditions, quite unusual in modern days ; he took the British flag to coasts where it had never before been seen. He had some experiences in Borneo, and was with the French Army of Occupation during the war in Tonkin. To name only some of his operations, it may be stated that he opened up a trade between Singapore, Celebes, the Spice Islands, Dutch New Guinea, and Indo-China, extended his energies to Siam, Java, China, and Japan, in which last-named country he spent a year, and subsequently visited Vladivostok. During the conquest of the Philippines he loaded a steamer with provisions, and managed to distribute his cargo among some thousands of Spanish troops, attacked by the insurgents on land and the Americans at sea. As the Author very truly says, both he and his father have lived through such strange scenes, and have been acquainted with so many extraordinary persons, that he must be one of the few men now living who possess the material to construct such a record as will be found in these volumes.

THE CONCISE KNOWLEDGE LIBRARY

Each volume in large cr. 8vo, half-bound leather and gilt,
400-800 pp., freely illustrated, 5s. per volume.

"Excellently arranged, beautifully printed, neatly illustrated, and sensibly and strongly bound."—*Pall Mall Gazette.*

A NEW VOLUME

In 1 thick volume, large crown 8vo, half-bound leather, 5s.

Photography

Edited by HENRY P. MASKELL

Assisted by eminent specialists including—

E. O. HOPPÉ, F.R.P.S. F. LOW.
W. F. SLATER, F.R.P.S. C. S. COOMBES, B.Sc.
J. LITTLEJOHNS. E. A. & G. R. REEVE.
Etc. Etc. Etc.

With Coloured Plates and Illustrations after Photographs by Alvin Langdon Coburn, J. Craig Annan, Will Cadby, Fredk. H. Evans, Rev. D. G. Cowan, J. W. Church, Lionel West, &c., besides Drawings and Diagrams.

Following the steps of its predecessors in the "Concise Knowledge Library," the volume on Photography will aim at presenting a complete and succinct synopsis of the Art in theory and practice. Each section will be dealt with by a writer well qualified by long experience and reputation, and the keynote throughout will be the combination of a popular treatment with all the information, hints, and formulæ necessary to the serious worker. Chapters will be included on the Manufacture of Dry Plates and Printing Papers. Photo-Engraving and Collotype, the latest developments of Colour Photography, Animated Photography, Micro-Photography, and the X-Rays. A considerable space will be devoted to Pictorial Composition, Portraiture, Architectural Work, and Retouching. Each process will be described from the beginning, and notes on home-made printing processes for the amateur will form a special feature. At the same time the book will contain abundance of matter to interest the humble owner of a cheap magazine or roll-film hand camera.

In short, the size, complete character, and up-to-date illustrations of the "Concise Knowledge Photography" promise to secure for it a very high place among works on the subject, while excellence in printing and binding, together with its low price will commend it to a place on the bookshelf of both professional and amateur photographers.

VOLUMES ALREADY PUBLISHED.

1.—NATURAL HISTORY. With nearly 800 pages and 530 original illustrations. **Mammals, Reptiles, Fishes,** etc., by R. LYDEKKER, F.R.S., V.P.G.S **Birds,** by R. BOWDLER SHARPE, LL.D. **Insects** by W. F. KIRBY, F.L.S. Other branches by B. B. WOODWARD, F.L.S., F.G.S., F. A. BATHER, M.A., F.G.S., W. GARSTANG, M.A., F.Z.S., R. KIRKPATRICK, and R. I. POCOCK.

2.—ASTRONOMY. The **History of Astronomy,** and The **Solar System,** by AGNES M. CLERKE. **Geometric Astronomy,** by A. FOWLER, F.R.A.S. The **Stellar Universe,** by J. ELLARD GORE, F.R.A.S With over 600 pages and 104 illustrations, including a beautifully produced Frontispiece in Rembrandt Intaglio.

3.—A History of the World from Earliest Historical Time to the Year 1898. By EDGAR SANDERSON, M.A., Author of "History of the British Empire," "The British Empire in the Nineteenth Century," etc. Over 800 pages, with numerous maps specially drawn for the work.

From Rhodesia to Egypt

Including an ascent of Ruwenzorie, and a
short account of the Routes from Cape Town
to Broken Hill, and Lada to Alexandria.

By THEO KASSNER, F.R.G.S.

Author of "Gold Seeking in South Africa," " A Geological Sketch Map
of the De Kaap Goldfields," " Geological Survey Map
of Southern Transvaal," etc., etc.

With numerous illustrations from original photographs and 3 maps.
In demy 8vo, cloth gilt and gilt top, **12s. 6d.** *net.*

This book contains a most interesting account of a journey from
Cape Town to the North of Africa. The first chapter is devoted
to a survey of the district between the Cape and Broken Hill, and
the rest of the book comprises a description of a journey on foot
through Eastern Congo and parts of German and British East
Africa. Mr. Kassner tells of his adventures with the native races
generally, including some of the cannibal tribes. He also gives
an account of the wild animals he encounters, and he includes
a graphic description of an ascent of Mount Ruwenzorie. The book
further contains a study on sleeping sickness, and chapters on the
development of the Congo and other parts of Africa.

Compiled by A. C. R. CARTER

The Year's Art, 1911

THIRTY-SECOND YEAR OF ISSUE

A concise Epitome of all matters relating to the Arts of
Painting, Sculpture, Engraving and Architecture, and to Schools
of Design which have occurred during the year 1910, together
with information respecting the events of 1911.

Crown 8vo, cloth 5/= *net.* **Over 630 pages with Illustrations**

Growing bigger annually. It is also growing better. . . . For
those who have to do with art and artists the volume is simply
indispensable, and it is valuable not only for current use, but as a
record. In short, we do not know what we should do without it."
—*Athenæum.*

Hutchinson's **1/=** Net Library
OF STANDARD COPYRIGHT BOOKS.

MESSRS. HUTCHINSON & CO. have pleasure in announc-
ing a new series of reprints of popular standard books at
the price of ONE SHILLING net. Each work is complete in
one volume, is printed in clear type on good paper and tastefully bound in art cloth, with gilt top and photogravure
frontispiece. They are light to handle and portable in size.

1 A Diplomatist's Wife in Japan

BY MRS. HUGH FRASER

" We do not hesitate to say that never before have the more
charming aspects of Japan been so attractively presented, and with
a clear conscience we can repeat to all lovers of the Island Empire
of the East that the possession of this volume will provide them
with a perennial feast."—*Athenæum*.

2 Five Fair Sisters

An Italian Episode at the Court of Louis XIV.

BY H. NOEL WILLIAMS

Author of "Madame Recamier and her friends," etc.

" From cover to cover it is crammed with exciting incidents,
romantic adventures, elaborate intrigues, and episodes of love,
jealousy and poisoning, all of which occurred in very fact, a feast
of thrilling romance narrated with a satisfying fullness of detail,
irresistibly entertaining and piquant. There is not a dull page in
the whole book. It is a book which everybody should get and read
and unfailingly enjoy."—*Tribune*.

3 Napoleon

BY PROFESSOR DR. MAX LENZ

" This is one of the most masterly studies of Napoleon which
have appeared in English. Probably it is the very best short book
upon its subject which we have in this country. Written by a
German, translated by an Englishman, with all the spontaneous
force of an original author, it gives a vivid, complete and yet dis-
criminating view of a man whose commentators have hitherto been
passionately hostile or passionately adulatory and consequently
obscure."—*Tribune*.

Hutchinson's **1/-** Library

4 Ruskin and His Circle
BY ADA EARLAND

" Miss Earland's delineation of the great artist and critic is intensely and undeviatingly sympathetic : its effect is that of the presentment of a personality of rare beauty and majesty. Right through the book we are, in truth, in great company. Millais, Rossetti, Carlyle, Morris and Burne-Jones, Miss Mitford and the Brownings, Elizabeth Siddal and Kate Greenaway, and the beautiful Lady Mount-Temple—such are a few of the figures into whose company Miss Earland takes us once again ever-willing visitors."

—Pall Mall Gazette.

5 In the Strange South Seas
BY BEATRICE GRIMSHAW
Author of " From Fiji to the Cannibal Islands," etc.

" One of the most fascinating books of modern travel that have appeared for many a long day. Her good humour pervades her style of writing, which is invariably bright, crisp and splendidly descriptive. In every respect this is a book to get and to read."—*Daily Telegraph.*

6 Louise de La Vallière
BY JULES LAIR

" For him, and consequently for his readers, ' the little La Vallière ' is not merely a Royal mistress like another, but a definite, and even a sympathetic human being. When we close the book we understand her and feel very sorry for her. There is a simple sincerity of emotion in her story, and the emotion, no less than the facts, is reflected in M. Lair's admirable narrative."—*Times.*

7 Richard Jefferies
A Biographical Study
BY EDWARD THOMAS
Author of "The Heart of England," etc.

" The mind and work of Jefferies can be portrayed, and Mr. Thomas has done it admirably, in a way not unworthy to rank with the spiritual self-revelation in his author's own beautiful ' Story of My Heart.' "—*Times.*

8 A Princess of Intrigue
Madame de Longueville and Her Times
BY H. NOEL WILLIAMS
Author of " Five Fair Sisters," etc.

" Mr. H. Noel Williams has packed an amazing quantity and variety of entertaining information between the covers of 'A Princess of Intrigue,' a vivid picture of the life of the French Court of her day—the period of Mazarin and Anne of Austria. Mr. Williams' great aim is to arrest and hold the attention of his readers. In this he is entirely successful."—*Outlook.*

Edward the Peacemaker

The Story of the Life of
King Edward VII. and his Queen

Told by W. H. WILKINS, M.A., F.S.A.

Author of "The Love of an Uncrowned Queen," etc.

AND BY OTHER WELL-KNOWN BIOGRAPHERS

WITH 782 BEAUTIFUL ILLUSTRATIONS
including 21 coloured Plates

Demy 4to, in two handsome volumes, cloth richly gilt and gilt edges,
8s. *net each.*

This is undoubtedly the best record of the late King's life that has been published, and the illustrations comprise very many fine drawings made specially for the work, and a vast number of reproductions of pictures by great painters, choice engravings and new photographs

---

BOOKS FOR THE COUNTRYSIDE

Uniform in size, shape and price

Each in (7½ × 5) richly gilt rounded corners, **5s.** *net.*

By FRANK FINN, B.A. (Oxon.), F.Z.S., &c.

EGGS AND NESTS OF BRITISH BIRDS

With 20 coloured plates and many other illustrations including coloured and uncoloured illustrations of all the British Birds'-Eggs, reproduced from the actual eggs.

BIRDS OF THE COUNTRYSIDE

With 12 coloured plates, 118 illustrations from photographs printed on art paper, and numerous outline drawings.

PETS AND HOW TO KEEP THEM

With a large number of illustrations from photographs and 12 coloured plates

WILD FRUITS OF THE COUNTRYSIDE

By F. EDWARD HULME, F.L.S., F.S.A., &c.

Author of "Butterflies and Moths of the Countryside," etc., etc.

With 36 coloured plates by the Author, and 25 illustrations from photographs on art paper.   Uniform with "Birds of the Countryside."

HUTCHINSON'S

New 6s. Novels

Each in Crown 8vo, Cloth Gilt

A most important novel which has been eagerly awaited
by the public for some years.

Adrian Savage

By LUCAS MALET

Author of "The Wages of Sin," "Sir Richard Calmady,"
"The Far Horizon," etc.

The action of the novel takes place partly in Paris, partly in
the rich residential quarter of a certain South of England watering-
place ; and covers, in time, two of the earliest years of the present
century. It recounts the fortunes of a young man of letters, an
Anglo-Frenchman, and the sentimental complications in which he
finds himself involved. It touches on modern developments in
religious thought, in art, and the position of woman. It is a novel
of character rather than of incident, though it contains some strongly
dramatic scenes. It may be said to have a happy ending, in as
far, at least, as the hero is concerned.

Lilamani

A Study in Possibilities

By MAUD DIVER

Author of "Captain Desmond, V.C.," "The Great Amulet," etc.

In this novel Mrs. Diver breaks fresh ground, both as to setting and types of character. The action of the story takes place in the South of France, on Lake Como, and in Surrey. But though the setting is not Indian, the interest centres in a high-caste Hindu girl, who has broken purdah and come to Europe with her father to study medicine. At Antibes she meets Nevil Sinclair, a baronet's son, with a gift for painting, which has been thwarted by his father's wish that he should devote himself to politics and the life of a country gentleman.

The first part of the book depicts the idyll of their courtship and ultimate marriage, in defiance of obvious difficulties on both sides, the greatest being the girl's complete break with her country and permanent loss of caste. How Lilamani works out her own and her husband's salvation the reader must find out for himself.

Moll o' the Toll Bar

By THEODORA WILSON WILSON

Author of " Bess of Hardendale," etc.

A stirring tale of romance and adventure in Cumberland during the rough starvation days of the Napoleonic wars, when law and order in country districts was as the people made it. Moll o' the Toll Bar, who is quite unaware of her real parentage, lives with her grandfather—a queen of the countryside, owing to her strong personality. Harry Brackenthwaite, grandson to Lady Brackenthwaite has returned from the wars to discover his dead uncle's heir. Mysterious sheepstealing is being carried on, in which Moll, her grandfather and Harry Brackenthwaite become involved in a very horrible manner. The story works out the discovery of the sheepstealing mystery and Moll's identity.

Mrs. Thompson

By W. B. MAXWELL

Author of " Seymour Charlton," " The Guarded Flame," " Vivien," etc.

This is a purely realistic novel, in which the author traces step by step the life of a woman of strong character, temperament and emotions. Throughout her story she has shown nothing but evidences of unusual power, until a crisis, or snapping point, is reached, and then she displays an almost unusual weakness, and, in consequence, commits a great mistake and throws herself into a sea of troubles. The main interest of the book lies in the series of events which follow the mistake, and her efforts to avert its results. The mistake occurs, as is natural in the case of a really strong woman, when she surrenders herself to an overwhelming love.

Mac's Adventures

By JANE BARLOW

Author of " Irish Idylls," " Bogland Studies," " Irish Neighbours," etc.

The stories in which these adventures of Mac Barry are related have hitherto appeared disconnectedly, and are here for the first time collected and chronologically arranged. It is thought that they gain considerably thereby, both as a whole and in parts. For although each story is to a certain extent independently complete when brought together, they acquire an atmosphere not separately attainable, which to Mac's personality, seen from varying points of view, and developed in different circumstances, gives an increased distinctness and consistency, so that he stands out a more solid and substantial figure. It is interesting to state that Mr. Swinburne expressed his delight with Mac and acknowledged him as one of his dearest and most cherished friends.

Some Happenings of Glendalyne

By DOROTHEA CONYERS

Author of "The Strayings of Sandy," etc.

Eve O'Neill, a rich heiress, is suddenly ordered by her guardian, the O'Neill of Glendalyne in Ireland, to come to live with him. He is a religious recluse and possessed of considerable wealth. She finds the place steeped in neglect, the house stripped of furniture, and the garden a wilderness, while everywhere are signs of colossal extravagance. The novel contains the fascinating mystery of a lost heir, who is found by the heroine, and her love story gives the book an additional interest. There is some hunting in the wild rough country ; the author introduces a good deal of Irish life and racing and describes the love affair of Madge Green, the trainer's niece.

Half a Truth

By RITA

Author of "Calvary," "Saba Macdonald," "Peg the Rake," "Souls," etc.

That "Half a Truth is ever the blackest of Lies" is the subject of this versatile author's new novel. The story commences in America and the three principal characters claim American nationality. The fact that Mrs. Humphreys has recently visited the United States probably accounts for the excellent study she has given of the millionaire Patrick Maddison and his wife Octavia. The latter is one of the most sympathetic and admirable portraits ever drawn by living author, and few could read the conclusion of her faithfulness and devotion to an unworthy husband with unmoved susceptibility.

The Irish portion of the story possesses all "Rita's" distinctive skill and charm and peculiar insight into national characteristics, The book is a virile, enthralling and admirable piece of work that will rank the writer still higher on the rôle of popular authors.

A True Woman

By BARONESS ORCZY

Author of " The Scarlet Pimpernel," "The Elusive Pimpernel," etc.

The story of a woman into whose humdrum existence there suddenly enters the element of a tragedy, the prologue of which tells of an extraordinary and unaccountable crime committed in Paris, which presently, by a strange sequence of events, finds its counterpart in London. It is the true woman's connection with the perpetrator of the crime that forms the nucleus of the book. The story itself is a romantic one of love with a modern setting.

The Dawn of All

By ROBERT HUGH BENSON

Author of "The Light Invisible," " None Other Gods," etc.

This is a kind of companion volume—though in no sense a sequel—of the " Lord of the World." In the " Lord of the World " the author worked out what seemed to him would be the development of human history a hundred years hence, if irreligion prevailed along the lines it is following at present. In the " Dawn of All " he pursues the other " cross road," and sketches the world as it appears to him it would be should Catholicism be triumphant. He discusses freely, in the persons of his characters, and represents in their adventures the problems and accusations that surround the path of religion ; and the book winds up to a dramatic close that will make some people certainly very angry indeed. The book, therefore, is fully as much an attempt to challenge as to persuade.

The Vision of Balmaine

By G. B. BURGIN

Author of " The Shutters of Silence," etc.

In " The Vision of Balmaine," Mr. G. B. Burgin makes an entirely new departure with his hero, a man whose conceit is so colossal that he imagines the world could not possibly get on without him. It is only when he suffers for another man's crime and thus expiates a sin of his early youth, that he becomes human, and, in the depth of his despair, sees " The Vision," which influences the whole of his after-life. A very pretty love interest lightens the mystic's grief at his own shortcomings. This powerful story will provide a surprise for those who have only studied Mr. Burgin in his lighter moments.

The Princess of New York

By COSMO HAMILTON

Author of " The Infinite Capacity," " Adam's Clay," etc.

Mr. Cosmo Hamilton's new novel is called " The Princess of New York," because the heroine is the daughter of the Steel King. How she comes to Europe for the first time, meets a charming young Oxford man on board ship, who afterwards goes to her rescue when, by a series of accidents, she has fallen into the hands of a family of titled cardsharpers ; how she is wanted by the police for an illegal act in the performance of which she was the innocent instrument, and is rushed out of London in a commandeered motor car of the Oxford man and spends forty-eight hours with him, like Paul and Virginia, between two haystacks are only a few of the exciting and romantic incidents with which " The Princess of New York " is crowded.

New **6/-** Novels.

A NEW NOVEL
By
H. DE VERE STACPOOLE
Author of "The Blue Lagoon," etc.

The Ship of Coral

A West Indian Romance

"The Ship of Coral" is Mr. Stacpoole's fourth tropical romance, and perhaps his most important book. In this story Mr. Stacpoole has done for the West Indies and Caribbean Sea what in "The Blue Lagoon" he did for the Pacific. Blueness and great spaces of sunshine, an islet off the Caicos, Martinique with its palms and Ceiba trees, St. Pierre the modern Pompeii with all its beauty and charm are the backgrounds in the "Ship of Coral" for one of the most poetical love stories ever written.

The Hand of Venus

By Dr. J. MORGAN DE GROOT

Author of "The Bar Sinister."

In this story the author tells how a statue of Venus, fashioned by the hand of the great Greek sculptor Phidias, comes to play an important part in the life of Ventimore a modern English artist. By means of a curious clue the image is discovered buried in a field in the outskirts of Rome, where the scene of the novel is partly laid. How the artist's fate was influenced by the hand of the statue must be left for the author to tell in his own words. The book has a powerful plot, and a strong love interest.

Flaws

By JANE BARLOW

Author of " Bogland Studies," " Irish Neighbours," &c.

The characters who appear in the novel " Flaws " are drawn
ess preponderantly from the Irish peasant class than is the case in
many of the author's stories. Its scene is laid partly in a Home
for Indigent Ladies, maintained near an Irish village, by a fortune
made in the United States ; and partly in an inland southern county,
where much purturbation was caused among the inhabitants of a
remote hamlet by the imagined discovery of an amateur astronomer.
Another incident is the stratagem adopted by a sort of ' handy-man '
for the protection of his late master's daughter from a hardly less
imaginary danger.

The Real Mrs. Holyer

By E. M. CHANNON

Author of " A Street Angel " and " The Authoress. '

The readers of this author's previous novel, " The Authoress,"
will remember how deftly the plot was unravelled, and how skilfully
one's sympathy was enlisted in the pathetic figure of the heroine
with all her faults. In this new story will be found most of these
excellent features that combined to make the success of her earlier
work. There is plenty of incident and there are some powerful
character-studies. But the mystery which is part of the story
is unsolved until the end is reached, when the puzzling question is
answered as to whom is the real Mrs. Holyer.

Hutchinson's New 2/- Net Series.

In Crown 8vo.   Cloth Gilt.

They and I

By JEROME K. JEROME
Author of " Paul Kelver," " Three Men in a Boat," &c.

" This is Mr. Jerome's peculiar vintage, sparkling with spontaneous gaiety, and rich in the deeper tone which suggests itself from time to time behind the sparkle. The author is said to have described the work as a more mature ' Three Men in a Boat.' That is just what it is."—*Evening Standard*.

Seymour Charlton   540 pages

By W. B. MAXWELL
Author of " Vivien," " The Guarded Flame," etc.

" It is a grand story, one to enchant, to hold the attention, to read and re-read for its many charms. . . . It is a splendid novel ; it ought to be very popular."—*Daily Telegraph*.

" ' Seymour Charlton ' is on a large scale, running to more than 530 closely printed pages. Mr. Maxwell takes his work seriously, and he has given us a very fine and careful study, interesting in every page, carefully and patiently studied throughout. It is not at all likely that we shall see any better novel than this during the winter season. It is a pleasure to keep company with a high-minded and scrupulous artist like Mr. Maxwell."—*British Weekly*.

Calvary

By " RITA "
Author of " The House Called Hurrish," " Peg the Rake," &c.

One is accustomed to surprises from the pen of this versatile writer, but in this novel she takes her reader by storm. The story itself is alive with human interest, and the characters seem to live. One strange and mystical being, known as " The Wanderer," would alone create interest enough to be pursued through the book with eager zest.

. NEW VOLUMES .
HUTCHINSON'S 1s. NET NOVELS

Each in Cr. 8vo., Cloth Gilt, with coloured wrappers.

Petticoat Government   BARONESS ORCZY

The Necromancers   R. H. BENSON

Kingsmead   BARONESS VON HUTTEN

Torn Sails   ALLEN RAINE

The Ladies' Paradise   EMILE ZOLA

A Winnowing   R. H. BENSON

The Mysteries of Marseilles
EMILE ZOLA

VOLUMES NOW BOUND IN CLOTH GILT.

The Strayings of Sandy
DOROTHEA CONYERS

A Spirit in Prison   ROBERT HICHENS

The Three Brothers   EDEN PHILLPOTTS

A Double Thread
ELLEN THORNEYCROFT FOWLER

Tatterley   TOM GALLON

Confessions of a Ladies' Man
WM. LE QUEUX

I Forbid the Banns F FRANKFORT MOORE

1s. NET BOOKS.

Each in crown 8vo, cloth gilt, coloured paper wrapper

The Elusive Pimpernel
By BARONESS ORCZY

200th thousand

Author of "The Scarlet Pimpernel," &c.

This novel contains further exciting incidents in the life of the Scarlet Pimpernel during the French Revolution after the King's death. It is about the same length as "The Scarlet Pimpernel," and most of the characters in that novel reappear in the new book—especially Chauvelin, the French agent.

Some new personages also appear on the scene.

A Welsh Singer
By ALLEN RAINE

355th thousand

Author of "A Welsh Witch," "Torn Sails," &c.

Allen Raine's novels have now reached a sale totalling over TWO MILLIONS. This, her most popular novel, is sure of a huge reception.

The *Daily Mail* says : "Wales has waited long for her novelist, but he seems to have come at last in Allen Raine, who, in his perfectly beautiful story, 'A Welsh Singer,' has at once proved himself a worthy interpreter and exponent of the romantic spirit of his country."

The Story of an African Farm
By OLIVE SCHREINER

111th thousand

The demand for this wonderful novel (which unquestionably is Olive Schreiner's masterpiece) in the more expensive editions has been enormous.

The Soul Market
9th edition

"England's Own Jungle."

By OLIVE CHRISTIAN MALVERY
(Mrs. Archibald Mackirdy)

"Her book is more interesting than any novel, for there are life-stories on every page. It is like a novelist's sketch-book—full of suggestive incidents and outlines of character, anecdotes, epigrams, out-of-the-way facts. Humour and pity, tragedy and mirth, tread in each other's steps. She says she does not expect her book to be popular ; I, on the other hand, prophesy that it will be read and talked about a great deal."—*Evening News.*

Each in crown 8vo, with attractive paper covers in three colours.

This—My Son

By RENÉ BAZIN

One of the most stirring and human novels that has been written by the popular author of that successful book, " The Nun."

"BRIMFUL OF HUMOUR."

Green Ginger

By ARTHUR MORRISON

Author of " Tales of Mean Streets," etc.

" It is long since we laughed so much over ludicrous situations. We are always heartily and wholesomely entertained. Should prove something more than the success of a season. It is assuredly one of the funniest books that we have had for some time."— *Daily Telegraph.*

Virginia of the Rhodesians

7th edition

By CYNTHIA STOCKLEY

" Deserves more than moderate praise. It is smart, acidulated and very clever indeed."—*Daily Mail*

"Will remind the reader of some of the best work of Mr Kipling."—*Newcastle Leader.*

The author's recent book, " Poppy : a South African Girl," has met with a considerable success, nine editions having been called for within a short time of its publication.

The City

By FREDERICK CARREL

Author of " The Adventures of John Johns," etc.

" A novel of such power as to stand well in comparison with Zola's ' Argent,' but the treatment of it is more expert and spontaneous. The hold the novel takes on you is surprising."— *Illustrated London News.*

1s. NET BOOKS—*continued.*

Each in crown 8vo, with attractive paper covers in three colours.

The Heart of a Child

**Being passages from the early life of
Sally Snape, Lady Kidderminster.**

By FRANK DANBY

"A work of art. Sally is a delightful acquaintance."—*Times.*
"Sally is a real woman, and Frank Danby is heartily to be con
gratulated."—Mr. W. L. Courtney in the *Daily Telegraph.*
"To say that 'The Heart of a Child' justifies its title is already
to give it high praise. Sally has our sympathy from first to last.
A delightful book."—*Manchester Guardian.*

Servitude

By IRENE OSGOOD

"Servitude" is really a very notable achievement in the
creation of atmosphere. The story of devotion and adventure
which is pursued through these thrilling pages would in itself recom-
mend the book to the lover of keen and vibrant romance, but the
setting is of such unusual lustre that the most lasting impression
comes from it. 'Servitude' is a book which is likely to prove more
than a nine days' wonder."—*Morning Post.*

Nor all your Tears

By MAUD H. YARDLEY

"Mrs. Yardley is to be complimented on so notable a step forward towards higher honours in the field of fiction. She shows in-
creasing dramatic power, has a pleasing style and a grip of the art
of characterisation."—*Bystander.*

Redemption

By RENÉ BAZIN

"Redemption" is an able study of the shop girl, who may
differ a little in a provincial French city from the London type, but
who in the main is the same ; the refinements, the difficulties, and
the temptations of this class are perfectly and sympathetically con-
ceived and described."—*Globe.*

HUTCHINSON'S SELECT NOVELS UNIFORM EDITION

Each in crown 8vo, handsome cloth gilt, 3s. 6d.

Hutchinson's 7d. Novels.

A new series of successful copyright works of fiction, printed in clear, readable type on good paper, and tastefully bound in art cloth, with gold lettering.

In foolscap 8vo, with designed title page and frontispiece.
ON ART PAPER.

PRISONERS
>>> By MARY CHOLMONDELEY.
>>>>>> Author of "Red Pottage," &c.

MY LADY FRIVOL
>>> By ROSA N. CAREY.
>>>>>> Author of "Mollie's Prince," &c.

INTO THE HIGHWAYS AND HEDGES
>>> By F. F. MONTRÉSOR,

A RISING STAR
>>> By DAVID CHRISTIE MURRAY,
>>>>>> Author of "A Rogue's Conscience," &c.

THE MAN WHO WON
>>> By Mrs. BAILLIE REYNOLDS,
>>>>>> Author of "A Dull Girl's Destiny," &c.

THE UNDER SECRETARY
>>> By WILLIAM LE QUEUX,
>>>>>> Author of "The Confessions of a Lady's Man," &c.

TOMMY AND CO.
>>> By JEROME K. JEROME,
>>>>>> Author of "They and I," &c.

THE ONE WHO LOOKED ON
>>> By F. F. MONTRÉSOR,

THALASSA
>>> By Mrs. BAILLIE REYNOLDS,
>>>>>> Author of "The Man Who Won," &c.

THE GAMBLERS
>>> By WILLIAM LE QUEUX,
>>>>>> Author of "Confessions of a Ladies' Man."

LADY ELVERTON'S EMERALDS
>>> By DOROTHEA CONYERS,
>>>>>> Author of "The Strayings of Sandy," &c.

LITANY LANE
>>> By Mrs. BAILLIE SAUNDERS,
>>>>>> Author of "Saints in Society," &c.

AT THE CROSS ROADS
>>> By F. F. MONTRÉSOR,

BY ORDER OF THE CZAR
>>> By JOSEPH HATTON,
>>>>>> Author of "In Male Attire,." &c
>>>>>> 21st Edition.

Hutchinson & Co.'s New 6d. Novels.

263	WICKED SIR DARE	...	...	...	... Charles Garvice
264	THE SLAVES OF ALLAH	...	...	... G. B. Burgin
265	WYNDHAM'S DAUGHTER	...	...	... Annie S. Swan
266	UNDER THE THATCH ...	...	...	... Allen Raine
267	THAT STRANGE GIRL ...	...	...	... Charles Garvice
268	THE LADY OF THE CAMEO	...	...	... Tom Gallon
269	THE GUARDIANSHIP OF GABRIELLE ...	...	... E. Everett-Green
270	A WHITE MAN ...	...	...	...	... E. M. Royle
271	MISS ESTCOURT	...	...	...	... Charles Garvice
272	A SIMPLE SAVAGE	...	...	...	... G. B. Burgin
273	THE MISCHIEF OF THE GODS	...	... Bertha Clay
274	FRANK SINCLAIR'S WIFE	...	...	... Mrs. J. H. Riddell
275	A SENSE OF HUMOUR ...	...	...	... { Beryl Faber & Cosmo Hamilton
276	NELLIE ...	...	...	...	...	... Charles Garvice
277	VERONIQUE	...	...	...	...	... Florence Marryat
278	THE MYSTERY OF THE ROYAL MAIL	... B. L. Farjeon
279	A STORMY VOYAGER ...	...	...	... Annie S. Swan
280	MY LOVE KITTY	...	...	...	... Charles Garvice
281	THE KING OF FOUR CORNERS	...	... G. B. Burgin
282	NOT IN SOCIETY	...	...	...	... Joseph Hatton
283	MARRIAGE BY CAPTURE	...	...	... Bertha Clay
284	VIOLET ...	...	...	...	...	... Charles Garvice
285	THE MYSTERY OF JOHN PEPPERCORN	... Tom Gallon
286	THE LADY OF SHALL NOT	...	...	... E. Everett-Green
287	ANTHONY WILDING	...	...	...	... Rafael Sabatini
288	MISS BETTY'S MISTAKE	...	...	... Adeline Sergeant
289	AS IT HAPPENED	...	...	...	... Ashton Hilliers

Hutchinson's 6d. Novels

Well printed on good paper in clear readable type.

Hutchinson's Sixpenny copyright Novels stand easily ahead of all other similar reprints.

ALREADY PUBLISHED.

HUTCHINSON'S SIXPENNY NOVELS—*continued.*

HUTCHINSON'S SIXPENNY NOVELS—*continued*.

ALREADY PUBLISHED

HUTCHINSON'S SIXPENNY NOVELS—*continued.*

ALREADY PUBLISHED

Printed in Great Britain
by Amazon

25251059R00229